Be
Mindful
of Us

Be
Mindful
of Us

PRAYERS TO
THE SAINTS

Anthony F. Chiffolo

Liguori
LIGUORI, MISSOURI

To Lisa and Rusty,
the saints in my life

Published by Liguori Publications
Liguori, Missouri
http://www.liguori.org

Library of Congress Cataloging-in-Publication Data

Chiffolo, Anthony F., 1959–
   Be mindful of us : prayers to the saints / Anthony F. Chiffolo.— 1st ed.
      p. cm.
   Includes bibliographical references and index.
   ISBN 0-7648-0380-8 (pbk.)
   1. Christian saints—Prayer-books and devotions—English. 2. Devotional calendars—Catholic Church. I. Title.

   BX2166.C45 2000
   242'.76—dc21   99-053659

The author and publisher gratefully acknowledge permission to reprint/ reproduce copyrighted works granted by the publishers/sources listed on pages 303–8.

Book design by Debbie Skaggs

Printed in the United States of America
04 03 02 01 00 5 4 3 2 1
First edition

Come to their assistance, all ye Saints of God; gain for them deliverance from their place of punishment; meet them, all ye Angels; receive these holy souls, and present them before the Lord.

John Henry Newman,
Meditations and Devotions

O heavenly patron, in whose name I glory, pray ever to God for me that he may strengthen me in my faith, establish me in virtue, and guard me in conflict, so that I might overcome all evil and attain to everlasting glory with you. Amen.

Traditional

Great friends of God, Holy Helpers, humbly saluting and venerating you, I implore your help and intercession. Bring my prayers before the throne of the Most Holy Trinity, so that I may experience in all the difficulties and trials of life the mercy of the eternal God, the love of the incarnate divine Son, and the assistance of the Holy Spirit; that despondency may not depress me when God's wise decree imposes on my shoulders a heavy burden. Above all, I implore your assistance at the hour of death. Help me then to gain the victory over the temptations and assaults of Satan, and to leave this world hopefully trusting in God's mercy, to join you in heaven, there to praise God for ever and ever. Amen.

Traditional

Contents

Introduction

As I ponder the hundreds of saints whose names appear between these pages, I realize how personal this book has become.

Originally, it was to be a compilation of prayers composed by other people, but I quickly discovered that while many, many people have implored the intercession of Saints Peregrine and Rita, for example, my research uncovered no prayers addressed to Saint Solange or Blessed Fra Angelico. This left most of my calendar blank. But I soon understood where the Spirit was leading and realized that this book would be more of a writing project than I had anticipated.

Another frustration was that I could often find prayers to several saints with the same feast day—indeed, I think it's safe to say that no saint has a unique feast day—but space permits the inclusion of only one per day. So I have embraced those saints with whom I feel a certain commonality. The reader will find a number of favorites like Saints Francis of Assisi, Elizabeth Ann Seton, John of the Cross, and Hildegard of Bingen, but many more that may be unknown to her or him, such as Saint Aelred of Rievaulx, Blessed Josephine Bakhita, or Blessed Jeremiah of Valachia Kostistk. I have made a conscious effort also to pray to saints and blesseds from all around the world and from all cultural and economic circumstances, because their understanding that all people are God's children speaks so strongly to the spirit of inclusiveness I attempt to live out in my own life. Finally, I have composed prayers to many whom Pope John Paul II has beatified and canonized; most of them are of the modern era, and their lives and spirituality are more accessible to me than those of some of the ancient saints and martyrs.

In making my selections I certainly faced a problem many
have encountered before, including the eminent theologian
Karl Rahner, who composed the following prayer:

> Saint Thomas, I must confess to you that at first
> it was somewhat difficult to hunt for and then to
> address one particular saint in the silent
> immeasurability of God (I could do it in relation
> to all the saints). But perhaps it is precisely that
> single correct choice that comes to one after much
> difficulty!
>
> So I ask of you (using the traditional formula,
> the precise meaning of which I shall not ponder
> right at the moment): Grant that you will inter-
> cede for me with God, insofar as all saints stand
> for all other saints, among whom even poor sin-
> ners like myself belong—grant me your interces-
> sion so that even if only from afar I may become
> a little like you.... (*Prayers for a Lifetime*, ed.
> Albert Raffelt. New York: Crossroad, 1984.)

Rahner's words speak eloquently to me, for I choose to
pray to saints whom I emulate, whose lives or spirit are so
attractive to me that I would like to become a little more
like them in some way. And I daresay the words that I use in
the prayers I have composed reveal this longing of my soul.

As well, the words of my prayers reflect my own varying
spiritual states over the many months of research and writing, for I wrote directly and honestly from my heart. As I
peruse these prayers, I feel again the longing for human sym-
pathy, the pain of injury or insult, the quest for a sure answer, the fatigue of unfinished business, and the exaltation
of a shared love. And I know that in my writing I have also
been praying. My hope is that my words will inspire you,
the reader, to pray along with me.

Be
Mindful
of Us

January

Mary,
the Mother of God

Mary, Mother of Jesus and of those who participate in his priestly ministry, we come to you with the same attitude of children who come to their mother.

We are no longer children, but adults who desire with all our hearts to be God's children.

Our human condition is weak, that is why we come to ask for your motherly aid so we are able to overcome our weakness.

Pray for us so that we can, in turn, become people of prayer.

We invoke your protection so that we may remain free from all sin.

We invoke your love so that it may reign and we will be able to be compassionate and forgiving.

We ask for your blessing so we can be like the image of your beloved Son, Our Lord and Savior, Jesus Christ. Amen.

MOTHER TERESA OF CALCUTTA

first century: Mary was betrothed to Joseph when the angel Gabriel appeared to her, asking her to be the mother of our Lord. Her fiat changed the history of the world.

—JANUARY 2—

Saints Basil the Great and Gregory Nazianzen

BASIL: PATRON OF RUSSIA AND HOSPITAL ADMINISTRATORS

O holy saints, the great friendship you shared is an inspiration to us. You studied together, became monks together, became bishops together, and eventually both joined the ranks of the great Fathers of the Eastern Church. The age in which you lived was difficult and dangerous for people of faith, and you depended upon each other for support and inspiration. O great saints, bless us, that we may find friendships that are supportive and loving, as yours was. Pray for us, that we may have friends who love us unconditionally and yet support us on our path to God. Inspire us with the courage to profess our faith as fearlessly as you did, in the face of opposition and even death. Help us, that we may persevere in seeking God's will. We ask this through Christ our Lord. Amen.

Basil: 329–379: Born at Caesarea in Cappadocia, he was one of the greatest of all bishops, having defended his huge see of Caesarea against the Arian heresy. Because he established the first monastery in Asia Minor, he is regarded as the father of all Eastern monks.

Gregory: c. 329–390: Born in Cappadocia, he read law for ten years in Athens but joined Saint Basil and was later ordained. Consecrated bishop, Gregory refused a diocese, but then reluctantly accepted the see of Constantinople. After a few months he resigned and retired. For his writings, particularly directed against the heresy of Arianism, he was named a Doctor of the Church.

—JANUARY 3—

Saint Geneviève

PATRON OF PARIS; INVOKED AGAINST
DROUGHT, FEVER, FLOODS,
AND THE PLAGUE

Most holy Saint Geneviève, during times of danger you raised your voice to negotiate, to lead, and especially to pray. For you, prayer was the beginning and the ending of everything you did, enabling you to accomplish remarkable things. Sometimes, dear saint, I forget to pray. Sometimes the situations I face look so bleak that I despair of prayer's efficacy. And sometimes, I admit, I do pray, but prayer doesn't seem to help. It is easy to forsake my prayers, and so, Geneviève, I ask you to nudge me to pray when I forget. Remind me of the desperate situations that you survived through the power of prayer, of the remarkable power of prayer in your life. Keep me from despair, and teach me to conquer fatalism. Help me to bring all things to the Lord in prayer, always, but especially when the situations I face look hopeless. I pray in Jesus' name. Amen.

c. 422–c. 500: Noted for her accurate prophecies and her remarkable abilities at prayer, Geneviève convinced Childric, chieftain of the invading Frankish tribes that occupied Paris, to release his captives. She negotiated successfully with Clovis, another Frankish chieftain, also. She later organized a squad to bring in boatloads of food during a famine, and the prayers she led protected Paris from Attila the Hun. Even after her death, prayers invoking her name have continued to protect Parisians from the plague, drought, and epidemic.

—JANUARY 4—

Saint Elizabeth Ann Seton

O Blessed Elizabeth Seton, shining today in splendor in the sight of all the nations because of your faithfulness to the promises made at your baptism, look lovingly upon your own people, who boast of you as their first flower of sanctity! Obtain for them from God the grace that they may preserve their most sacred inheritance which is fidelity to the Gospel, firmness of faith, and enthusiastic charity, so that they may joyfully fulfill their own particular vocation. And protect the whole Church, offering her the example of your warm-hearted generosity and love which carried you onward from one degree of glory to another to the final glory of today.

POPE JOHN XXIII

1774–1821: Born in New York, Elizabeth married and became involved in social work, helping to found the Society for the Relief of Poor Widows with Small Children. Widowed, with five children to raise, she became Roman Catholic, was ostracized by her family, and moved to Baltimore. The school she founded was the beginning of the far-reaching Roman Catholic school system in the United States. She was also the first superior of her order, the Sisters of Charity, which was the first American religious society. She is the first American-born saint.

—JANUARY 5—

Saint John Neumann

O Servant of God, Saint John Neumann, obtain for me an ardent love of God, that will detach me from the love of created things and from myself, to love [God] alone and to spend myself for [God's] glory. Obtain for me also the special favor *(mention request)*, which I now ask through your intercession with God.

O Servant of God, Saint John Neumann, obtain for me a true love of my neighbor, that will make me do good even to those who have offended me. Obtain for me also the special favor *(mention request)*, which I now ask through your intercession with God.

O Servant of God, Saint John Neumann, obtain for me a tender devotion to the Passion of Jesus Christ, to the Blessed Sacrament, and to my dear Mother Mary. Obtain for me also the special favor *(mention request)*, which I now ask through your intercession with God.

O Servant of God, Saint John Neumann, obtain for me above all the grace of final perseverance and the grace always to pray for it, especially in time of temptation and at the hour of death. Obtain for me also the special favor *(mention request)*, which I now ask through your intercession with God.

THE NATIONAL SHRINE OF SAINT JOHN NEUMANN

1811–1860: Born in Bohemia, John emigrated to America, where he worked as a pastor for twenty-four years, most of the time as a Redemptorist missionary. After he had become bishop of Philadelphia, he founded the Third Order of Saint Francis of Philadelphia, a congregation of religious women.

—JANUARY 6—

Blessed André Bessette

Blessed Brother André, your devotion to Saint Joseph is an inspiration to us. You gave your life selflessly to bring the message of his life to others. Pray that we may learn from Saint Joseph, and from you, what it is like to care for Jesus and do his work in the world. Amen.

TERRY MATZ

1845–1936: A member of the Holy Cross Brothers, André surprised the archbishop of Montreal by asking permission to build a chapel to Saint Joseph on the mountain near Notre Dame College. The archbishop assented, as long as André stayed out of debt. Beginning with nickels and dimes he collected as donations for giving haircuts to boys, André progressed with his project. When he finished the small shrine, he began a basilica on the mountain to express his great devotion to Saint Joseph. Brother André never saw the basilica finished, but he didn't mind starting small and giving as much of himself as he could for as long as he could.

—JANUARY 7—

Saint Raymond of Peñafort

PATRON OF LAWYERS AND LAW SCHOOLS

Holy Saint Raymond, the Lord gave you many gifts —of longevity, languages, legal understanding, and administration—and you used your gifts wisely, for God's glorification. Help me to accept the gifts the Lord has bestowed on me, to use them to the fullest of my abilities and not to squander what I have been given. Help me also to realize that the future is not something I will merely inhabit: it is something to create, and in this creative work, my only limitations are my own efforts. Pray for me, then, that I will accomplish the great things that God wants me to do. I ask this through Jesus, our Savior. Amen.

1175–1275: A kinsman of the kings of Aragon, Raymond joined the Dominican Order and preached to the Moors and the Albigenses. He was called to Rome by Pope Gregory IX to be his confessor and was also charged with codifying canon law. Later, he was chosen master-general of his order.

—JANUARY 8—

Saint Gudula of Brussels

PATRON OF BRUSSELS

O Saint Gudula, your devotion to the daily Eucharist is cause for joy and inspiration. Inspire in me the devotion to commune with our Lord daily at Mass, and teach me to appreciate the great gift of holy Communion.

As well, pray for all people who are unable to participate in the Eucharist. If religious persecution or political proscriptions be the cause, please pray for the spirit of tolerance and freedom. If sickness be the cause, please pray for healing. If shortages of priests or deacons be the cause, please pray that more will answer the call of the Lord to ordination. If geographical considerations be the cause, please pray for more accessible transportation systems. Beseech the Lord, I implore you, to overcome these obstacles, so that the people of God can partake of the grace present in the Eucharist. In Jesus' name I pray. Amen.

died 712: The daughter of Saint Amalberga, Gudula was educated at Nivelles, Belgium, by Saint Gertrude, her godmother.
After Gertrude's death, Gudula led a life of prayer, fasting,
and almsgiving. Many miracles have been attributed to her.

—JANUARY 9—

Saint Adrian of Canterbury

Saint Adrian, you felt yourself unworthy of the honors of the episcopacy, knowing in your heart that
God had other important work that only you could
accomplish. Help me to listen to my heart, that I
may learn not to seek after the honors other people
think I should pursue but rather dedicate myself to
the work that is true and meaningful for me. Pray
that the Lord not only strengthens my interior voice
but speaks to me himself about the path I should
follow. Bless me as I make difficult decisions, dear
saint. I pray for special guidance in the matter of
(mention request), which perplexes me so that I don't
know what to do. Ask the Lord to clarify my
thoughts, that I may choose rightly. Amen.

died 710: A native of Africa, Adrian became abbot of Nerida,
near Naples. Chosen to be archbishop of Canterbury, Adrian
declined, but he accompanied Saint Theodore of Tarsus,
whom he served as adviser and assistant instead. Adrian
became abbot of Saints Peter and Paul, and under his super-
vision this school attracted students from all over Christendom.

—JANUARY 10—

Saint Peter Orseolo

O Saint Peter, you took your great success in the world so lightly, cherishing in your heart a secret hunger for closeness to God. Teach me, I pray, to pause occasionally in my great rush through the day's tasks, that I may listen to what my heart is telling me about the choices I'm making and the life I'm living. Inspire me to trust my heart's desire, and ask the Lord to grant me the courage to make changes when they are necessary. Remind me to give consideration as well to all the people in my life who might be affected by such changes, that I may remember them and treat them with charity. Most of all, help me to trust in the Lord and to have faith that what he is calling me to do will be for the good of all. I ask this through Christ our Lord. Amen.

928–987: Peter married, became admiral of the Venetian fleet at a young age, then became Doge of Venice, one of the city's greatest, and guided the Republic through dangerous political crises. Then he disappeared for two years, only to reveal himself as a monk in the Benedictine abbey at Cuxa, Spain, where he served as sacristan. He retired after some years to live as a hermit in the wilderness, and his reputation was such that his tomb became a great place of pilgrimage.

—JANUARY 11—

Saints Ethne and Fedelm

O holy saints, Ethne and Fedelm, you were unafraid to question the great teacher of Ireland about matters with which you were unfamiliar. Inspire in me the curiosity that prompted your questions about God. Pray for me that I may always have a searching attitude that wonders where I might find, know, and love God and God's sons and daughters. As well, bless me with the courage to approach teachers, ministers, or leaders who have information that I desire. Help me to learn from them and, perhaps, even to teach them what I might know that they do not. Most of all, keep me from arrogance, that I may never believe myself to have all the answers. I implore your help in the name of the Trinity, God, Son, and Holy Spirit, who animates the universe with Love. Amen.

fifth century: According to legend, Ethne and Fedelm were the daughters of King Loegaire of Connacht. Upon encountering Saint Patrick at a well, they questioned him about his God. The women found his answer, echoing the Celtic understanding of the Creator as being inseparable from the universe, and his explanation of the Trinity so wonderful that they passed on to the next life immediately. They were buried nearby, as wells served as the traditional Celtic entry into the other world.

—JANUARY 12—

Saint Marguerite Bourgeoys

Dearest Saint Marguerite, God called you to leave your country to extend the kingdom of heaven by educating people in the Christian way of life. Inspire me by your example and assist me with your prayers, that I may proclaim by my words and actions the presence of Jesus to all who seek paths that lead to God. Help me to respond with love and compassion to the special needs of the Church in my time. Guide all teachers and educators as they enable others to grow in knowledge, wisdom, and Gospel values. Send me your spirit so that I may follow your example in my presence and service among those who are needy and poor in my time. And pray for me that I may live in openness to the Spirit and that I may respond with courage to God's call in my daily life. I implore your help in the name of Jesus. Amen.

1620–1700: Marguerite left France for the newly founded colony of Ville Marie, now Montreal, in Canada, where she opened the first school for the children of the native people and the French colonists. She also founded the Congregation of Notre Dame, the first uncloistered community of women in the new world.

—JANUARY 13—

Saint Hilary of Poitiers

O holy Saint Hilary, you knew that the Gospels offer no support for a sunlit holiness that encounters no problems. You knew that Christ did not escape at the last moment, but you also knew that Christ did live happily ever after—after a life of controversy, problems, pain, and frustration. Like many saints, dear Hilary, you simply had more of the same. Pray for me, then, when I encounter difficulties in my life. Remind me that life's challenges are opportunities for me to learn and to grow in the love of Jesus. Inspire me to persevere, to keep my eye on the ultimate goal, which is life with Jesus.

As well, dearest saint, when others challenge my faith, implore the Lord to strengthen me in my beliefs. Ask the Spirit also to give me the words to say, so that I may meet my detractors and any doubters with the love and wisdom of Jesus, and so bring them to respect our Lord and my love for him. I ask this in the name of Jesus, who told his disciples not to worry about what to say, for he would provide them with the words to speak. Amen.

died c. 368: Born of noble but non-Christian parents, Hilary became bishop of his native Poitiers. For his campaign against the heresy of Arianism, he was exiled to Phrygia. Eventually, he was allowed to return. He is a Doctor of the Church.

—JANUARY 14—

Blessed Peter Donders

Blessed Peter, Apostle of the Poor, knowing poverty firsthand, you did not hesitate to embark upon a life of service to the poor. You showered the Lord's wonderful mercy and loving care upon slaves, native peoples, and people with leprosy—those most terribly oppressed members of society. By your example and prayers, inspire me to serve my outcast neighbors in like manner, and serve the Lord by bringing his loving care to those who are in the greatest need in society. This I pray through Christ our Lord. Amen.

1809–1887: From Tilburg, the Netherlands, Peter felt called to the missionary life but lacked the resources for a seminary education. A patron provided financial aid, and Peter went to Surinam (Dutch Guiana) after his ordination to minister to slaves and native peoples. Then he worked in Batavia with people sick with leprosy. He fell ill, but because of his work there, the Redemptorists asked him to join their congregation. He returned to Batavia to minister selflessly to people with leprosy until his death.

—JANUARY 15—

Saint Ita of Limerick

Holy Saint Ita, you who from a young age learned from the angels the meaning of the Holy Trinity, pray to the Lord for me that I may have true faith in

God, that I may lead a simple life, and that I may live generously. Teach me how to turn my spirit to these three things that most please God. As well, I pray you, help me to tame my mouth when it hates people, my heart when it harbors resentments, and my pride when it trusts in wealth. Help me, I implore you, to overcome these three things that most displease God. Most of all, dearest Ita, help me to understand the Trinity, that I may truly love my neighbors with the love that joins God, Jesus, and the Spirit together. I pray in the name of Jesus, our Lord. Amen.

died c. 570: A native of Drum in County Waterford, Ireland, Ita founded the convent of Hy Conaill, in County Limerick, and soon attracted large numbers of women. Her life is noted for her devotion to the Holy Trinity.

—JANUARY 16—

Blessed Joseph Vaz

Blessed Joseph, you combined the virtues of your own heritage with the radiance of Christ to serve the needs of your adopted people. Pray for me, that I may discern what's best in my own heritage and what's best among the other cultures and traditions I encounter. Give me courage to abandon what is comfortable but useless or harmful. And help me to embody all good as I strive to serve God and God's people in whatever place, culture, tradition, or society I find myself. I ask this in Jesus' name. Amen.

1651–1711: Born in Goa, India, of the Brahmin caste, Joseph was raised a Christian and was ordained. He ministered in Ceylon (now Sri Lanka), working in disguise to preach and console the faithful, who were being persecuted by Dutch colonial authorities. He was imprisoned for a time, until the king interceded for his release. Joseph is honored as the Apostle of Ceylon.

—JANUARY 17—

Saint Anthony of Egypt

PATRON OF BASKET WEAVERS, BRUSH MAKERS,
BUTCHERS, DOMESTIC ANIMALS, GRAVEDIGGERS,
SWINE; INVOKED AGAINST ECZEMA AND
"SAINT ANTHONY'S FIRE" (ERGOTISM)

O glorious Saint Anthony, who, upon hearing only one word of the holy Gospel while assisting at the divine liturgy, abandoned the riches and ease of your father's house, your native land, and the world, in order to retire into the wilderness; who, notwithstanding the heavy burden of years and the ravages of a lifetime of penance, did not hesitate to leave your solitude and go up to Alexandria in Egypt to openly reproach the impiety of heretics and to strengthen the wavering faith of Christians, as a true confessor of Jesus Christ, eager to receive the palm of martyrdom, had your Lord permitted it; ah, get us the grace to be ever zealous in the cause of Jesus Christ and of his Church, and to persevere even to the end of our days in our adherence to Catholic truth, in the observance of his commandments, in the practice of his counsels, and in the imitation of your virtues; that so, having faithfully followed your example here on earth, we may come to marvel at your glory in heaven and to be partakers of the same, through all the ages. Amen.

THE RACCOLTA

251–356: The patriarch of all monks, Anthony, born in upper Egypt, was a wealthy man who gave all his property to the poor and went to live as a hermit. He established communities of hermits in the desert—the first to establish the monastic life as we know it today. He became famous and was in great demand as an adviser.

—JANUARY 18—

Blessed Christina Ciccarelli

Most Blessed Christina, during your lifetime people from all spheres of society implored your intercession on their behalf, seeking cures for all sorts of sicknesses. Now look with favor upon me also, I implore you, as I pray for your intercession on my behalf. Bless me with your healing power, and ask the Lord to send his Spirit of healing to me also, that I may be cured of my affliction *(mention request)*. Help me as well to imitate your spirit of obedience, that I may learn to discern the will of God, particularly as it concerns my health, accepting the work of Divine Providence and following where our Lord leads. I ask this in the name of our Lord Jesus Christ, whose Spirit continues to bring healing to his people. Amen.

1481–1543: Named Mattia, Christina was born in Abruzzi, Italy, and entered the Augustinian monastery of Santa Lucia in Aquila. She was soon elected abbess, becoming famous for her sanctity, her visions, and her ability to obtain miraculous cures. She had two notable ecstasies: During the first, on the feast of Corpus Christi, she levitated, and a sacred Host in a golden pyx radiated from her breast. During the second, on Good Friday, she experienced our Lord's passion during a vision that lasted until the following day.

Saint Wulfstan of Worcester

Holy Bishop Wulfstan, God gave you the faith and courage to help those who were in captivity. Like our Lord Jesus, you worked to set the captives free. Pray now for all those who remain in bondage or oppression, and send the spirit of freedom to political prisoners, slaves, and hostages. As well, pray for those who are enslaved to drugs, alcohol, sex, money, or other addictions. Most of all, be with those who are oppressed by poverty, that they may come to the Lord's table of plenty and emerge into the true freedom of the kingdom of heaven. I ask this through Jesus Christ our Lord, who lives and reigns forever and ever. Amen.

died 1095: When William the Norman conquered England in 1066, he replaced all the native Anglo-Saxon bishops with Normans, with the exception of Wulfstan, bishop of Worcester, who was known for his wise governance. Wulfstan became one of the king's most trusted advisers, serving as bishop for thirty-two years. He is best remembered for his care of the poor and his opposition to the slave trade in western England.

Saint Sebastian

PATRON OF ARCHERS, ATHLETES, DOCTORS, HARDWARE, PIN MAKERS, THE POLICE, AND SOLDIERS; INVOKED AGAINST THE PLAGUE

O Saint Sebastian, you were blessed to serve as an example to your fellow soldiers, bringing the Gospel to them by curing illness, converting, and baptizing. Pray that our soldiers may, like you, know the love of Christ. Pray also that through your intercession they may become models of service, and that they may share Christ's love with all. Amen.

died c. 288: One of the most renowned of the Roman martyrs, Sebastian was an officer in the imperial army. When he was discovered to be a Christian, he was tied to a tree and shot with arrows, then clubbed to death. The basilica built over his tomb is one of the seven principal churches of Rome.

—JANUARY 21—

Saint Agnes

PATRON OF VIRGINS AND GIRL SCOUTS

O courageous Saint Agnes, the Lord performed miracles to preserve the chastity you had dedicated to him. Intercede for all women and men who have taken vows of chastity, that the Lord may strengthen them in their chosen way.

As well, in these times when rapes and threats of violence are all too frequent, defend all people from sexual and other physical assault. Pray that the Lord will send legions of angels to protect those threatened with violence, performing miracles if necessary to keep them from harm. And pray also for all those who do not know the Lord and seek pleasure instead in sexual brutality; bring them the assistance they need to be healed of their afflictions. In Jesus' name I pray. Amen.

died c. 304: A Roman maiden, aged twelve or thirteen, Agnes was martyred for refusing to marry the governor's non-Christian son. Her symbol is the lamb.

—JANUARY 22—

Saint Vincent Pallotti

We wish to offer a very special and confident prayer to you, our own Saint Vincent Pallotti, glory of the Roman clergy, now shining in all the splendor of your virtues....We beg you, who were an indefatigable apostle, a director of consciences, an inspirer of holy enthusiasms, magnificent in your many and varied activities, to kindle with new fervor all ministers of the Lord and these precious collaborators of the Catholic apostolate; make them ready and eager to answer every appeal from their brothers. Always and everywhere the "salt of the earth and the light of the world" intent on spreading "the good odor of Christ." May they be apostles of truth, love, and mercy, and educators of exemplary Christians, consoling the humble and poor in the light that streams from Christ, the Good Shepherd, Savior of souls and peoples. Amen, Amen.

POPE JOHN XXIII

1795–1850: A priest who devoted himself to pastoral work, Vincent organized schools for tradespeople so that they could better work at their crafts, as well as evening classes for farmers and unskilled workers. He founded two congregations and helped establish a missionary order in England and several colleges to train missionaries. He is included among the incorruptibles.

—JANUARY 23—

Saint Emerentiana

Dear Saint Emerentiana, you gave your life for Christ even though you were barely a new member of the Church. Remind us of the strength of new faith,

that we "older" members of the Church may remember what our faith was like when we were
younger. Teach us to look to our "younger" members for renewal, and to allow them to lead us in
rededicating our lives to the love of God. As God
may speak to us from even the youngest voices in
our midst, pray that we may open our hearts to learn
from all. As well, bless all catechumens, that they
may boldly proclaim the faith they feel so fervently—
and that they may never become lukewarm. In Jesus'
name. Amen.

died 304: According to legend, Emerentiana, while still a
catechumen, was found praying at the tomb of her recently
martyred foster-sister Saint Agnes, and the mob stoned
Emerentiana to death when she professed her Christian faith.

—JANUARY 24—
Saint Francis de Sales
PATRON OF EDITORS, JOURNALISTS,
AND WRITERS; INVOKED AGAINST DEAFNESS

Saint Francis, you who were a great defender of the
faith, send your spirit to me when my faith is weakened. Show me the way of Truth when I find myself
lost amid errors and temptations. Gift me with your
eloquent voice whenever I must give witness to
Christ.

O dear Saint Francis, above all, help me to follow your example of gentleness and love, so that
the love of God may shine through me to all the
world.

As well, dear saint, bless my work in publishing,
that I may bring truth and joy to people through
the printed word. In Jesus' name I pray. Amen.

1567–1622: From his native Savoy he was sent as a missionary to the Protestants in the Chablais. On the basis of his success, he was eventually made bishop of Geneva. With Saint Jane Frances de Chantal he founded the order of Visitation Nuns. He is a Doctor of the Church, and his works include *Treatise on the Love of God* and *Introduction to the Devout Life.*

—JANUARY 25—

Saint Paul
The Conversion

PATRON OF GREECE, MALTA, ROPE MAKERS, TENTMAKERS, AND UPHOLSTERERS

O glorious Saint Paul, who, from being a persecutor of the Christian name, became its most zealous apostle, and who, to carry the knowledge of Jesus, our divine Savior, to the uttermost parts of the earth, joyfully suffered prison, scourgings, stonings, shipwreck, and all manner of persecutions, and who finished your course by shedding the last drop of your blood: obtain for us the grace to accept, as favors bestowed by the mercy of God, the infirmities, sufferings, and misfortunes of this life, that we may not grow slack in our service of God by reason of these vicissitudes of our exile, but that we may the rather show ourselves ever more devoted. Amen.

Pray for us, Saint Paul the Apostle, that we may be made worthy of the promises of Christ.

THE RACCOLTA

c. 3–c. 67: Born at Tarsus, Paul was a Pharisee, a Roman citizen, and a tentmaker. He took an active part in the stoning of Saint Stephen and attempted to stamp out Christianity, but after his miraculous conversion on the road to

Damascus he preached Christ to the Gentiles, establishing churches and surviving dangers of all sorts. Legend holds that Paul was beheaded in Rome.

—JANUARY 26—

Saint Paula of Rome

PATRON OF WIDOWS AND WRITERS

Holy Saint Paula, your example of simple and peaceful living inspired others in the Holy Land to dedicate their lives to the Lord. We implore you now, intercede for justice and peace in the war-torn Holy Land—and in all places ravaged by war and violence. Pray that all people may reject the evil of violence and may come to understand the power of love. Protect especially those who are helpless in the face of war—the children, the seniors, the sick— and ask God to keep them from harm.

O holy saint, pray also for all widows and widowers, that they can come to realize that their lives still have purpose, that God still has a good plan for them and good work for them to accomplish. Help them to run to our Lord, casting their cares upon him and relying as well upon the strengthening power of the Holy Spirit. In Jesus's name we pray. Amen.

born 347: Widowed with five children, Paula learned from Saint Marcella how to live simply. Paula ministered with Saint Jerome and, with her daughter Saint Eustochium, built a hospice, monastery, and convent in Bethlehem.

Saint Angela Merici

Dear Saint Angela, you are an example of prayerful and dedicated service to God's people. May your prayers help us to live the Gospel as witnesses to God's presence in the world. Teach us to overcome the obstacles of prejudice, selfishness, and fear, and show us that God is present to all people. Help all missionaries and teachers to spread God's reign by word and action. Show us how to trust in the presence of the Spirit, and pray that God will grant us the grace to know and live the Word. We ask this through your intercession and the intercession of all your faithful followers who now live with God. Amen.

1474–1540: Angela devoted herself to the care of sick women and to the education of girls. Joined by several companions, she founded the Institute of Saint Ursula, the first order of women specifically dedicated to teaching.

—JANUARY 28—

Saint Thomas Aquinas

PATRON OF SCHOLARS, THEOLOGIANS, AND PENCIL MAKERS

Saint Thomas, God called you to spend most of your life in academic pursuits, first as a student, and then as a professor of theology. In your work as a teacher, you desired to help your students apply what they learned to their lives, in order to grow in holiness. You realized that knowledge is meant to draw people closer to God. In your teaching you sought to communicate the truth, desiring to help your students become better Christians.

Pray for all students. Pray for those who may have difficulty in their studies, as well as for those who can study with ease. Pray that they may all be open to the truth, and always seek to better understand it. May they grow in knowledge so as to know God better and to be able to serve their brothers and sisters as the Lord desires. Saint Thomas, pray especially for theologians, that in their studies and research they may come to a deeper knowledge of revealed doctrine in keeping with the mind of the Church. May their lives reflect the holiness of the Word of God, which they seek to more fully understand.

MARIANNE LORRAINE TROUVÉ, F.S.P.

c. 1225–1274: Born in Rocca Secca, Italy, Thomas spent his life in teaching in France and Italy. His principal works are *Summa contra Gentiles* and *Summa Theologica*, a work so vast that because of it Saint Thomas is called the Universal Teacher. He is a Doctor of the Church.

—JANUARY 29—

Blessed Boleslawa Maria Lament

O Blessed Boleslawa, you set yourself apart by showing great sensitivity to human misfortune. I implore you, then, to continue to intercede on behalf of all those who are suffering now, particularly those who are displaced or made cold or hungry or tired by the vagaries of war. I ask your special blessing on the people of *(mention request)*: ask the Lord to bring them all that they need, but especially ask the Lord to comfort them with his boundless love. And help me discover what I myself might do to ease the sufferings of these, your children. The burden seems

so massive, and my ability to help so small—inspire
me, that I may know how I may be of service. I ask
for your blessing upon all my efforts, in the name
of our Lord, Jesus Christ. Amen.

1862–1946: From Lowicz, Poland, Boleslawa founded the
Missionary Sisters of the Holy Family, concentrating her
ministry on the forgotten suffering people of the modern
world. She also worked ceaselessly to improve relations
between Roman Catholics and the Orthodox faithful in
Poland.

—JANUARY 30—

Saint Bathildis

Saint Bathildis, who suffered the indignities of slavery yourself, we implore your intercession to free
all those enslaved today—those enslaved by poverty, by sickness and pain, by prejudice, by ignorance, and yes, those actually forced to perform slave
labor, even in our time. As the Lord came to set
captives free, so, we implore you, beg him to eman-
cipate all who still suffer from slavery's degrada-
tion.

O holy Saint Bathildis, pray also for those whose
dignity is demeaned and diminished in our society,
especially unborn children, people with disabilities,
people who are terminally ill, and all those who face
prejudice in their lives. Pray for us all, that we may
accept with joy the diversity of God's created people
and treat all of our brothers and sisters with God's
love and peace. We ask this through Jesus, our great
emancipator. Amen.

died 680: Sold as a slave to a mayor in France, this English girl attracted the love of King Clovis II, who married her. When her husband died, she served as regent of their sons. She also promoted the release of captives destined to slavery. Finally, she entered the monastery of Chelles, choosing to work at the lowliest of tasks.

—JANUARY 31—

Saint John Bosco

PATRON OF APPRENTICES AND EDITORS

O glorious Saint John Bosco, who in order to lead young people to the feet of the divine Master and to form them in the light of faith and Christian morality heroically sacrificed yourself to the very end of your life and founded a proper religious institute destined to endure and to bring to the farthest boundaries of the earth your glorious work, obtain also for us from our Lord a holy love for young people who are exposed to so many seductions in order that we may generously spend ourselves in supporting them against the snares of the devil, in keeping them safe from the dangers of the world, and in guiding them, pure and holy, in the path that leads to God.

THE RACCOLTA

1815–1888: John's lifelong work was the education of boys, and the congregation he founded, the Salesians, grew rapidly and spread throughout Europe and the foreign missions. He also founded the Daughters of Mary Auxiliatrix for the education of girls.

February

Saint Brigid of Kildare

PATRON OF IRELAND, NEW ZEALAND,
MILKMAIDS, FUGITIVES, NEWBORNS,
NUNS, AND POULTRY RAISERS

Dear Saint Brigid, you gave to the Christian world the foundations of education for the laity and the opportunity for women of Ireland to use their energies and intellect in a way previously not open to them. An "ascetic with a smile," you helped lay the foundations of a golden age of learning and missionary endeavor. We pray you to continue to be a beacon of light and courage to all women who labor to lead others in the freedom of the Gospel. Pray that we receive the grace to remain open to growth all the days of our lives. Help us to meet difficult personalities with patience and understanding. And teach us to let love be the measure of our giving, in the fullness of God's being. We ask this in Jesus' name. Amen.

c. 450–c. 525: Among the most venerated of Irish saints, Brigid was born in Faughart, became a nun at an early age, and founded the monastery of Kildare, becoming the spiritual mother of Irish nuns for many centuries.

—FEBRUARY 2—

Venerable Francis Mary Paul Libermann

O Venerable Francis, the Heart of Mary moved you to respond to the Spirit and seek baptism. You also sought ordination, despite the epilepsy that many in the Church felt disqualified you from holy orders, and started a congregation to minister to the most neglected of all. Inspire me with that same courage and perseverance to follow the will of God despite all obstacles. Pray that I may rise above my limitations, physical or otherwise, that I may allow the Holy Spirit to use my infirmities to proclaim God's glory. And send me your spirit of generosity and enthusiasm for spreading the Good News. I ask this through Christ our Lord. Amen.

1802–1852: The son of a rabbi, Francis converted but was barred from the priesthood by his epilepsy. Nevertheless, he was retained as a spiritual adviser and novice master of the Eudists. Ordained at the age of thirty-nine, he took control over their missions in West Africa. He was elected superior general of the Congregation of the Holy Spirit, and his commentary on the Gospel of Saint John is considered on a par with the writings of Saint John of the Cross and Saint Teresa of Ávila.

—FEBRUARY 3—

Saint Aelred of Rievaulx

Dearest Saint Aelred, you sought only "to love and to be loved," and your only happiness was to make others happy and to cultivate close friendships and loving relationships with everyone you met. Bless us then, dear saint, with your spirit of friendship and love, that we, clasping one another's hands, may share with you and with one another the joy of friendship, human and divine, and may draw many others to God's community of love. Dear Aelred, teach us to be the type of friend that we ourselves would like to have. Teach us to cherish the friends we have already, blessing them with our attention and encouragement and support. And bless us with like friends, that we ourselves may enjoy a circle of trusted people who will love and care for us.

As well, pray for all those who find themselves friendless today. Bless them with friendship, and inspire us to befriend them when they cross our path.

Saint Aelred, in the sweet spirit of friendship, pray for us. Amen.

1110–1167: A Cistercian monk, Aelred was abbot of Revesby in Lincolnshire and then of Rievaulx. The author of *On Spiritual Friendship* and *The Mirror of Charity*, he was known for his gentleness with his monks.

—FEBRUARY 4—

Blessed Maria de Mattias

Blessed Maria, faith enabled you to discover in the cross of Jesus and in the gift of his precious blood the incentive and strength for your apostolic commitment. Obtain for us from God an increase of living faith, and help in our present need.

Blessed Maria, you expressed your adoration of the blood of Jesus through your prayer and loving service of the "dear neighbor." Obtain for us from God a strengthening of our hope, and that grace for which we have great need.

Blessed Maria, yours was a radical and joyous response to God, who so loved the world that God gave the only begotten Son for our salvation. Obtain for us an increase of love for God and neighbor, together with the grace for which we ask with confidence.

MISSIONARIES OF THE PRECIOUS BLOOD

1805–1866: Born in Vallecorsa, Italy, Maria was inspired by Saint Gaspar del Bufalo to found a congregation of women, the Adorers of the Blood of Christ.

—FEBRUARY 5—

Saint Agatha

PATRON OF WET NURSES,
BELL-FOUNDERS, AND JEWELERS

Holy Saint Agatha, the world knows little about you save that you prayed to the Lord, "Possess all that I am—you alone." May your prayer inspire me to offer my all to the Lord, no matter how little that might be and no matter the cost. Teach my heart to love Jesus so completely that I hold nothing back from him. And on that day when I face my Creator, ask the Lord to strengthen my faith, so that I may profess him Lord and Savior. Thus I implore you, in the name of Jesus, from whom you withheld nothing. Amen.

died c. 250: Born either at Catania or Palermo, Sicily, Agatha suffered martyrdom at Catania. According to legend, she was handed over because of her faith to a prostitute, and her breasts were cut off. Saint Peter was said to have cured her, but she died in prison. Her intercessions have preserved Catania from the eruptions of Mount Etna.

—FEBRUARY 6—

Saint Paul Miki
and Companions

O blessed saints, Japanese martyrs for the faith, pray for me, that I may have the faith to follow Jesus and the courage to profess Christ always.

Saint Paul Miki, pray for me.

Saint Francis, pray for me.

Saint Cosmas Takeya, pray for me.

Saint Peter Sukejiro, pray for me.

Saint Michael Kozaki, pray for me.

Saint James Kisai, pray for me.

Saint Paul Ibaraki, pray for me.

Saint John of Goto, pray for me.

Saint Louis Ibaraki, pray for me.

Saint Anthony, pray for me.

Saint Peter Baptist, pray for me.

Saint Martin of the Ascension, pray for me.

Saint Philip of Jesus, pray for me.

Saint Gonzalo Garcia, pray for me.

Saint Francis Blanco, pray for me.

Saint Francis of Saint Michael, pray for me.

Saint Matthias, pray for me.

Saint Leo Karasumaru, pray for me.

Saint Bonaventure, pray for me.

Saint Thomas Kozaki, pray for me.

Saint Joachim Sakakibara, pray for me.

Saint Francis, pray for me.

Saint Thomas Dangi, pray for me.

Saint John Kinuya, pray for me.

Saint Gabriel, pray for me.

Saint Paul Suzuki, pray for me.

O holy saints, martyrs for Jesus, pray for me, now and at the hour of my death. Amen.

died 1597: Paul Miki was one of twenty-six Christians crucified on a hill overlooking Nagasaki by the forces of the Japanese shogun Hideyoshi. A Japanese native, educated as a boy in the Jesuit school, Paul treasured his vocation to spread the Gospel and was approaching ordination. Speaking out before his execution, he asked that his blood fall on his fellows "as a fruitful rain." His fellow martyrs were Japanese, Spanish, Mexican, and Indian; the youngest among them was only twelve.

—FEBRUARY 7—

Saint Aegidius Mary of Saint Joseph Pontillo

Holy Saint Aegidius, you sacrificed your time and energies in face-to-face confrontations with pain and suffering. Indeed, you are the patron of those who are despised because of sickness. So I implore your intercession on behalf of those very people, the people who are too poor to afford medical care, who have to take care of themselves or rely upon the occasional charity of kind souls. Protect them, and bring them healing. Most of all, bring them love, that they may know through me and my neighbors that God has not abandoned them but has sent them what they need. And keep me mindful of my responsibility to be my brothers' and sisters' keeper. Through Christ our Lord. Amen.

1729–1812: Born in Taranto, Italy, Aegidius made his living as a rope maker until he was accepted as a lay brother with the Discalced Friars Minor of Saint Peter of Alcántara. As a porter in Naples, he had many opportunities for charitable acts. He was busy every day with the wounded or sick, and he sought out those who were forced outside the city, particularly people with leprosy.

—FEBRUARY 8—

Blessed Jacoba de Settesoli

Blessed Jacoba, you ministered to those who served Lady Poverty, supporting them as they spread the Lord's Gospel. Send me your spirit of charity, that I too may offer alms unstintingly, seeing in all people, but especially the homeless and the hungry, the face of God.

Pray also that I may find good friends, godly friends, people who will support me in my spiritual journey, and people who will benefit from my friendship. Bless me and my friends, that our friendships may be mutually loving and supportive. Through Christ our Lord. Amen.

died 1273: A noblewoman, Jacoba offered hospitality to Saint Francis when he came to Rome. When her husband died, she couldn't enter the Poor Clares because she had to care for her sons, so she became a Third Order Franciscan.

—FEBRUARY 9—

Saint Miguel Febres Cordero

Saint Miguel, holy scholar, you never hesitated to present the truth to your students. Teach me to discern the truth in all things, for I am sometimes confused about what is true and what is false. Reveal to me particularly the truth of faith, for my mind sometimes cannot wrap itself around the mysteries of Christianity nor accept what seems to me inexplicable in our faith. Help me to accept the truth revealed within me, the truth that comes from God within, the truth that God whispers in my heart and to my soul. And help me most of all, dear saint, to use my new doubts in a positive way, that I may continue to search for what is true. I ask this in the name of Jesus, Lord of Truth. Amen.

1854–1910: Born in Ecuador to a prominent family, Miguel did not walk until he was five because of his malformed feet, and then only because he received a heavenly vision. Miguel was the first native Ecuadorian to become a Christian Brother, and he became a gifted teacher. A famous researcher, he was admitted to the Academies of France, Ecuador, and Spain. He was in Spain during the revolution of 1909, and his exertions on behalf of his novices led to his death from pneumonia shortly afterward. He is listed among the incorruptibles.

—FEBRUARY 10—

Saint Scholastica

PATRON OF RAIN; INVOKED AGAINST CHILDHOOD CONVULSIONS

Loving daughter of God, dearest Saint Scholastica, your love was stronger than adherence to rule, and God heard your prayer because of your great faith. Pray likewise for all those who have received the gift of prayer and charity. Teach us to live by the law of love. Remind us to pray and to trust in God's care for us. Ask the Lord to send us the grace to be always people of prayer and to do our work with reverence and creativity. And implore God's kindness upon all families, that they may grow closer in love and trust of one another. This we ask through Jesus our Lord, God's incarnate Word. Amen.

died c. 550: Sister of Saint Benedict, Scholastica became a nun and lived near Montecassino under her brother's direction. She is regarded as the first Benedictine nun.

Saint Lazarus of Milan

Saint Lazarus, you never lost sight of your duty to lead and serve your people. Despite mortal dangers, your trust in God and faith in public prayer never wavered, and your followers, in emulating you, were able to maintain their faith during perilous times. Your story reminds me of the power of personal example, and so I ask for your blessing upon the example I set for others. Other people may base their opinion of Christians upon what I do or say, so help me to live a life worthy of the name I bear. I ask this through our Lord, Jesus Christ, whose name we bear. Amen.

died c. 450: Archbishop of Milan, Lazarus was the mainstay of his flock during the invasion of the Ostrogoths. He is believed to have developed the Rogationtide litanies.

Saint Ethelwald of Lindisfarne

Saint Ethelwald, you had such love and reverence for God's Word that you had the Book of Gospels decorated with the finest of precious metals and stones. Instill in me a similar love for the Word of God, and remind me that it is more valuable than any collection of gold or jewels. Teach me to read it daily, and help me to learn from God's Word the way of love. I pray in the name of Jesus our Lord, the Living Word. Amen.

died c. 740: Ethelwald was one of Saint Cuthbert's chief helpers. Prior and then abbot of Old Melrose in Scotland, Ethelwald finally succeeded to the see of Lindisfarne. He commissioned Saint Bilfrid to embellish the famous Lindisfarne Book of Gospels with gold, silver, and precious stones.

—FEBRUARY 13—

Saint Prisca

Holy Saint Prisca, you and your husband, Aquila, were the first couple-ministers, traveling fearlessly with Saint Paul and proclaiming the Word by his side. Send graces down to all couples who minister together, that their lives may witness to the love possible between two people who enter into faithful, committed relationships. And bless their ministry, that they may witness to the love Jesus Christ has for all people.

Dear Saint Prisca, pray also for those people whose marriages suffer from a lack of agreement on matters of faith. Bless them with a willingness to be open to their partner's viewpoint, and keep them from falling into inflexibility. Remind them that God loves all people of all faiths. This I pray through Jesus Christ our Lord. Amen.

first century: Prisca and her husband, Aquila, a tentmaker, having been banished from Rome by an edict of Claudius, met Saint Paul in Corinth. Over the next several years they traveled and preached with Paul, living for a while in Ephesus and eventually returning to Rome. According to tradition, Prisca and Aquila were martyred in Rome. The Eastern churches celebrate their feast on February 13; in the West, their feast is July 8.

—FEBRUARY 14—

Saints Cyril and Methodius

PATRONS OF THE CZECH REPUBLIC, SLOVENIA, EUROPE, AND THE SLAVS

O Saints Cyril and Methodius, who brought the faith with admirable dedication to peoples thirsty for the truth and the light, let the whole Church always proclaim the crucified and the Risen Christ, the Redeemer of [humankind]!

O Saints Cyril and Methodius, who, in your hard and difficult missionary apostolate always remained deeply bound to the Church of Constantinople and to the Roman See of Peter, bring it about that the two sister Churches, the Catholic Church and the Orthodox, having overcome the elements of division in charity and truth, may soon reach the full union desired!

O Saints Cyril and Methodius, who, with the sincere spirit of brotherhood, approached different peoples to bring to all the message of universal love preached by Christ, bring it about that the peoples of the European continent, aware of their common Christian heritage, may live in mutual respect for just rights and in solidarity, and be peacemakers among all the nations of the world!

O Saints Cyril and Methodius, who, driven by love for Christ, abandoned everything to serve the Gospel, protect the Church of God: me, Peter's successor in the Roman See; the bishops, priests, men and women religious, men and women missionaries, fathers, mothers, young men, young women, the poor, the sick, and the suffering; may each of us, in the place in which Divine Providence has placed us, be a worthy "laborer" of the Lord's harvest! Amen!

POPE JOHN PAUL II

Cyril: died 869: A priest in Greece, he was sent with his brother into Moravia as a missionary. He died in Rome.

Methodius: died 847: Having built a monastery on the island of Chio as a retreat, he was summoned to Constantinople by Saint Nicephorus. After years of persecution, Methodius was named Patriarch of Constantinople.

—FEBRUARY 15—

Saint Claude de la Colombière

O Saint Claude, your devotion to the Heart of Christ was a source of balance and spiritual strengthening for Christian communities so often faced with increasing unbelief. As you helped spread devotion to Jesus' Sacred Heart in your time, inspire me today with the same devotion, that I may center my life around Christ's presence. Teach me as well to rely on Jesus' mercy and forgiveness, and to fly into his arms and allow him to embrace me with his love. I ask this in the name of Jesus, our Lord, who died on our behalf for the forgiveness of all sins. Amen.

1641–1682: A Jesuit and superior of Paray-le-Monial College in Paris, Claude was Saint Margaret Mary Alacoque's spiritual director and coadjutor in propagating devotion to the Sacred Heart of Jesus. He later served as chaplain to the Duchess of York during the reign of King Charles II of England; falsely accused of conspiracy to bring Roman Catholicism back to England, he never recovered from the tortures he received at the hands of the English and spent his last few years in poor health at Paray-le-Monial, a so-called "dry" martyr for the faith.

—FEBRUARY 16—

Blessed Joseph Allamano

Dear Blessed Joseph, you received an ardent desire
to cooperate in God's plan of universal salvation,
educating priests and serving as father of missionaries. Pray that I may grow in the same zeal as to
give up even my own life for the sake of my brothers and sisters and to dedicate my life for the good
of all. Help me to respond to the Lord's call to bring
the Good News to all the nations. Most of all, inspire me to seek God above all else. I pray this
through Jesus Christ our Lord. Amen.

1851–1926: From Castelnuovo d'Asti, Italy, Joseph suffered
from hemoptysis (coughing up blood). Nevertheless, he was
ordained. He was the founder of the Consolata Missionary
Fathers, which during his lifetime labored in Africa and
North and South America, running hospitals, dispensaries,
schools, and seminaries. He also founded the Consolata
Missionary Sisters, at the request of Pope Saint Pius X.

—FEBRUARY 17—

Seven Founders of
the Order of Servites

O blessed saints, brothers who devoutly venerated
the Virgin Mary, infuse in me the piety of your own
spirit, which led you to adopt a life of prayer, peace,
and service apart from the strife of the times in which
you found yourselves. Help me to devote myself to
prayer, bless me with peace, and reveal to me the
ways I may serve my sisters and brothers.
  Saint Buonfiglio Monaldo, pray for me.
  Saint Alexis Falconieri, pray for me.
  Saint Benedict dell'Antella, pray for me.

Saint Bartholomew Amidei, pray for me.
Saint Ricovera Uguccione, pray for me.
Saint Gerardino Sostegni, pray for me.
Saint John Buonagiunta, pray for me.
O holy saints of God, pray for me, that I may
discern the way to make my life decisively centered
in Christ. Amen.

On the Feast of the Assumption, 1233, the Blessed Mother
appeared to seven members of a Florentine Confraternity
gathered in prayer. Seven years later, these noblemen of Florence decided to withdraw to a solitary place for prayer and
service to God. They adopted the rule of Saint Augustine
and the name Servants of Mary.

—FEBRUARY 18—

Blessed Fra Angelico

PATRON OF ARTISTS

Most Blessed Fra Angelico, your artistic masterpieces
mirror your religious life and speak eloquently of your
virtue and your interior union with Christ. Teach me,
I pray, how I may allow my own spiritual nature to
emerge in the work that I do. My work is not artistic
as yours was, nor is it even remotely religious; nevertheless, I want to please God with what I do, and my
spirit wants to express itself through what I do. So
even if my work is mundane and even sometimes te-
dious, remind me that God is pleased when what I do
brings blessings to other people. Remind me to find
joy in the small accomplishments, in the tiny blessings, and, sometimes, even in the beautiful gestures I
bring to others people's lives. I ask your blessing in
the name of our God, Creator of all beauty. Amen.

c. 1387–1455: Named Giovanni da Fiesole, Fra Angelico
was one of the greatest religious painters of all time. A Do-

minican priest, he lived in Fiesole, Florence, Cortona, and Rome and completed art for Popes Eugenius IV and Nicholas V. In addition to his angelic paintings, he was known for his remarkable virtue.

—FEBRUARY 19—

Saint Conrad of Piacenza

Most glorious Saint Conrad, you were bold in accepting responsibility for your own actions. The fallout ruined you, at least as the world judges success and failure, but you, dear saint, used the opportunity for the glory of God, and the results were wonderful.

O Conrad, when I am tempted to abandon my duties and avoid my responsibilities, strengthen my faith, that I may accept what is mine and do what is right with conviction. Encourage me when I fear the consequences, and help me to cast my cares upon the Lord's providence, believing that his love will care for me beyond my wildest imaginings and that he will never abandon me. And when the outlook of my actions looks bleak beyond repair, bless me with the faith of trusting in the Lord to bring all things well again. In the name of Jesus, our providence, I pray. Amen.

1290–1354: A nobleman of Piacenza, Conrad caused a destructive conflagration during a hunting trip, and an innocent peasant was condemned to death as the perpetrator. Conrad publicly confessed his responsibility for the disaster when he saw the man on the way to being executed, forfeiting all his fortune to make restitution. Conrad and his wife then decided to enter the religious life; she became a Poor Clare, and he a Third Order Franciscan. Seeking seclusion, Conrad retired to a hermitage near Syracuse, Sicily, spending his life in prayer and in the care of the sick.

—FEBRUARY 20—

Blessed Elizabeth Bartholomea Picenardi of Mantua

Blessed Elizabeth, you left a life of ease to devote yourself to serving God's children, and your life of servanthood is for me a beacon in a world that glorifies self-centeredness. Encourage me to examine my life, that I may discern where it falls short of God's plan, that I may discover what particular work God is calling me to follow. Show me the folly, the inevitable dissatisfaction of self-indulgence. Teach me the joys of servanthood, that I may see Christ in all people and serve them, and him, with love. O Blessed Elizabeth, pray for me. Amen.

1428–1468: Born to a noble family, Elizabeth entered the third order of the Servites. Several young girls banded together to live in community under her direction. She was known for her humility, gentleness, and supernatural gifts.

—FEBRUARY 21—

Saint Peter Damian

O holy Saint Peter, Christ and the service of his Church were the first love of your life. Pray for me, that I may so love Jesus that I give myself entirely to him. Pray also that in so doing I cast off my selfish ways and dedicate myself entirely to serving the Church, particularly those members of the human family who are so often neglected—the homeless, the sick, the imprisoned. Show me how I may help them, and how I may lead others to help them.

Saint Peter, I pray also that you will intercede on behalf of all orphans. Please, dear orphan saint, provide for their every need. Help find them loving homes. Bring them people who will serve as loving parents and raise them as their own. I ask this through Christ our Lord. Amen.

1007–1072: Born at Ravenna, Italy, Peter was orphaned and left in the charge of a married brother who ill-treated him, but another brother took over and paid for his schooling. Peter joined the Benedictines and became a model monk and eventually abbot. He was called to be cardinal-bishop of Ostia and served several popes on various delicate international missions. Due to his prolific and profound theological writings he was named a Doctor of the Church.

—FEBRUARY 22—

Saint Margaret of Cortona

PATRON OF PROSTITUTES

Glorified Saint Margaret, who did not spare your body, make us ashamed of our cowardly pampering. God promised you while you were on earth that he would show mercy to anyone who asked for it through your intercession, so give us one spark of your love for the crucified Christ, to ignite our cold hearts. Help us to live as if we understood the meaning of life. And ask Jesus to shower his Divine Mercy upon us. Amen.

1247–1297: Born in Tuscany, Margaret was a farmer's daughter who became mistress to a young nobleman. In his sudden death she saw God's judgment and publicly confessed her sins. She became a Franciscan tertiary and founded a convent and a hospital.

Saint Polycarp of Smyrna

Remember, O most holy Saint Polycarp, that your work as bishop is not at an end. You taught your flock to follow Jesus, and your personal example inspired others to share in your martyrdom. I ask, therefore, for your blessing, that I may learn from you what it means to follow Jesus, and that I may not shrink from the sometimes dire and sometimes fatal cost of discipleship. In times of trial and persecution—and they come with too frequent regularity, dear saint—implore the Lord on my behalf, that he will strengthen me and give me courage. Help me to be, like you, a fine and loving and Christian example to others.

Be my guardian and protector, dear saint. Hear my prayer, and grant me the graces I now ask of you *(mention request)*. O Saint Polycarp, pray for me. Amen.

died 156: As bishop of Smyrna, Polycarp, with his friend Saint Ignatius of Antioch, was the link between the apostles and subsequent generations of Christians. Polycarp was burned alive, along with twelve of his own disciples.

—FEBRUARY 24—

Blessed Josepha Naval Girbes

Dear Josepha, your disciples filled cloistered con-
vents, yet you knew you were not called to that type
of religious life yourself. You who were so discern-
ing, teach me, I pray, to discern my own particular
calling. Teach me to listen to the voice of God speaking in my heart, that I may know what God intends
for me to do with my life. As well, pray that when it
does come I may have the courage to follow the call
wherever it may lead me. Strengthen me, that I may
be true to my own truth, that I may be true to the
purpose for which God made me. I implore your
intercession especially regarding *(mention request)*,
for a decision is required, yet I am perplexed about
what to do. Please pray for me, that God will guide
me in this decision. I ask your help in Jesus' name.
Amen.

1820–1893: Born near Valencia, Spain, Josepha took a vow
of perpetual virginity and became a Third Order Carmelite,
working to prepare other young women in her area for
marriage or religious life. A learned mystic, Josepha took
advantage of the time she spent teaching embroidery to also
teach catechism and prayer. She is honored also for fostering many religious vocations.

—FEBRUARY 25—

Saint Walburga

PATRON OF CROPS; INVOKED AGAINST COUGHS, FRENZY, AND THE PLAGUE

Dearest Saint Walburga, lily of purity and model of humility, I bring my humble prayer to you. You are still working miraculous cures among God's people, so I implore you to intercede with the Lord on my behalf, that I may obtain the miracle that I so desperately desire, if it be God's will. *(Mention request.)*
Pray also that I may, like you, despise the pomps and vanities of the world. Pray that I may, like you, make an entire offering of myself to our Lord. Pray that I may, like you, faithfully serve God in perfect love. Help me also that I may become, like you, an example of faith well lived to all those I encounter. Pray for me, O holy Saint Walburga, that I may be made worthy of the promises of Christ. Amen.

died 779: Sister of Saints Willibald and Winebald, Walburga became a nun and followed Saint Lioba to Germany. She became abbess of Heidenheim, and her relics were translated to Eichstätt, where remarkable cures are ascribed to the fluid exuding from the rocks upon which her shrine rests.

—FEBRUARY 26—

Blessed Isabelle of France

Dear Blessed Isabelle, you chose a life of solitude so that you could commune in prayer with our Lord. Send me your spirit, that I may set aside time out of the day to talk to God. Pray for me to give myself to Jesus more often, so that I may know him more and more.

O Isabelle, remind me also to share of my bounty with those who serve the Lord. And intercede on behalf of religious everywhere, so that they may not suffer from lack of the necessities of life. Help particularly women religious, that their retirement years may be filled with joy and sufficiency. To that end, inspire me and all young persons to attend to the needs of our elder religious. In Jesus' name I pray. Amen.

1225–1270: Daughter of King Louis VIII of France and Blanche of Castile, Isabelle was a gifted student who chose a life of seclusion and prayer. She also founded a convent for Poor Clares, supporting them with income from her properties, though she herself was too ill to keep the rule. She is known for her ecstasies in prayer.

—FEBRUARY 27—

Saint Gabriel of Our Lady of Sorrows

O holy Saint Gabriel, God taught you to have the sorrows of our most dear Mother in perpetual remembrance. Through her, God glorified you with the fame of holiness and miracles. By your intercession and example, then, help me in my suffering and pain, that by sharing the pain of Our Lady of Sorrows I may be blessed with her maternal protection. Ask her to pray for me to her Son, that I may thus be saved. Amen.

1838–1862: Born Francis Possenti at Assisi, Gabriel joined the Passionist Fathers and died of consumption six years later. He was noted for heroic self-denial in small things.

—FEBRUARY 28—

Blessed Daniel Brottier

O Blessed Daniel, apostle of Christ, the Lord filled you with faith, love, and missionary zeal, giving you the strength to lighten the burden of many human sorrows. With unselfish love you served soldiers during the Great War and ministered to war orphans afterward.

We pray you, continue to send your blessings upon all those who serve in armies, navies, and military forces throughout the world. Ease their loneliness, protect them from harm, and shower them with God's love. Inspire us to reach out with hospitality and love to soldiers, sailors, and all those who wear the military uniforms of their countries.

As well, we pray you, continue to send your blessings upon all those children who have lost their parents. Ease their loneliness, protect them from harm, and shower them with God's love. Inspire us to reach out with tenderness and love to all orphans and to provide them with food, clothing, shelter, and a place to call home.

O Blessed Daniel, pray for us, that we may be made worthy of the promises of Christ. Amen.

1876–1938: After becoming a Holy Ghost Father and serving as a missionary in Senegal, Daniel became a legend in the French Army, serving as chaplain on the front lines during World War I. Afterward, he directed the orphanage at Auteuil, France, transforming a collapsing institute into a center that raised thousands of boys.

March

—MARCH 1—

Saint David (Dewi)

PATRON OF POETS AND WALES

David, show me the way to make even small tasks and humdrum activities occasions for prayer. Kindle in me the love of God so that even when I am doing nonspiritual work I will be able to keep the spirit of prayer and have a strong awareness of the divine presence.

TOM COWAN

fifth–sixth centuries: The son of Saint Non, who was raped by a local ruler, David studied with Saint Paulinus on an unidentified island. He established monastic communities in many places and in time founded the great monastery at Mynyw (Menevia) in the remote southwestern part of Wales. The place, now called Saint David's, followed an exceedingly austere rule and became a veritable nursery of saints.

—MARCH 2—

Blessed Charles the Good

Blessed Charles, you fought for justice and championed the poor against the wealthy. You were one of the first to enact policies of preferential option for the poor, but for this you were martyred. Holy

Charles, intercede on behalf of the poor today. Inspire authorities and legislators and voters, that they and we may support a preferential option for the poor. Protect us and them from all opposition. Ask the Lord to soften our hearts, that we may not be greedy, selfish, and mean-spirited men and women who refuse to share the bounty we enjoy from God, but that we may come to understand what God wants of our plenty. Teach us to share joyfully and to trust that the Lord's providence will provide all that we will need. Amen.

died 1127: Son of Saint Canute of Denmark, Charles fought in the second Crusade and succeeded Robert II as Count of Flanders. Charles's rule was a continuous defense of the poor against profiteers, both clerical and lay. Called "the Good" by popular acclamation, he was murdered in the church of Saint Donatian at Brugges by a conspiracy of the wealthy whom he had offended.

—MARCH 3—

Blessed Katharine Drexel

Blessed Katharine, God called you to share the message of the Gospel and the life of the Eucharist with the poor and oppressed among Native and African-American peoples. Through your intercession, may we grow in the faith and love that will enable us to be united as brothers and sisters in God. Teach us to do peacefully at each moment what ought to be done. Show us how to pray to the Heart of Jesus. Explain to us how to put God's love into action. Help us to trust in the universal and eucharistic presence of the Lord. And ask Jesus to lead us in his footsteps, opening us to the presence of the Spirit and turning our words and actions to peace and love. Amen.

1858–1955: Heir to a Philadelphia banking fortune,
Katharine decided to dedicate her life and her resources to
the education of Native American and African-American
children. She founded the Sisters of the Blessed Sacrament
for Indians and Colored People and established Xavier University in New Orleans.

—MARCH 4—

Saint Casimir

PATRON OF POLAND AND LITHUANIA;
INVOKED AGAINST THE PLAGUE

Saint Casimir, Patron Saint of Lithuania, intercede
for us before the Almighty so that God will grant us
the grace that our hearts be enflamed by an ardent
faith and love of one another; that our youth com-
prehend the beauty of a chaste and virtuous life;
and that the parental Providence of God may lead
our entire nation down the path of devotion to God's
commandments toward peace and prosperity. Amen.
Saint Casimir, pray for us.

TRADITIONAL

1458–1483: The second son of King Casimir IV of Poland,
Casimir was expected to expand the kingdom by seizing
the crown of Hungary, but, refusing, he was imprisoned by
his father. After a short time, he was released, and he devoted the rest of his life to prayer and study.

—MARCH 5—

Blessed Jeremiah
of Valachia Kostistk

Most Blessed Jeremiah, you are the first Romanian
to ascend officially to the honors of the altar. With
your ministry to the poor and abandoned, to the

nobles and religious, you brought together the power elite and the outcasts, the rich and the poor, the East and the West. Inspire me with your spirit of bridge-building, that I may be an example of inclusiveness, that my actions may never exclude or be interpreted as exclusive by anyone. Help me to work for understanding among groups and inclusiveness for all at God's table and banquet of grace, as well as in society. Teach me the way of acceptance, and help me to teach others the ways of reconciliation and coexistence. I ask this in the name of our Lord, who sought out the outcasts of his society to embrace them in his kingdom. Amen.

1556–1625: Born in Zaro, Romania, Jeremiah became a Franciscan and traveled to Naples and the surrounding region, startling the people there with his selfless imitation of Christ. He ministered to the sick and abandoned but also provided medical care to bishops and nobles. His reputation for wise counsel attracted people from all walks of life. Jeremiah stands as the historical symbol of the bridge between East and West.

—MARCH 6—

Saint Colette

Holy Saint Colette, you did not shrink from accomplishing the task Brother Francis assigned to you, despite terrible opposition and personal persecution. I implore you, then, to be with me when I face jobs that seem overwhelming. Pray for me, that I may find the strength and courage to persevere despite all obstacles, and that I may have the wisdom to discern ways to overcome all opposition. And intercede for me, that I may win over my opponents with grace, love, and truth.

As well, Saint Collette, pray for all religious or-

ders, that they may remain true to the loving example of their founders. If need be, ask the Lord to
send them reformers, so that they can find their way
back to Jesus. And at all times, be with them in spirit,
so that all religious may remember your example and
be inspired to recommit themselves to the way of Jesus,
which is the way of love. In Jesus' name. Amen.

died 1447: Having entered the Third Order Franciscans,
Colette had a vision in which Saint Francis told her to reform the Poor Clares. She encountered much opposition in
this mission, but her perseverance enabled her to enact reforms and found seventeen new houses of Poor Clare observance. She was noted for her deep prayer life.

—MARCH 7—

Saints Perpetua, Felicity, and Companions

Dear Perpetua, even as the hour of your death approached, you were concerned with the welfare of
others and comforted your father with these words:
"It shall happen as God shall choose, for assuredly
we depend not on our own power but on the power
of God." Dear saint, these words are also a comfort
to me, for there are many circumstances in my life
over which I seem to have no control. Help me, then,
to offer my life to God, that I may loosen my
stranglehold on things of this world and abandon
my worries. Strengthen me in my resolve to cast my
cares on the Lord, to trust in his love, which surely
will never abandon me. And even if I must suffer
pain and death for his sake, may I be assured that
he—and you, dearest saint, and all your companions—will be with me, comforting me and guiding
me into paradise. Amen.

died 203: Perpetua was a young married woman of good social position. Felicity, also married, was a slave. Together with a number of catechumens they were imprisoned at Carthage and refused to renounce their Christian faith, despite the impassioned pleas of Perpetua's father. All were sent to the public games in the amphitheater, where Perpetua and Felicity were beheaded and the others killed by beasts.

—MARCH 8—

Saint John of God

PATRON OF BOOKSELLERS, HOSPITALS, NURSES, AND PRINTERS; INVOKED AGAINST ALCOHOLISM AND HEART DISEASE

Saint John of God, heavenly patron of the sick, I come to you in prayer to seek your help in my present sickness. Through the love that Jesus had for you in choosing you for the sublime vocation of serving the sick, and through the tender affection with which the Blessed Virgin Mary placed upon your head a crown of thorns as a symbol of the sufferings you would undergo in the service of the sick to attain to your crown of glory, I beg you to intercede for me to Jesus and Mary that they may grant me a cure, if this should be according to the will of God.

How patiently you bore the sufferings of your own disease! Teach me to carry with cheerful resignation the cross that God has given me. Let me never complain or lose courage. Help me to understand that suffering is a very important means of sanctifying my soul, of atoning for my many sins, and of reaping a plentiful harvest of merit for heaven. I trust in your great love for the sick and in the power of your intercession to help them. Help me, good Saint John, and beg the God whose name you bear to touch me as he touched the sick while on earth, that through his almighty power health may return to my body. And as you derived strength in your own sufferings from the crucifix, so may I find in it the strength I need, that I may be able to say what you did to Jesus crucified: "Lord, thy thorns are my roses and thy sufferings my paradise."

Good Saint John, lover of those who suffer and special patron of the sick, I confidently place before you my earnest petition. *(Mention request.)*

I beg you to recommend my request to Mary, the Mother of Sorrows and Health of the Sick, that both Mary and you may present it to Jesus, the Divine Physician.

Saint John of God, patron of the sick and beloved of Jesus and Mary, pray to them for me and obtain my request.

REV. LAWRENCE G. LOVASIK, S.V.D.

1495–1550: From Portugal, John worked as a shepherd, soldier, peddler, superintendent of slaves, vendor of religious books, and at various other jobs until a sermon of Blessed John of Ávila led to his conversion. However, John of God was so fervent that people thought him mad. Finally, he settled in Granada and founded a hospital. This was the beginning of the new Order of Brothers Hospitallers (Brothers of Saint John of God).

—MARCH 9—

Saint Catherine of Bologna

PATRON OF ARTISTS

O Catherine, help me to imitate your virtues, to love Christ and his word, to love the Mass as my daily bread, and to love my brothers and sisters. Intercede for me, to request the grace I am seeking. *(Mention request.)* I know that no one who has turned to you for help has been disappointed; therefore, I put my humble supplication in your hands. I ask this in the name of Jesus Christ, our Lord. Amen.

1413–1463: Catherine took the veil of the Augustinians, who later became Poor Clares, and served as novice-mistress and then abbess in Bologna. Spending her life praying for sinners, she received amazing visions from God and committed her mystical experiences to writing. She is among the incorruptibles.

—MARCH 10—

Blessed Elias del Socorro Nieves

O Blessed Elias, you trusted totally in God; despite the many obstacles that delayed your vocation, you believed in your calling and persevered in your quest to serve God's people. When things do not go the way I have planned, I must admit, dear Elias, that I get impatient and testy. And I wonder why God doesn't intervene to clear away the obstacles, so that I can get on with God's work. Help me understand, Elias, that God's timetable is not necessarily the same as mine. Teach me patience, that I may take the longer view and look to eternity. And inspire me to persevere, that I may continue to pursue that special vocation given to me, no matter what it is, and no matter how long it may take to begin it. And once I do begin, inspire me to continue in it, with love and joy in the knowledge that it is a special and unique gift from God. I pray in Jesus' name. Amen.

1882–1928: Elias was parochial vicar of La Cañada de Caracheo, where he won the respect of the people. When Mexican authorities restricted religious services and the activities of priests, Elias moved to the hills and began a clandestine ministry. He was captured and eventually shot, caught up in the Mexican reign of terror.

—MARCH 11—

Saint Eulogius of Cordova

You put yourself at risk, Saint Eulogius, to protect a child of the faith, and you both met death on behalf of the truth. Teach me, dear saint, what things are more important than life and death. Inspire me with your love of truth, with your spirit of sacrifice, with your love of God and God's children. Most of all, encourage me in my encounters with people who are newly learning about the love of God, that my actions and words may welcome all people into the kingdom of God and may model God's unconditional love for all creation. Through Christ our Lord. Amen.

died 859: A prominent priest during the height of the Moorish persecution of Christians, Eulogius wrote *Exhortation to Martyrdom* and *Memorial of the Saints* for the encouragement of his fellow Christians. Having protected Leocritia, a convert from a noble Moorish family, from her irate parents, Eulogius himself was discovered and beheaded for the faith.

—MARCH 12—

Saint Maximilian of Rome

Saint Maximilian, you refused to serve two masters. Help me to evaluate the activities of my own government with the eyes of faith, so that I may know when I am being asked to do something opposed to the love of God. Bless me, that I may always know God's truth and that I may always follow God's calling, even if it contradicts what officials or politicians or even other citizens expect of me. Pray that I may have the courage to follow Christ instead of the crowd, despite the consequences. Help me also not to be too quick to judge others for their decisions, for we are all possessed of different knowledge and different callings. I ask your special intercession about *(mention request)*, for I am troubled in spirit and implore your guidance. In the name of Jesus our Lord. Amen.

died 295: Little is known of this Roman soldier who refused to continue his military service. As a Christian, Maximilian felt that he was called to pacifism. As well, he could not worship the emperor or the Roman gods, as he had consecrated his life to Jesus Christ. He was executed for "impiety."

—MARCH 13—

Saint Rodriguez

Saint Rodriguez, your life demonstrates the harm that can occur when religious practices divide families. Intercede, we pray, on behalf of all interfaith families, that these family members may learn to respect and honor one another's beliefs. Help all to learn from one another the truths that are not exclusive to particular religious practices or systems. And help all families to approach closer to the Divine, that they may love all their members as brothers and sisters and as children of God. In the name of God, who transcends religious differences and denominational lines. Amen.

died 857: A priest in the area of Cordova, Spain, Rodriguez was beaten senseless by his two brothers when he tried to break up a violent quarrel between them. His Muslim brother than carried Rodriguez through the streets and proclaimed that he had embraced Islam. When Rodriguez recovered from his injuries, he escaped, but he was hauled before the judge on the charge of abandoning Allah. Though he had never himself abandoned Christianity, he was imprisoned and, eventually, beheaded, along with Saint Solomon.

—MARCH 14—

Saint Matilda of Saxony

Holy Saint Matilda, you gave up your inheritance from your loving husband, living austerely in order to keep peace among your children; yet despite your example of loving forgiveness, your sons continued to quarrel. Pray that we may heed a mother's plea for peace among her children. Teach us to lead simple lives, so that we may not argue over money or worldly goods or any passing fancies. Send us your spirit of forgiveness and charity, so that we may live together amicably, forgetting past hurts and overlooking potential offenses. We pray for your intercession for better relationships among family members. Through Christ our Lord. Amen.

895–968: Wife of the German king Henry the Fowler, Matilda was known for her generosity and founded, among others, the Benedictine abbeys of Nordhausen, Pöhlde, Engern, and Quedlinburg. When her husband died, she suffered much at the hands of her sons, Otto and Henry, by whom she was despoiled of her possessions.

—MARCH 15—

Saint Clement
Maria Hofbauer

PATRON OF VIENNA

O Saint Clement, most faithful disciple of Jesus our Redeemer, from your tenderest infancy you regarded our Holy Catholic Faith as your only treasure and were solicitous to strengthen it in the hearts of the faithful with wonderful zeal and to make it known among all people. Obtain for us the grace to imitate your example and to learn to esteem the precious gift of the true faith above every other gift. Teach us to conform our actions to its holy maxims so that, placing in the practice of faith all our glory, we may exultingly repeat your words: "We confess, we are sinners, and devoid of every virtue; but we glory in the fact that we are children of the Holy Catholic Church."...

O Saint Clement, most loving disciple of Jesus our Redeemer, animated with the most ardent charity, you lived for God alone and made yourself all to all, to gain all for Jesus Christ. Persecutions and dangers, temptations and sufferings were not able to diminish your charity. Obtain for us, we implore you, at least a spark of your most burning love for God and our neighbor. Assist us by your prayers to be so united in harmony and charity that we may always love our Redeemer Jesus Christ and his Immaculate Mother, follow him steadfastly until death, and finally praise and bless him for all eternity.

Pray for us, that we may be made worthy of the promises of Christ.

THE REDEMPTORISTS

1751–1820: From Tasswitz, Moravia, Clement worked as a baker, became a hermit, and joined the Redemptorists. He went as a missionary to Warsaw, working among the poor and building orphanages and schools. Expelled by Napoleon, Clement returned to Vienna, eventually establishing a Roman Catholic college and revitalizing the religious life of the German nations.

—MARCH 16—

Saint Abraham Kidunaia

Abraham, if you were alive today on the streets of
our cities, we would treat you like a dirty, homeless
man. Most of us would shun you. Many would fear
you. Give me the insight to look at the homeless as
human beings like myself. Let me see in them the
same potential for prayer, devotion, and gentleness
that is in all of us. Help me to help them.

TOM COWAN

died c. 366: Leaving a wealthy home and a promising marriage, Abraham lived as a hermit in a desert near Edessa.
He was ordained and appointed to Beth-Kiduna, a town he
completely converted to Christianity.

—MARCH 17—

Saint Patrick

PATRON OF IRELAND AND NIGERIA;
INVOKED AGAINST SNAKES

We salute you, O great and glorious Saint Patrick,
Apostle of Ireland, ornament and glory of Christianity. We salute you, great saint, cherub of wisdom
and seraph of divine love. We rejoice at the favors
our Lord has so liberally bestowed on you.

Grant that we may imitate your perfect detachment from creatures, your confidence in God, your
abandonment to the divine will, your humility, obedience, and charity, your generosity in the practice
of virtue, and your great zeal for souls. And having
had the happiness of walking in your footsteps here
below, may we one day enjoy with you the bliss of
heaven.

RICHARD CARDINAL CUSHING

c. 389–c. 461: A Romano-Briton, Patrick was carried off as a slave to Ireland but escaped after six years. Having been consecrated a bishop, he returned to Ireland to take up missionary work and convert the Irish to Roman Catholicism.

—MARCH 18—

Saint Cyril of Jerusalem

Saint Cyril, when I am tempted to think of the lives of the saints as simple and placid, untouched by controversy, I think of your life and the difficulties you faced. Unjustly accused, you endured long exile from the home you loved. Nevertheless, you persevered and held fast to your faith, and in the end the Lord rewarded your love with a place near him in paradise.

So, dear saint, when I think that my life is too difficult, when enemies seem to pursue me on all sides, when danger forces me to quit my home and abandon all things that I love, pray for me. Bless me with the long view, that I may transcend the problems of the day and remember that God has a master plan, though I may never be able to discern it in this life. Help me to trust, and inspire me to persevere. Most of all, intercede for me, that God will send the Holy Spirit to me when I am feeling most desperate, to bear me up on eagle's wings. I pray in Jesus' name. Amen.

c. 315–387: Born near Jerusalem, Cyril became patriarch of the city from 350 until his death, though he spent seventeen of those years in exile, accused of siding with the Arian heresy. His instructions on Christian doctrine, addressed to catechumens, are gems of theological literature, for which he was named a Doctor of the Church.

—MARCH 19—

Saint Joseph

PATRON OF CARPENTERS, FATHERS, LABORERS,
HAPPY DEATH, HOUSE HUNTING, AUSTRIA,
BELGIUM, CANADA, MEXICO, PERU, VIETNAM;
INVOKED AGAINST COMMUNISM AND DOUBT

Be mindful of us, O blessed Joseph, and intercede
on our behalf with your reputed Son; and secure for
us the favor of your most holy Virgin Spouse, the Mother
of him who lives and reigns with the Father and the
Holy Spirit, world without end. Amen.

SAINT BERNARDINE OF SIENA

O Saint Joseph, whose protection is so great, so
strong, so prompt before the throne of God, I place
in you all my interest and desires. O Saint Joseph,
do assist me by your powerful intercession, and
obtain for me from your divine Son all spiritual
blessings, through Jesus Christ, our Lord. So that,
having engaged here below your heavenly power, I
may offer my thanksgiving and homage to the most
loving of fathers. O Saint Joseph, I never weary of
contemplating you and Jesus asleep in your arms; I
dare not approach while he reposes near your heart.
Press him in my name and kiss his fine head for me
and ask him to return the kiss when I draw my dying
breath. Amen.

TRADITIONAL

first century: Spouse of Mary and foster-father of Jesus, Joseph was a carpenter. Little else is known about him for certain. His story appears in the Gospels of Matthew and Luke.

—MARCH 20—

Saint Cuthbert of Lindisfarne

PATRON OF SAILORS

Saint Cuthbert, you know homesickness well, the feeling of not being in the proper place, of not having found your home in the world. Help me to recognize my home in the world and my place in life, and to accept it and plant myself in peace when I arrive. Teach me as well to recognize the places where and the people with whom my soul comes alive, places and people that open my spirit wide, that free my spirit to be my true self. Most of all, be mindful of me when I worry about not having arrived home yet, that I may, with your help, learn to inhabit and enjoy all the world as my sometime home until I arrive joyfully at my eternal home in heaven. I ask your blessing through Christ our Lord. Amen.

died 687: Cuthbert tended his father's sheep until joining the monastery at Melrose. He was eventually consecrated abbot-bishop at the Celtic monastery on Lindisfarne. One of the most famous of English saints, he was renowned as a wonder-worker, and his shrine at Durham was one of the most frequented during the Middle Ages.

—MARCH 21—

Saint Enda of Arranmore

Enda, show me how important it is to be always mindful of eternity and not to get lost in the fads and fashions of the modern world. The fashionable quickly passes, and only the spirit endures. May I

remember this, and keep, at least in my imagina-
tion, a little island of protection around me where
the eternal values never get lost.

TOM COWAN

died c. 590: On the barren Isle of Arran, against the advice
of all his family, Enda built the great monastery of Killeany,
for he considered this island to be his "place of resurrection." He lived there until his death, establishing monastic
practices for the many students who followed him and becoming spiritual director to men and women who came for
his advice.

—MARCH 22—

Saint Lea

Holy Saint Lea, you exchanged your rich attire for
sackcloth and ceased to command other people so
that you might obey all. You were willing to be considered a fool on earth so that you might attend the
wedding feast of the Lamb of God. Help me to re-
frain from seeking the favors of the world and to
renounce all that is carnal. Teach me well that it is
impossible to follow both the world and Jesus. Inspire me to a life of wise renunciation, for my body
will soon be dust, and all my possessions as well,
and nothing will last except my eternal soul, which
I cast upon the Lord, our Savior. Amen.

died 384: Little is known about Lea except that upon the
death of her husband, she joined the community of Saint
Marcella. She ultimately became the superior of the community and spent her life in serving the nuns.

—MARCH 23—

Blessed Sibyllina Biscossi

O most Blessed Sibyllina, pray for all people who are blind, that if it be the Lord's will, they may receive a restoration of their sight. But if this is impossible, bless them, that they may glimpse the light of heaven, as you did, and take heart in the struggle to cope with their infirmity. Strengthen them in their day-to-day coping with a sight-oriented society, and help them to make their way through the world. Inspire them also, as they encounter uncharitable attitudes or prejudices, to repay insult or injury with the love God has for all people. Pray that God will make them, and all people with disabilities, beacons of light and love in a world darkened by prejudice and discrimination. We ask this in the name of Jesus, who brought sight to the blind and acceptance to the outcasts. Amen.

1287–1367: Orphaned and blinded at an early age, Sibyllina prayed to Saint Dominic for restoration of her sight. Instead, she received a vision of the light of heaven and understood that her reward would be great in eternity. By the age of fifteen, she began to receive mystical graces and chose a life of seclusion, living beneath the Dominican church. From her room she counseled others about sin, forgiveness, and the Holy Spirit. She is one of the incorruptibles.

—MARCH 24—

Saint Gabriel the Archangel

PATRON OF CHILDBIRTH, DIPLOMATS, MESSENGERS, POSTAL WORKERS, STAMP COLLECTORS, TELEPHONE AND TELEVISION WORKERS

O Angel truly strong, strengthen, guide and protect us, you who by your embassy did usher even God himself to earth, most strong of all, who having carried off the spoils and having routed the strongly armed one that for so long a time had exercised destructive tyranny over us, did rescue us from slavery and restore us to the Liberty of the [children] of God!

SAINT ALOYSIUS GONZAGA

One of the three angels named in the Bible, Gabriel appears in the Book of Daniel and the Gospel of Luke. He appeared to Our Lady to announce that God had chosen her to be the mother of our Lord. He is called the Angel of the Annunciation.

—MARCH 25—

Saint Dismas, "The Good Thief"

PATRON OF CRIMINALS, THIEVES, AND UNDERTAKERS

Dear Saint Dismas, beg of God for us, not the recompense we deserve, but the labor that is necessary for the deserving of everlasting life—in a word, the cross. You who discovered that Christ is the paradise of crucified souls, help us to know that in our cross we find the assurance of Christ's kingdom. Help us to die sweetly in him, renouncing all for him, and loving him until our last breath, in order to have eternal life. Happy Thief, who entered at once into paradise, remember your likeness and assist us in meriting the Love that you loved. Poor Pensioner on the mercy of a moment, help us to realize that we may at any auspicious moment pick sanctity out of the gutter with God's grace. Lucky Saint, to die beside the Living God and to see the infinite merits he won at such a cruel price, beg of him for us a profound trust in that largess!

MARIE C. COMMINS

first century: Dismas is the name given by tradition to the repentant thief, to whom Jesus, upon the cross, promised paradise. Though legendary tales abound, nothing is known about him for certain outside of the Gospel.

—MARCH 26—

Saint Ludger

Holy Saint Ludger, despite your many offices and good works, you never neglected your prayers and spiritual exercises. As I go through my often frenetic days and nights, remind me to pause for several moments now and then, that I might remember the Lord. Nudge me when I forget to thank God, and keep me mindful of the wonderful things the Holy Spirit accomplishes in my life. Help me recall with joy the words of our Lord, his lessons and stories, his example, and, above all, his sacrifice. O Saint Ludger, pray for me. Amen.

died 809: A Frisian by birth, Ludger was educated under Saint Gregory in the abbey school of Utrecht and under Blessed Alcuin in England. Returning home as a missionary, he worked chiefly in Westphalia. When the Saxons expelled all priests, he went to Rome, then to Monte Cassino. Charlemagne sent Ludger back to Friesland, where he had considerable success. Ludger was eventually consecrated bishop of Münster.

—MARCH 27—

Blessed Francis Fa'a di Bruno

Dear Blessed Francis, the Holy Father named you "a giant of faith and charity," and indeed, you accomplished so much during your lay service to the people of God. Inspire me with the wisdom and desire to help my sisters and brothers, that I may learn how to include charitable service among my daily activities. You who were one of the leading mathematicians and astronomers of your era, teach me as well how to combine my faith with today's scientific knowledge, that I may never cease to marvel at the wonders of the Lord's creation. I pray, bless all students and teachers in this way too.

Most Blessed Francis, pray for me. Amen.

1825–1888: The youngest of twelve children, Francis entered the army of Piedmont, becoming a captain and eventually studying in Paris, where he earned his doctorate in mathematics and astronomy. Then he resigned his commission and returned to Turin to teach at the university. But as a member of the Saint Vincent de Paul Society, his focus was on charitable work, and he showed special concern for the safety of women and girls, establishing schools, retirement homes, and other charitable institutions. He eventually founded the Sisters of Our Lady of Suffrage and of Saint Zita to aid in his ministry. He did not seek ordination until the final years of his life.

—MARCH 28—

Blessed Joseph Sebastian Pelczar

Blessed Joseph, you exhibited extreme courage in the face of the horrors of war, never abandoning your people but strengthening and leading them during a time of dreadful crisis. I pray, then, for your intercession on behalf of all leaders, whether civil, military, or religious. Inspire them with the spirit of service, that they may remember that their purpose as leaders is to serve those entrusted to them. Imbue them with compassion and wisdom, and open their hearts to God's love. I pray especially for the leaders in *(mention request)*, whose leadership is sorely tested at this time. Ask the Lord to be with them in a special way, that they may bring his peace and love throughout the land. As well, I pray for your blessing whenever I am called upon to lead, that I may follow the fine example you set, and that I may look to the Lord's perfect example of leadership. I ask this in the name of Jesus, the Good Shepherd. Amen.

1842–1924: Joseph was born in Korczyna, Poland, and raised devoutly in a troubled time. He founded the Servants of the Most Sacred Heart of Jesus and was eventually consecrated bishop of Przemysl, inspiring his people during the horrors of World War I. When the Russians entered his diocese in 1915, burning churches and imprisoning priests, Joseph led his clergy, nuns, and people in aiding the wounded and oppressed. He is revered particularly for his saving grace during severe oppression.

—MARCH 29—

Saint Joseph
of Arimathea

PATRON OF FUNERAL DIRECTORS

Holy Saint Joseph, I thank you because you have shown me how to live up to my convictions. You overcame your fear and "came out of the closet," revealing your great love for Jesus at the very moment when his closest friends had abandoned him, at the very moment when being known as a friend of Jesus was the most life-endangering reputation to possess. Help me also to "come out of the closet" and profess my love for Jesus. Help me as well to "come out of the closet" in other ways too, that I may be truthful in all things with all people, that I may have no secrets, and that I may express my true self with integrity and without fear, no matter the consequences. Dear Joseph, strengthen me to meet disapproval with love, and help me to rely upon the Lord's approval and support. I pray in the name of Jesus, your dear though sometime secret friend. Amen.

first century: Afraid to reveal himself as a disciple of Jesus, Joseph took courage after the Crucifixion and asked Pilate for Jesus' body. With the help of Nicodemus and the women who followed Jesus, Joseph laid the perfumed body in his own new tomb. Little else is known of him, though legends abound.

Blessed Maria Restituta Kafka

O Blessed Maria, your courage and love of Christ helped you to profess your faith even in the face of mortal danger. You kept the cross of Christ in your heart; imprint it, I implore you, in my heart also, that I may never forget the love my Lord bears for me, and that I may have the courage to follow him no matter where my faith may lead me. I pray, as well, that you might intercede on behalf of all Christians who are currently in grave mortal danger because of their faith. Protect them, and inspire them to hold fast to the love of Jesus, from which nothing can ever separate us. I ask this in the name of Jesus, our loving Savior. Amen.

1894–1943: Raised in Vienna, Maria entered the Franciscan Sisters of Christian Charity, serving as a surgical nurse for two decades. An ardent opponent of Hitler, Maria placed a crucifix in every room of a new hospital wing. She was arrested in 1942 for plotting high treason against Hitler and was offered freedom if she would give up her religious life. Refusing, she was condemned to death. Appeals for leniency were refused, and she was decapitated. While awaiting her death, Maria distinguished herself by caring for the other prisoners.

Blessed Mother Maria Skobtsóva

O Blessed Maria, while you lived among us, you showed us that obedience to the will of God is the path to the kingdom of heaven. Though the world was engulfed in war and had forgotten the ways of God, you never ceased to care for the sick, the homeless, the weak, and the spiritually lost. You did not let the coldness of hatred enter into your being but showed compassion toward all God's children. Now, O faithful witness of Christ our God, look down from your heavenly abode upon those who raise their voice to you in prayer. Intercede for us before the throne of God, that we may be strengthened in love for God and love for our neighbor. Grant us the grace to see God's image in every human being. Through word and deed, you taught us to be patient in suffering, joyful in time of adversity, and to put one's trust in God's providence at all times, at every place, and in each circumstance during our lifetime. Grant us to see our countless voluntary and involuntary sins. Renew our faith and trust in the living God and God's forgiveness. At the hour of our death, take us by the hand, granting us the courage to stand before the awesome judgment seat of Christ. May we be counted worthy of the joy of the eternal kingdom awaiting all those who love Christ with their whole hearts. Amen.

CANTOR RAYMOND J. MASTROBERTE

1891–1945: Born into an aristocratic family in Riga, Latvia, Maria married and bore two children. She also served as mayor, but in 1923 fled to Paris, where she had her third child and assisted destitute Russian refugees. Maria became a nun in 1932, and her house became a center for works of mercy and the birthplace of Orthodox Action. When the Nazis occupied Paris, she did all things possible to protect her Jewish neighbors. The Gestapo arrested her in 1943, sending her to Ravensbrück concentration camp, where she took the place of a Jewish prisoner who was to be sent to the gas chamber and died in her place.

April

Saint Valéry

O Saint Valéry, like Brother Francis of Assisi and some few others, God gifted you with the ability to talk with the animals. Thank you for your example. Remind me, as I move through this modern, human-created world, that the real world of nature surrounds me at all times. Teach me to tread lightly upon the natural world, to reverence both birds and insects and reptiles and all of God's creatures, as well as the plants and water and air that sustain all life, including my own. Keep me mindful of my own God-given stewardship of nature, and help me to understand how to nurture this wonderful world. Bless my efforts to recycle, to conserve, to educate. Most of all, remind me now and then to rest from my activities so that I may sit and simply commune with nature for a few moments.

O Saint Valéry, pray for me. Amen.

died c. 622: A monk under Saint Columbanus at Luxeuil, then a missionary in what is now northern France, Valéry became the abbot-founder of Lencone at the mouth of the Somme. He was known for his ability to talk with animals and commune with nature.

—April 2—

Saint Francis of Paola

PATRON OF MARINERS: NAVAL OFFICERS, SAILORS, AND SEAFARERS

In the silence of the evening, on our knees, we, those living aboard ship and those buried in the depths of the ocean, pray to you with all our soul, holy protector.

O Francis of Paola, who came barefooted from a hermitage to the glory of the altar in the footsteps of Jesus:

Let the night pass clear and peaceful for those who are resting, and for those who are keeping watch.

Let everyone, before going to sleep, make the sign of the Cross, in the love of the Lord and the forgiveness of his law.

Let every ship keep to its course and each sailor keep faith in the departures here below, and the arrivals in paradise.

Hold back the winds and calm the storms: in the hour of danger, spread your cloak, bring all to safety.

Comfort our loneliness with the voice of happy memories, the hope of tomorrow, the certainty of a safe return.

Light up the stars and the hearts of the wanderers and those who are the lost at sea and in life, who do not see the light, do not find the way.

Bless our country, bless our home. Bless us all: those who are working on ships for daily bread and those who are awaiting the holy charity on the bottom of the sea.

In Jesus' name we pray. Amen.

"MARINERS' PRAYER," MINIM FATHERS

1416–1507: At the age of fourteen, Francis settled as a hermit on the sea coast. Many disciples followed him, and their community at Paola eventually became the new order of

Minim Friars. At the direction of Pope Sixtus IV, Francis traveled to France to assist the dying King Louis XI, remaining in France afterward.

—APRIL 3—

Saints Agape, Chionia, and Irene

O holy Saints Agape, Chionia, and Irene, the horrible deaths inflicted upon you raise conflicting emotions within me. Certainly, I admire your great courage and your boundless faith in God's love. But I am also angry about what happened to you, that your mere possession of certain writings was enough for the authorities to condemn you to death. How grateful I am to live in a society where I am free to read and believe what I want. Yet how sad I am to know that intolerance and hatred of difference still flourishes, even in my open society, even among people who are educated and progressive. So dear saints, I implore your intercession on behalf of all who suffer from prejudice and intolerance; protect them from all harm, that they may go about their business in peace. As well, intercede on behalf of all those who still cling so tightly to their prejudices; ask the Lord to infuse them with the wisdom to understand that God's way is the way of love and acceptance, not the way of fear and hate and discrimination.

I pray especially for *(mention name)*, a victim, like yourselves, of intolerance and prejudice.

Saints Agape, Chionia, and Irene, pray for us. Amen.

died 304: Agape, Chionia, and Irene were three sisters who, with several companions, were burned alive for the Faith at Salonika under the persecutions of Emperor Diocletian.

—APRIL 4—

Saint Benedict the Moor

O holy Saint Benedict, people loved you because of
your humility and kindness, and you returned their
love. Pray for me, that I may always see the image
and likeness of God in every person I encounter, re-
gardless of their social position, wealth, health, age,
race, sex, sexual orientation, or religion. Teach me
to see the beauty and miracle of each person for
whom Christ died.

As well, dear saint, help me to accept my share
of the daily chores. Remind me that even the most
menial tasks are not beneath me. Pray that I may
humbly take on what must be done. I ask your blessing in the name of Jesus, who taught his disciples to
be servants of all. Amen.

1526–1589: Born of African parents near Messina, Sicily,
Benedict first became a hermit and then joined the Friars
Minor of the Observance at Palermo as a lay brother. Nevertheless, he was appointed guardian and novice-master of
the friary. Though he excelled at both offices, his heart was
in the kitchen, where he worked in his old age.

—APRIL 5—

Saint Vincent Ferrer

PATRON OF BUILDERS

O Saint Vincent, glorious worker of miracles, who
in your lifetime converted so many sinners by
preaching the last judgment, grant that we too, by
meditating on the four Last Things, may be enabled
to obtain from Almighty God through your intercession the healing of all our spiritual maladies. Let
your heart be tender toward us, O mighty saint;

stretch forth your hand over us, and obtain for us
those graces for the welfare of both soul and body,
which we so earnestly ask of you. Amen.

THE RACCOLTA

c. 1350–1418: A native of Valencia, Vincent entered the
Dominican Order. He was adviser to the king of Aragon
and the Avignon pope at that time. To heal the papal schism,
Vincent traveled through Spain, France, Switzerland, and
Italy, preaching penance, working miracles, and converting
thousands. When he realized that the Avignon party was in
the wrong, he worked to bring them into obedience to the
legitimate pope. Vincent is credited with healing the schism.

—APRIL 6—

Blessed Pierina
(Petrina) Morosini

Dear Pierina, you are a symbol of purity in a modern world of rampant violence and suffering, and
your selfless service to others reminds me of my responsibility as a Christian. Intercede, I implore you,
to protect those members of society who are most
helpless yet most often victimized: children, women,
the sick, the homeless, the poor. As well, help me to
work to end violence. Encourage me to speak up in
the face of violence and victimization; and inspire
me to discern the times when I am myself a victim,
so that I may seek the help that I need. I ask your
special blessing upon *(mention name)*, who has suffered from violence; heal *her/him*, and remind *her/
him* of Jesus' undying and unconditional and healing love. In the name of Jesus, who is Love, I pray.
Amen.

1931–1957: Raised in the Roman Catholic faith, Pierina came from a poor Italian village and took private vows of poverty, chastity, and obedience. As well, she was a member of the Catholic Action organization. She was raped and beaten to death by an assailant.

—APRIL 7—

Saint John-Baptist de la Salle

PATRON OF SCHOOLTEACHERS

O glorious John-Baptist de la Salle, apostle of children and young folk, from the heights of heaven, be our guide and our patron. Offer your prayers for us and help us, that we may be kept free from every stain of error and corruption, and remain ever faithful to Jesus Christ and to the infallible head of his Church. Grant that we, practicing the virtues of which you were so wondrous an example, may be made partakers of your glory in heaven, our true country. Amen.

THE RACCOLTA

1654–1719: From Rheims, John-Baptist became canon of the cathedral there at a young age, yet he was touched by the plight of poor children and devoted his life and considerable fortune to their education. In the teeth of extreme opposition, John-Baptist succeeded in establishing his system of revolutionary educational principles. He is the founder of the Congregation of the Brothers of the Christian Schools.

—APRIL 8—

Saint Julie Billiart

Dearest Saint Julie, God blessed you with humility and wisdom in the midst of struggle and misunderstanding. Through you, many came to know God's love and concern. Through your intercession, may all threatened by revolutions and political unrest know the peace the world cannot give. Through your intercession, may all those who are injured and physically disabled receive courage. Through your intercession, may all who suffer misunderstanding as they follow the guidance of the Spirit know comfort. Help us all to use our gifts of nature and grace for God's glory. We ask this in the name of Jesus and his mother, Mary. Amen.

1751–1816: Born the daughter of a peasant farmer in Picardy, Julie took a vow of chastity at the age of fourteen and gave herself up to the service and instruction of the poor. Her health was soon destroyed, and she was helplessly crippled until cured miraculously. Her charitable activities developed into the Institute of Notre Dame, for the Christian education of girls, which grew quickly despite much opposition. Scandal caused Julie to move the motherhouse from Amiens to Namur, from where the congregation spread throughout the whole world.

—APRIL 9—

Saint Mary of Cleophas

Holy Saint Mary, you had such courage, following Jesus when his friends all abandoned him and standing by his mother despite the mortal danger of associating with him. Encourage me, then, to follow Jesus unstintingly, even when the environment is

hostile to faith. And intercede, I pray, on behalf of
all whose love for Jesus is prohibited by law or cus-
tom or social pressure. Strengthen their resolve, and
help them persevere, despite ridicule or punishment.
I ask your special blessing for the people of *(mention place)*, who face grave danger because of their
faith in Jesus. Protect them, and ask the Lord to
shower them with love, that they may know that he
will never abandon them. I ask this through Christ
our Lord. Amen.

first century: The wife of Cleophas (Cleopas) or Alpheus,
Mary followed Jesus during his ministry throughout Galilee and was present at the foot of his cross. She may be the
same Mary who was the mother of Saint James the Less
and Joses, who stood by the cross and went with Mary
Magdalene to the tomb on the third day. She is perhaps the
sister of the Blessed Virgin Mary. Little is known of her for
certain, despite many legends.

—APRIL 10—

Saint Michael
of the Saints

O glorious Saint Michael, seraph inflamed with the
most ardent love of Jesus in the Blessed Sacrament,
you spent your nights and days in his real Presence
and found there your dearest joys, so that you
swooned away for very love. Vouchsafe, I pray you,
to obtain for me a lively faith, a firm hope, and an
ardent love toward this inestimable Treasure, this
precious Pledge of glory everlasting; in order that I
may be able to be a fervent worshiper of Jesus in
the Blessed Sacrament, and thereby rejoice with you
to behold him face to face in an eternity of bliss.
Amen.

THE RACCOLTA

1591–1625: Born in Spanish Catalonia, Michael first joined the calced Trinitarians but passed over to join the discalced Trinitarians. Twice superior at Valladolíd, he was one of the greatest apostles of the holy Eucharist in seventeenth-century Spain.

—APRIL 11—

Saint Stanislaus Szczepanow

PATRON OF POLAND

Saint Stanislaus, our Patron, the protector of the whole country, help us, teach us to be victorious, teach us to attain victory from day to day. Patron of the moral order in our country, show us how we must attain it, by carrying out the work of indispensable renewal, which begins in [humankind], in every [person], which embraces the whole of society and all the dimensions of its life: spiritual, cultural, social and economic, spiritual and cultural, spiritual and material. Teach us this. Teach us and help us, you who are, together with the Queen of Poland of Jasna Gora and with Saint Adalbert, the Patron Saint of our country. Help us to attain this victory in our generation. Amen.

POPE JOHN PAUL II

1030–1079: From Krakow, Stanislaus excommunicated King Boleslaus the Cruel for his evil life, and in retribution the king himself killed Stanislaus while he was celebrating Mass. Pope Saint Gregory VII laid Poland under an interdict as a result, and Boleslaus fled the country, dying a fugitive.

—APRIL 12—

Saint Joseph Moscati

O holy Saint Joseph, your attendance at daily Mass
and your devotion to Mary fortified your work of
saving souls through your care for the body. I ask
that your prayers and example may inspire those in
the medical professions to serve their suffering patients with charity, understanding, self-sacrifice, and
devoted treatment, especially of the unfortunate and
the outcasts of our society. May their service honor
your example, and through you bring honor to God,
our life-giving Creator, with due reverence for the
sanctity of human life. Amen.

1880–1927: Born in Benevento, Joseph studied medicine,
becoming a teacher and researcher. Out of love for Christ
and charity for others he volunteered for military service
during World War I. He was able to blend his knowledge
and practice of medicine with his practice of the Catholic
faith, and his spiritual advice brought many of his patients
back to the sacraments.

—APRIL 13—

Blessed Margaret
of Castello

O Blessed Margaret, how motherly you were in your
care for others, despite your deep rejection by your
own mother and father. Your life demonstrates how
passionately God always wants every one of us, especially those unwanted by their parents. Intercede
for the pro-life movement of our time, that unwanted
babies may not be aborted, that those with disabilities will be cherished and nurtured, and that the

lives of the terminally ill will be protected and respected. Through Christ our Lord. Amen.

RONDA DE SOLA CHERVIN

died 1320: When Margaret was born blind, lame, dwarfed, and hunchbacked, her parents, ashamed, kept her birth a secret. Her father, afraid that she would reveal herself as his child, had her walled up in a church in the forest. Only with the help of a chaplain was the young child able to survive this horrible imprisonment—and develop a pious nature. When she was twenty, her parents abandoned her in the church at Castello, where she joined with the beggars until some of the poor people took her in. Soon becoming famed for her holiness, she was taken into a monastery but expelled because of her strictness in following the rule. Afterward, Margaret became a Third Order Dominican, ministering to the sick, the dying, and prisoners. Many miracles and wonders, including levitation, were attributed to her, and she is among the incorruptibles.

—APRIL 14—

Saint Ardalion

Saint Ardalion, as an actor, you enjoyed the gift of understanding human emotions. Teach me how to identify with other people by appreciating the depth of their emotions. Help me to put myself in their shoes, that I may better understand the "why" behind the "what" in their lives. As Jesus reminded his disciples to exhibit compassion, so too remind me to be compassionate with everyone whom I encounter today, that by my empathy for them they may come to glimpse the boundless love that God has for them. As well, dear saint, help me to discern false emotions, that I may help others by seeing and relating to the true person behind the facade. Amen.

died c. 300: An actor who pleased his audiences by ridicul-
ing Christians, Ardalion suddenly proclaimed himself a
Christian after receiving applause for one of his perfor-
mances. For his faith he was roasted alive in the public square.

—APRIL 15—

Blessed Damien de Veuster

Most holy Father Damien, your dedication and
unfailing devotion changed the way the world views
leprosy and the people who suffer from this disease. Inspire me with your fervent charity, that I
may change my view of people who are ill. Too often I recoil from sickness—and from those who bear
it—out of fear or repugnance of their disease or even
conceit about my own health. Help me to see people
who are ill or dying as individuals worthy of my
respect, kindness, courtesy, and care. Help me to
embrace them when I am faced with the opportunity,
that I may bring to them through my actions the
message of God's unconditional and all-accepting
love.

As well, I pray for your particular intercession
on behalf of *(mention name)*; bring your healing
spirit to *him/her,* that *he/she* may find comfort and
peace. In the name of Jesus, who healed and embraced the sick. Amen.

1840–1889: From Tremeloo, Belgium, Damien joined the
Congregation of the Sacred Heart (the Picpus Fathers) and
volunteered for the Hawaiian missions. When the royal
Hawaiian government exiled victims of leprosy to a remote
settlement on the island of Molokai, Damien volunteered
to minister to and care for these souls that society had cast
out. Father Damien died of leprosy himself, and he is revered in his adopted islands as the "Hero of Molokai."

—APRIL 16—

Saint Bernadette Soubirous of Lourdes

PATRON OF SHEPHERDS

O Saint Bernadette, pure and simple child, you who were privileged to behold the beauty of Mary Immaculate and to be the recipient of her confidence eighteen times at Lourdes; you who desired thereafter to hide yourself in the cloister of Nevers and there live and die as a victim of sinners: obtain for me that spirit of purity, simplicity, and mortification that will lead me also to the glorious vision of God and of Mary in Heaven. Amen.

THE CATHOLIC FAMILY BOOK OF NOVENAS

1854–1879: God chose this peasant child to reveal to the world the healing shrine of Our Lady of Lourdes in France. Bernadette suffered much on account of her visions of the Blessed Virgin Mary and joined the Sisters of Notre Dame at Nevers to keep out of the public eye.

—APRIL 17—

Saint Stephen Harding

Stephen, I wish I could be more spontaneous in my spiritual life, as you were on that spur of the moment when you stayed in France to be a monk. So often I am leery of acting spontaneously. Help me to be less controlling, less fearful, and to take reasonable risks for the sake of my spiritual growth.

TOM COWAN

died 1137: An English monk, Stephen migrated with Saint Robert to Cîteaux, becoming that monastery's third abbot.

As such, he was responsible for the original constitutions of
the Cistercians, as well as the Charter of Charity, and the
Cistercians owe to him their status as a new branch of the
Benedictines. Stephen received Saint Bernard and his companions and sent them to found Clairvaux.

—APRIL 18—

Blessed Marie
of the Incarnation
(Barbara Acarie)

PATRON OF EXTREME POVERTY

Blessed Marie, you loved the time you spent with
the Lord in contemplation, yet you also followed
the Lord's command to love his people by serving
them in their needs. Help me to balance these demands as you did, so that I may commune with the
Lord in silent prayer as well as in the person of his
people on earth. Teach me to use the graces I receive in solitude for the good of God's children. I
ask this in the name of Jesus, who went into the
desert to pray and then went into the midst of God's
people to heal and teach and spread the Good News.
Amen.

1566–1618: Married to an aristocratic lawyer, Marie had
six children and raised them all to be saints. She was noted
for her widespread charities, including feeding the hungry,
tending the sick, assisting old people, instructing those fallen
away from the faith, and bringing several orders of religious to France. She particularly helped the Carmelites, and
became a Carmelite lay sister herself. Her life was filled with
visions and ecstasies.

—APRIL 19—

Pope Saint Leo IX

Saint Leo, God gave you to the Church at a time when reforms were greatly needed. Your devotion to the Church and your desire to adhere to its teachings give us hope during these difficult times. Help us to remain faithful to the Gospel, and teach us to apply Gospel precepts to our debates about Church rules and reform. Help us to see Christ and the enduring truths of our faith as the true foundation of our Church, so that we cease to be so preoccupied with lesser issues. At the same time, we ask your blessing upon all those who do seek to reform the Church, that they may proceed with your wisdom and discernment in doing what is necessary. Remind them, and us, always to follow Jesus, who is the Way, the Truth, and the Life. Amen.

1002–1054: Born in Alsace, a cousin of the emperor Conrad the Salic, Leo was made bishop of Toul and eventually elected pope. He reformed the Roman curia, combated simony, and strove to prevent the schism between the Eastern and Western churches. Leading an army against Norman invaders, Leo was captured; he died soon after his release.

—APRIL 20—

Blessed Clare Bosatta

O Blessed Clare, whose life exemplified the spirit of sacrifice, teach me to follow your example in bringing the Gospel among the poor and abandoned and send me your spirit of dedication to the most needy. Show me also how to be patient in suffering and how to abandon myself completely to Divine Providence. Give me most of all your love for prayer, that I may serve my Lord by serving my sisters and brothers. Amen.

1858–1887: Born on the shores of Lake Como, Clare wanted to become a teacher but was rejected for her frailty and withdrawn personality. Instead, she began to minister to the needs of the poor and soon joined the Institute of Pianello to be "a contemplative in the heroic exercise of Charity." Under the direction of Blessed Aloysius Guanella, she was put in charge of a girls school at Dongo and later the Institute's new house in Como, where she served as teacher of novices and postulants, educator of orphans, and assistant of the aging. But her frail health led to her early death. She is noted as one of the first Daughters of Saint Mary of Providence.

—APRIL 21—

Saint Anselm of Canterbury

Anselm, give me the wisdom to hold onto the idea of human perfection even when I see so little evidence of it around me. May I keep a strong belief in God's own perfection, and a belief that each of us, who are made in [God's] image, contains at least a nugget of that perfection and probably much more. Help me to bring forth the best in my companions and neighbors, so that they too can make strides toward living a more perfect life.

TOM COWAN

1033–1109: Anselm left his native Piedmont to become a Benedictine at Bec in Normandy. From there he was appointed to the see of Canterbury, but he was exiled for resisting King William Rufus's encroachments on ecclesiastical rights. On the king's death he returned to Canterbury at the invitation of the new king Henry I, who sent Anselm into exile again, this time for his opposition to the question of investitures. Anselm eventually returned. Known as the Father of Scholasticism, he is a Doctor of the Church.

—APRIL 22—

Saint Opportuna

Saint Opportuna, you chose the monastic life, embracing God's special call to you. Bless me, that I too may embrace the way God is calling me to go, that I may be true to myself and true to what God wants of me. And as you practiced austerity and self-sacrifice out of love for God, help me to discern what special practices God might be calling me to embrace.

As well, intercede on behalf of all those whose callings seem to run contrary to expectations, especially *(mention name)*. Bless all people with hearts to discern God's plans and with the willingness and perseverance to do God's will despite opposition. Through Christ our Lord. Amen.

died c. 770: Born in Normandy, Opportuna, sister of Saint Chrodegand, bishop of Séez, entered the Benedictine abbey of Montreuil at an early age. She became abbess and was a great source of edification for the community. The murder of her brother affected her deeply, and she died soon after.

—APRIL 23—

Saint George the Great

PATRON OF ENGLAND, PORTUGAL, GERMANY,
CAVALRY, HORSES, EQUESTRIANS, FARMERS,
BOY SCOUTS, KNIGHTS, ARCHERS,
AND ARMORERS; INVOKED AGAINST
THE PLAGUE, LEPROSY, AND SYPHILIS

Faithful servant of God and invincible martyr, Saint George; favored by God with the gift of faith, and inflamed with an ardent love of Christ, you fought valiantly against the dragon of pride, falsehood, and

deceit. Neither pain nor torture, sword nor death
could part you from the love of Christ. I fervently
implore you for the sake of this love to help me by
your intercession to overcome the temptations that
surround me, and to bear bravely the trials that
oppress me, so that I may patiently carry the cross
that is placed upon me; and let neither distress nor
difficulties separate me from the love of our Lord
Jesus Christ. Valiant champion of the faith, assist
me in the combat against evil, that I may win the
crown promised to them that persevere unto the end.
Amen.

TRADITIONAL

died c. 300: A Palestinian soldier martyred during the
Diocletian persecutions, George figures prominently in legends of the period of the Crusades, and he was considered
the model of knighthood and the avenger of women. Little
is known about him for certain.

—APRIL 24—

Saint Fidelis of Sigmaringen

Thy name, Fidelis, doth proclaim
Thy living faith and doctrine's fame;
False teachers bow before thy word,
Thy blood bears witness to thy Lord.
    Let heaven's light, to thee we pray,
Within our hearts and minds hold sway;
Let faith and hope and holy love
Shine in us brightly from above.
    Through thee the halt, the lame, the blind,
New health and strength and light do find;
To speechless tongues, speech thou dost give;

Thou makest dying infants live.
  Let heaven's light, to thee we pray,
Within our hearts and minds hold sway:
Let faith and hope and holy love
Shine in us brightly from above.

THE RACCOLTA

1577–1622: Born Mark Ray in southern Germany, Fidelis practiced as a lawyer and came to be known as the advocate of the poor. After joining the Capuchins, he went as a missionary to the Swiss Protestants. His success raised the ire of Calvinists, and he was stabbed to death.

—APRIL 25—

Saint Mark

PATRON OF CATTLE BREEDERS, VENICE, NOTARIES, AND GLAZIERS; INVOKED AGAINST FLY BITES

Most holy Saint Mark, your inspired words record the life of our Savior, bringing the Good News to untold numbers in need of salvation each day. As well, the example of your life continues to inspire women and men to follow Jesus and dedicate themselves to God. Be with me then, I implore you, when my faith grows weak and my focus blurs. Bring me the Good News anew, and remind me again of what our Lord did out of love for us, out of love for me. Strengthen my faith, and help my unbelief. Most of all, pray that I may come to know Jesus as my personal friend, as you would have liked to have known him.

O saint, intercede also for those who have never heard of God. Inspire them with the desire to approach the Divine, and ask the Lord to send them messengers and teachers of God's love.

As well, I implore you to intercede on behalf of

those people who have turned away from God. Pray that Jesus will continue to shower them with his love, that he will continue to present them with opportunities to return to God's loving embrace. In this regard I pray especially for *(mention name)*. In the name of Jesus. Amen.

died c. 75: One of the four evangelists, Mark wrote his Gospel in Greek. Mark came from a levitical family, and the upper room of his mother's home was a meeting place for the apostles in Jerusalem. He traveled with Saints Paul and Barnabas and later became interpreter and secretary to Saint Peter in Rome. Tradition credits Mark with establishing the Church in Alexandria, Egypt, where he died a martyr.

—APRIL 26—

Saint Stephen of Perm

Stephen, help me develop a love of language like you had. So often we take words and literacy for granted. Even the alphabet seems so common that we hardly notice the shapes and designs in the letters we use every day. Teach me to watch how I speak and write, to take time to use language well, and to appreciate my language and those of other peoples as gifts from God.

TOM COWAN

died 1396: A Permiak who studied in Russia, Stephen returned to his native land east of the Volga and southwest of the Urals to minister to his people. Understanding that all languages have their own value, Stephen translated parts of Scripture and the liturgy into the Permiak language, even creating a new alphabet explicitly for the people of this region. He also founded schools where people could learn to read and write their own language. Stephen was made the first bishop of Perm for his work.

—APRIL 27—

Saint Zita

PATRON OF HOUSEMAIDS AND
DOMESTIC SERVANTS; INVOKED IN
THE SEARCH FOR LOST KEYS

O holy Saint Zita, many of us resent all menial labor as monotonous and unbearable. Some of us even substitute overly long hours of prayer and meditation for our household duties or employer's assignments. Pray for us, that we may accomplish all of our necessary chores with a spirit of generosity and joy. Teach us that everything we do is for a greater purpose, though we may not be able to discern God's plan at the moment. Show us that our littlest task is part of God's great tapestry of life, that whatever we do contributes in greater measure than we can ever imagine to the kingdom of heaven. Intercede for us, that we may come to enjoy life, and that if our lot is not what we would have it be, that we may strive with a cheerful spirit to improve our situation. We pray this through Jesus our Lord. Amen.

1218–1278: Zita was a servant for two generations of the wealthy Fatinelli family, and she was known for giving her own—and sometimes her employers'—food and clothing to the poor. Reputedly, angels and even the Blessed Mother waited on Zita. She is among the incorruptibles.

—APRIL 28—

Saint Louis Marie Grignion de Montfort

Dear Saint Louis de Montfort, lover extraordinary of Our Lady, in life you wanted only one thing, to bring souls to Mary's love. Your work of consoling the tempted, afflicted, and unenlightened has grown since your short life. Your Companies of Mary now bring vast numbers of souls to her, for God is not outdone in generosity. [God] has a capacity of rewarding in the manner deserved.

Pray for us to the Immaculata. May we be inspired to listen to her maternal pleadings for our full conversion to God! As Queen, standing at the right hand of her only-begotten Son, she obtains all she desires. Our Lord says to her, "Ask, my Mother: it would not be right that I should turn you away."

Dear Saint, you who spited yourself so unstintingly in order to reach the side of your loved Lord and Lady, "you are there" now, with portfolio and all credentials. Don't forget us. Help all to make the approved consecration, that they may abandon themselves completely to our compassionate God and his Mother. That is the sweet "secret of Mary" you tried to tell the world long ago: she is the safe, sane shortcut to Christ!

MARIE C. COMMINS

1673–1716: Louis founded the first establishment of the Missionary Priests of Mary, and his book *True Devotion to the Blessed Virgin* is well known. His emotional sermons aroused much opposition, yet he was a very successful missionary in Brittany.

—APRIL 29—

Saint Catherine of Siena

PATRON OF ITALY, NURSES, PHILOSOPHY,
AND UNMARRIED WOMEN; INVOKED AGAINST FIRE

Holy Saint Catherine, God gave you courage and
deep faith and strengthened you to challenge the
leaders of the Church of your day for the sake of
unity and peace. Pray that the Church may always
be open to God's grace and truth. Pray that all who
are estranged may be reconciled in Christ, our peace.
Pray for an openness to dialogue and reconciliation
within the Church and among all peoples. And bless
all those who challenge us in our complacency. Send
us the spirit of Jesus, so that we may truly love and
reverence one another, that we may be one family
united in Christ. Amen.

1347–1380: One of the greatest women of Christendom,
Catherine persuaded Pope Gregory XI to abandon Avignon
for Rome. She also wrote a great mystical work, her *Dialogue*. She is a Doctor of the Church.

—APRIL 30—

Blessed Marie
of the Incarnation
(Marie Guyard)

Blessed Marie, you found God among the most mundane circumstances, while you were working on the docks among the stevedores. Pray for me, that in my current situation, which seems so hostile to the spirit of God, the Lord may not abandon me. Intercede for me, that the Lord may open my heart to hear his voice. Teach me how to listen for the rush of the Holy Spirit coming into my daily life. Help me to remember the times God has touched me, and to keep my heart open to the recurring touch of Love. I ask this through our Savior, Jesus Christ. Amen.

1599–1672: The daughter of a baker in Tours, Marie married at seventeen, had a son, and was widowed two years later. At the age of thirty she joined the Ursulines, and ten years later went to Quebec to lay the cornerstone for the first Ursuline convent there. She compiled dictionaries in Algonquin and Iroquois, and she experienced mystical visions.

May

—MAY 1—

Saint Peregrine Laziosi

PATRON INVOKED AGAINST CANCER

O glorious wonder-worker, Saint Peregrine, you answered the divine call with a ready spirit. You left all the comforts of a life of ease and all the empty honors of the world, to dedicate yourself to God in the order of his most holy Mother. You labored zealously for the salvation of people, meriting the title of "Apostle of Emilia."

In union with Jesus crucified, you endured the most painful sufferings with such patience that you were healed miraculously. With a touch of the divine hand, your incurable leg wound disappeared.

Obtain for us, we pray, the grace to answer every call from God. Enkindle in our hearts a consuming zeal for the salvation of all people. Deliver us from the infirmities that so often afflict our bodies. And obtain for us the grace of perfect resignation in our sufferings. So may we, imitating your virtues and tenderly loving our crucified Lord and his sorrowful Mother, be enabled to merit glory everlasting in paradise. Amen.

DAUGHTERS OF SAINT PAUL

1260–1345: During his wild youth, Peregrine struck Saint Philip Benizi across the face. When Philip turned the other cheek, Peregrine was converted on the spot and joined the Servites. Later in life he was instantaneously cured of a cancer of the foot as a result of a vision.

—MAY 2—

Saint Zoe

Saint Zoe, holy martyr for the faith, you were humble enough to take the lead from your own sons, following their example of virtue, holiness, and steadfastness for the faith. The Lord calls all of us to become like little children so that we may enter the kingdom of heaven. Help all parents whose faith is weak, that they may humbly accept the simple faith of children, especially their own children. Pray for them, that their hearts may be opened to the great love their children have for them and for God. Intercede for all families, so that family members can be unified in their faith, a faith based not just on the minimum but on heroic love of God and neighbor.

As well, bless all parents who raise their children in the faith and love of God. Strengthen their resolve, and lay their efforts before the Lord, that he may look kindly upon them and reward the entire family with the gift of faith. We ask this through Christ our Lord. Amen.

died 140: Zoe and her husband, Hesperus, were slaves and Christians who with their two sons refused to participate in their master Catullus's pagan household rituals. The boys were cruelly tortured in front of their parents, inspiring Zoe and Hesperus to remain steadfast in the faith. All four were killed.

—MAY 3—

Blessed
Marie-Leonie Paradis

Blessed Marie-Leonie, in the spirit of Saint Thérèse of Lisieux, you sought out and followed the "little way" of simple and humble service to the servants of God. Your embodiment of Christ's fundamental attitude—"not to be served, but to serve"—is an inspiration to me. Remind me, when I seek the first place among my family or friends or when I start to think that they should do for me, that Jesus himself washed the feet of his disciples and calls me to do the same in his name. Bless me with that spirit of service, that I may know the joy of giving of myself for others. Through Jesus, our Lord. Amen.

1840–1912: From Montreal, Marie-Leonie entered the Holy Cross Sisters at Saint-Laurent at age thirteen. She served at St. Vincent's Orphanage in New York City and later as director of a group of sisters in Indiana. There she established the Little Sisters of the Holy Family. These sisters continue to care for clerical and episcopal households in Canada, the United States, and Honduras.

—MAY 4—

Saint Godehard
(Gothard)
of Hildesheim

Good Saint Godehard, you were an outstanding exemplar of Divine Love, embodying Jesus' exhortation to us to love our neighbors as ourselves. Inspire me to do more on behalf of my neighbors, particularly those who are less fortunate than I.

Encourage me to give of my plenty, to give of my time, to give of my energy, to give of my skills, that those in need may have enough food and clothing and shelter and education. As well, help me to rally my community, if necessary, to pay more attention to the needs of our neighbors.

In particular, bless *(mention name)*, who is in special need at this time. And bless *his/her* community, that they may respond with charity to the need in their midst. With reliance upon the Lord's providence, I pray for your blessing in this matter. Amen.

c. 960–1038: Godehard was instrumental in reintroducing the Benedictine Rule at Niederaltaich and was commissioned by Emperor Saint Henry II to revive the Benedictine observance in several German dioceses. He was eventually made bishop of Hildesheim, in which capacity he built and restored churches, fostered education, and erected a hospice for the poor and sick.

—MAY 5—

Saint Jutta of Kulmsee

Dear Saint Jutta, you knew in your heart the real worth of material possessions, using what you owned to help people in desperate straits. Please teach me the true value of my possessions, that I may loosen my grip on the things of this world and focus on the life to come. Inspire me to use what I own to help other people. Pray that I may unlearn my selfish habits and learn new habits of sharing— without thought for my own comfort, focusing on the real needs of others. The Lord taught that God will supply all our needs: share with me your secret of overcoming fear of want, of trusting God to supply what I require. In Jesus' name I pray for your blessing. Amen.

died 1260: Happily married to a nobleman, Jutta spent most of her time ministering to the poor. After her husband died and all her children entered religious orders, Jutta gave away all her possessions and begged in the streets. She settled in Prussia, living in a hermitage from where she taught all who came to her about coming to know God through illness, exile, and poverty.

—MAY 6—

Blessed François of Quebec
(Francis de Montmorency Laval)

Blessed François, you gave up wealth and title and comfort in your homeland to become a missionary of the wilderness. Like Abraham, you followed God's special plan for your life, so I ask you to pray for me, that I may hear and follow when God calls me. Teach me to wait patiently for the call, and help me to obey swiftly when it comes. Remind me that God would not ask me to do anything impossible for me to accomplish, for with God, all things are possible. I pray for your blessing, dear François, upon my waiting, and upon my responding. Amen.

1623–1708: François's inheritance of his family's estate interrupted his plans for ordination, but he persevered in his calling and was eventually consecrated bishop of New France. When he arrived in Canada, he was responsible for all of North America except for New England and the Spanish settlements. He promoted missions, discouraged the rampant liquor trade with Native Americans, erected a cathedral dedicated to the Immaculate Conception, and restored the shrine of Saint Anne at Beaupré. He also established the Roman Catholic school system in Canada. He was known as a "bishop according to God's heart."

—MAY 7—

Saint Nilus of Sora
(Nil Sorky)

O venerable father Nilus, blessed of God, our divinely wise instructor and teacher! Having withdrawn from the turmoil of the world for the sake of God's love, you chose to make your abode in the trackless wilderness and impenetrable forests. And having increased the children of the wilderness like a fruitful branch, you showed yourself to them as an image of every monastic virtue by word, writing, and manner of life....We beseech you, O you who are blessed of God: instruct us also...that we may love the Lord God with all our heart, please him alone and think of him alone, skillfully trampling underfoot those thoughts that drag us down, and may ever vanquish the assaults of the enemy...and plant in our hearts every virtue wherein you labored. Entreat Christ God that he illumine the minds and hearts of all...that they may see salvation, that he establish them in faith and piety, and in the doing of his commandments protect them from the deception of this world, and grant unto them and to us remission of sins, and bestow upon them, according to his true promise, all things they need for this transitory life. Yea, let those who abide in the wilderness and in the world live a life of inner stillness, in all piety and honor, and glorify him with mouth and heart, together with his unoriginate Father and his all-holy, good, and life-creating Spirit, always, now and ever, and unto the ages of ages. Amen.

ISAAC E. LAMBERTSEN

c. 1443–1508: Though little is known of his life, it is certain that from deep within the vast wilderness of northern Russia, Nilus called Russian monasticism back to simplicity, humility, prayer, and the basic teachings of the early Church.

—MAY 8—

Blessed Julian of Norwich

Blessed Julian, you rejoice that God is our Father, and you rejoice that Jesus is our Mother, and you rejoice that God is our Lord. You also taught that "all shall be well and all shall be well and all manner of thing shall be well." Pray that I take these words into my heart, that I learn to trust completely in God's goodness. Show me how to abandon myself to God's tender mercy. Through your intercession, may I come to know the joy of God's providential love and care. May I be united with God in prayer. May I come to live, move, and have my being in God alone. I ask this in the name of Jesus, our Savior and mother. Amen.

1343–1423: An unhappy child, Julian prayed for an early death. However, during an illness she received such clear visions of the passion of our Lord that she decided to become an anchoress and spend her time in spiritual reading. Her famous writing *Revelations of Divine Love* is a classic of English mysticism.

—MAY 9—

Blessed Marie Theresa of Jesus Gerhardinger

Blessed Marie Theresa, your order of teachers has been a pioneering influence in the development of education in countless European and American countries, and you continue to be a shining example for all Christian educators. Intercede on their behalf, I pray, that they may not shy from sacrifice or difficulties of any kind in order to fulfill God's work. I ask your blessing especially on *(mention name)*, a teacher whose love and wisdom made a great impression upon me during my youth. Bless also *(mention name[s])*, my *child's/children's* teacher(s); inspire *him/her/them* to teach as Jesus taught, with compassion and great insight into the needs of students. And bless all who work with difficult students, that they may have God's patience for the challenge. In the name of Jesus, our great rabboni, I pray. Amen.

1797–1879: Marie Theresa founded the School Sisters of Notre Dame in Stadtamhof, Germany. She eventually made her way to the United States to start new missions among the German immigrants, returning to Germany to direct the congregation as superior general and sending sisters to many lands.

—MAY 10—

Saint Solange

Most pure Saint Solange, your communication with the Lord was so remarkable that even the stars shone more brilliantly during your conversations. As I so long to converse with the Lord as you did, I implore you to send me your spirit of prayer. Teach me to talk to God as a friend, intimately, laying out all my joys and fears and needs and hopes. Teach me to listen too, that I may hear God speaking to me in my heart. And help me to have faith in the truth of God's words of hope and mercy and compassion and love. I ask you also to pray for *(mention request)*, who is having a difficult time praying; be with *her/him* during times of prayer, and carry *her/his* words to the Lord. I ask this in the name of Jesus, our Savior, who taught his disciples and all of us how to pray. Amen.

died c. 880: A poor shepherdess of the neighborhood of Bourges, France, Solange was murdered by a local lord for resisting his sexual advances. She was known for her ability to heal illnesses and advise people about the spiritual life and was noted for having a guiding star that shone more brilliantly when she was praying or meditating.

—MAY 11—

Saint Ignatius of Laconi

Most holy Saint Ignatius, humble brother, your hidden life of labor and poverty reveal to me the necessity of rooting pride from my mind and heart. Pour down upon me your blessings, that God may give me the grace and courage to be humble and to rely upon others for my needs. Inspire me to follow your example of doing humble, menial tasks well, all for the love of God. Help me to accept God's will in all things, but especially when it seems to require serving others' needs before my own, as this is a great challenge for me. Most of all, holy saint, help me to pray, that in communicating with God I may discern the direction my service should take. I ask this through Christ our Lord. Amen.

1701–1781: Born into dire poverty on the island of Sardinia, Ignatius entered the Capuchin monastery of Saint Benedict at Cuoncammino and led a life as a lay brother. He worked for many years in the weaving room and, for the last forty years of his life, begged his bread from door to door. He was known for his holiness, his deep prayer life, and his ability to cure illness.

—MAY 12—

Saint Pancras

PATRON OF CHILDREN, OATHS, AND TREATIES

O glorious Saint Pancras, who, in the flower of youth, which for you was especially rich in the promises of the world, renounced all, with true greatness of mind, to embrace the faith and to serve our Lord Jesus Christ in a spirit of burning love and profound humility; and who joyfully offered your life for him in a sublime martyrdom: now that you are all-powerful with him, hear our prayers. Obtain for us a lively faith that shall be a shining light upon our earthly path; an ardent love of God above all things and of our neighbor as ourselves; a spirit of detachment from the good things of earth and a contempt for the vanities of this world; the grace of true humility in the exemplary profession of the Christian life. We pray you in especial manner for all young men. Remember that you are the patron of youth; therefore, by your intercession, make all young men clean of heart and fervent in piety, and bring them safe to our Lord. Obtain for all of us the happiness of heaven. Amen.

THE RACCOLTA

died c. 304: A Phrygian of noble birth, Pancras sought baptism at the age of fourteen. When he thereupon proceeded to give all his possessions to the poor, the authorities, realizing that he was a Christian, had him arrested, and he was decapitated because he refused to renounce Christianity.

—MAY 13—

Saint Mary Domenica Mazzarello

Saint Mary Domenica Mazzarello, you who dedicated your entire life for the salvation of souls, inspire me, as I strive to save my own soul, to lead others to love Jesus and Mary, to spread the Good News of Christ's unfailing love to those I meet, and to be joyfully optimistic as I go about my daily tasks for the love of God and neighbor. I ask this through Christ our Lord. Amen.

DAUGHTERS OF MARY HELP OF CHRISTIANS

1837–1881: After almost dying from typhoid fever, Mary and her cousin gathered together the girls of their town—Mornese, near Genoa, Italy—to teach them dressmaking, as well as the art of loving God. Some of these girls formed the nucleus of the Institute of the Daughters of Mary Help of Christians, also known as the Salesian Sisters of Saint John Bosco. Mary was among the first professed sisters and is considered cofounder with John Bosco.

—MAY 14—

Saint Matthias

PATRON OF ALCOHOLICS;
INVOKED AGAINST ALCOHOLISM

Holy Saint Matthias, you were called to share in the mission of the apostles. By the help of your prayers, may we receive with joy the love Jesus shared with you and be counted among those he has chosen. We ask this through our Lord Jesus Christ. Amen. Saint Matthias, pray for us.

TRADITIONAL

first century: Chosen by lot to take the place of Judas Iscariot (Acts 1), Matthias was according to legend eventually martyred in Colchis. Supposedly, he evangelized in Ethiopia, where he was blinded and saved from death by Saint Andrew.

—MAY 15—

Saint Dymphna

PATRON OF ASYLUMS AND MENTAL-HEALTH
WORKERS; INVOKED AGAINST EPILEPSY,
INSANITY, AND SLEEPWALKING

Dearest Saint Dymphna, gracious patron of those suffering from afflictions of mind and body, I humbly implore your powerful intercession to Jesus through Mary, the Health of the Sick. Since you are filled with love and compassion for those who seek relief from their disorders, I beg you to show your love and compassion for me. The many miracles and cures that have been wrought by your prayers give me great hope that you will help me in my present needs. *(Mention request.)* O Saint Dymphna, young martyr of purity, the fervent faith and devotion of the many souls you have helped by your charity inspires me to entrust myself to your special care. I am confident of obtaining my urgent request, if it be for the greater glory of God and the good of my soul. Help me to bear my sufferings with patience and resignation. May my prayer for the consolation and the cure of my illness be granted through your intercession. Amen.

LEAFLET MISSAL COMPANY

sixth century: According to legend, Dymphna was the daughter of a pagan Celtic chief and a Christian mother. When her mother died, her father was determined to marry his own daughter, but Dymphna fled to Belgium. Her father found her and, when she continued to refuse his proposal, beheaded her.

—MAY 16—

Saint Brendan

PATRON OF SAILORS;
INVOKED AGAINST ULCERS

Saint Brendan, holy mariner fittingly called "God's Voyager," you zealously spread the Gospel through long and arduous voyages. Intercede for us with the "God of the waves," that we too may cherish the Gospel of salvation. Grant that through your intercession we may be led safely through all perils of the sea until we come to the land of eternal life. Through Christ our Lord. Amen.

DAUGHTERS OF ST. PAUL

c. 435–c. 583: Educated under Saints Ita, Finnian, and Gildas, Brendan was a great founder of monasteries, chief among which was Clonfert. He gave his monks a rule of remarkable austerity. Brendan is best known for his voyages, and he is said to have reached the American continent. Legends of Brendan's voyages were popular throughout Europe and can be said to have influenced the history of exploration.

—MAY 17—

Saint Paschal Baylon

PATRON OF SHEPHERDS

Paschal, illustrious is thy name,
    But brighter glows thy virtue's fame;
With many a sign thy works are crowned;
    Through thee God's gifts to [us] abound.
From heaven look down, we humbly pray,
    On us who seek thine aid this day;
Remove the evil that we dread,
    And grant us what we ask instead.
And when to heaven's high feast we go,
    The nuptial robe on us bestow,
That Christ our strength and food may be,
    In death and for eternity.
From heaven look down, we humbly pray,
    On us who seek thine aid this day.

THE RACCOLTA

1540–1592: Born of peasants in Aragon, Paschal started life as a shepherd. As a Franciscan lay brother, he spent his life mainly as doorkeeper in different friaries in Spain. He was known for his intense love for the Eucharist.

Blessed Blandina Merten

O Blessed Blandina, you know what it is to suffer intense pain, the type of pain that never leaves and that never gives one pause to rest. Help me in my pain, for it is more than I feel I can bear. O Blandina, intercede for me, I implore you, that God may ease my pain. O Blandina, I try to follow the "little way" of bearing all for love of God, the way that you followed so successfully, but I fear myself unable to continue—the pain is too much. I think only of it— I cannot think of anything else—I cannot do anything. O Blandina, ask the Lord for a pause—a breath—a short cessation of pain—that I may repose in his love and recover for a moment. Then I feel that I might go on. Dear Blandina, thank you for your prayers on my behalf. Amen.

1883–1918: From Duppenweiler, Germany, Blandina entered an Ursuline convent. Her life was filled with intense physical suffering, but she bore her pain in calm silence and continued her teaching vocation, out of concern for her students, until her death.

Saint Joaquina Vedruna de Mas

Dear Saint Joaquina, you who followed your parents wishes and married, despite your own calling to the religious life. On behalf of all children whose parents cannot or will not understand the deepest desires of the heart, I beg your intercession. Send your spirit to these children, that they may not despair. Ask the Lord to send the Holy Spirit to them, that they may know his unconditional love. Help them, that they may hold fast to their dreams—and persevere—as you did.

I beseech you, be with those parents also. Pray that the Lord, who called the children to himself, will send his Spirit to these parents, so that they too will call their own children back. And pray with me that all parents may learn to love their children unconditionally, may accept their children for who they are, and may not attempt to force a parent's wishes upon any of them. I ask this through our Lord Jesus Christ. Amen.

1783–1854: A Spanish lady, Joaquina was the wife of Teodore de Mas, of the Spanish nobility, who died in the Napoleonic wars. Joaquina then retired to Vich, where she founded the Institute of the Carmelite Sisters of Charity, now prominent throughout Spain and South America.

—MAY 20—

Saint Bernardine of Siena

PATRON OF ADVERTISING AND PUBLIC RELATIONS; INVOKED AGAINST HOARSENESS AND LUNG DISEASE

You who so deeply loved Jesus, Mary, and Joseph, dear Saint Bernardine, my special advocate and example, model of Christian modesty, restorer in our times of piety and holy living, present my prayers, I beseech you, to the Holy Family, and implore that, together with piety and the fear of God, holy purity of soul and body may reign in all Christian families and in all children of our Mother, the holy Roman Church. Amen.

THE RACCOLTA

1380–1444: A great preacher, Bernardine restored strict observance in the Franciscan Order, especially in the matter of poverty. Called "the people's preacher," he spread devotion to the Holy Name of Jesus.

—MAY 21—

Saint Eugene de Mazenod

Dear Saint Eugene, your embodiment of the hallmarks of the true Christian—courtesy, respect for the dignity of others, and fidelity to the truth—even in the face of violent antagonism, continues to inspire Christians throughout the world. O Ambassador of the Faith, I pray for your intercession in the great religious conflicts that are spreading violence in the world today. Whether the opposing parties are Catholics or Protestants, Jews or Muslims, Communists or Buddhists—intercede in the name of peace, dear saint. Give your spirit of diplomacy to leaders involved in the conflict, that they may learn the art of dialogue and may work tirelessly to bring about peace. I pray especially for *(mention request)*, that the parties involved may learn to look upon their opponents as sisters and brothers. I ask this through Christ our Lord, the Prince of Peace. Amen.

1782–1861: Born in Provence, Eugene was the last in his noble line, but he sought ordination and served in parishes in his region, where he ministered to the faithful in the aftermath of the French Revolution. He founded the Congregation of the Oblates of Mary Immaculate and succeeded to the see of Marseilles. As archbishop, Eugene declared apostolic freedom again and again in the face of civil powers trying to repress the Church in France. He was made a Peer of France, a testament to his ability to maintain the faith without alienating those with opposing views. He died just before he was to be consecrated cardinal.

—MAY 22—
Saint Rita of Cascia

PATRON OF DESPERATE CASES; INVOKED
AGAINST BLEEDING, INFERTILITY, LONELINESS,
TUMORS, AND UNHAPPY MARRIAGE

Saint Rita, valiant woman, model of Christian and religious life, blessed advocate, whom Providence has given us to win for [God] our earthly hearts, example of earnest and childlike prayer, I come before you with full confidence in your powerful intercession before our crucified Lord and his blessed Mother, whom you never petitioned in vain. I earnestly implore you to obtain for me the grace to be abandoned to the will of God, to share in your love for [God], and to imitate the virtues of which you gave so perfect an example. Listen to my prayer, blessed Rita; show that you are truly the patroness of desperate cases by obtaining the favor that I ask. In return I will sing your praises and strive to imitate your virtues. Saint Rita, advocate of the impossible, pray for me. Saint Rita, patroness of desperate cases, pray for me. Saint Rita, help me.

O glorious Saint Rita, you who so wonderfully participated in the passion of Christ, obtain for me the grace to suffer the pains of this life, and protect me in all my needs.

TRADITIONAL

1381–1457: Born into a peasant family, Rita married a brutal and dissolute husband. After his death, she entered an Augustinian convent, where she experienced visions and received a seemingly thorn-induced wound in her forehead.

Saint Euphrosyne
of Polotsk

Saint Euphrosyne, friend of the poor, help me to remember that many others in the world need my help. Though the Lord may have called me to a particular station in life, he does not want me to neglect the poor, the homeless, the hungry, the sick. Pray for me, that I may have a spirit of compassion and charity for those in need. Pray for me, that I may rise above my own selfishness and learn to recognize—and take care of—the pressing needs of other people.

O holy saint, help me also to remember that my own brand of spirituality is not the only brand around. Teach me to respect the wonderful spiritualities of other traditions, that I may learn from them and thus deepen my relationship with the Lord. Ask him to grace me—and everyone—with a spirit not only of tolerance but also of gracious acceptance and embracing love. I ask this through Christ our Lord. Amen.

died 1173: The daughter of Prince Svyatoslav of Polotsk, Euphrosyne entered a monastery at the age of twelve and later became a solitary at the Church of Santa Sophia. The money she earned by copying books was used to care for the poor. She also founded a monastery for women. She died during a pilgrimage to Jerusalem but is buried in Kiev.

—MAY 24—

Blessed Louis
Zephyrinus Moreau

Blessed Louis, your understanding of the needs of others was blessed, enabling you to serve one and all with tact and grace. Bless me, that I too may understand what my loved ones, friends, and colleagues may need most, and that I may find the best way to have their needs met. Particularly, bless me in my service as a leader, that I may pay attention to the wants and needs of those who have been entrusted to my care. Remind me to keep them first in my thoughts; remind me that my job is to care for them. This I pray in Jesus' name. Amen.

1824–1901: A native of Bécancour, Canada, Louis was eventually named bishop of St. Hyacinthe. He dedicated a new cathedral, sponsored religious communities, and promoted education. He also founded the Sisters of St. Hyacinthe, dedicated to helping priests and religious with their administrative duties.

—MAY 25—

Saint Madeleine
Sophie Barat

Dearest Saint Madeleine, despite personal illness and difficulties, you persevered in your calling, dedicating yourself to the education of women and founding a congregation dedicated to Jesus' Sacred Heart. Bless all those responsible for the education of children, and pray that all children may come to know God's love and concern through the love and respect given to them. Pray that all administrators may share in your gift of wisdom and moderation. Pray that all teachers may become great lovers of humility and recognize God as the source and giver of all that we are and possess. And pray that we have "no memory but to remember, no heart but to bless, no strength but to serve." This we ask in the name of Jesus. Amen.

1779–1865: Born in Burgundy, France, Madeleine founded the Society of the Sacred Heart, to educate girls who were growing up without the Faith after the turmoil of the French Revolution.

—MAY 26—

Saint Philip Neri

PATRON OF ROME

O holy Apostle of Rome, you accepted your divine calling to convert and sanctify souls in the city of Rome, which had become lukewarm and corrupt. Indeed, you transformed Rome in your own lifetime. I implore you, therefore, to convert and sanctify my soul, for I too have become lukewarm in my love for the Lord. I too am a sinner, falling far short of the person God has called me to be. I too need your transforming spirit to pray for me, to rescue my soul for God. O great Saint Philip, you who were able to bring an entire city to holiness, ask the Lord to enlarge my heart with love, as yours was enlarged, and to accept the gift of my most humble love. This I ask through our Lord Jesus Christ. Amen.

1515–1595: Born in Florence, Philip founded the Congregation of the Oratory in Rome. He lived simply, served all, and influenced all those he encountered to follow Jesus.

—MAY 27—

Saint Augustine
(or Austin)
of Canterbury

PATRON OF ENGLAND

Holy Saint Augustine, great apostle of England and renowned apostle to the Gentiles, you were a glorious defender of the faith and a worthy confessor of Christ our Lord. Pray for us, that we may also faithfully witness the Gospel to the world. In all dangers of losing the faith, and especially in the hour of our death, help us by your intercession. That our faith may never cease, make intercession for us. That our hope may continually increase, make intercession for us. That we may perpetually love God with a sincere heart, make intercession for us. And that we may never lose the grace and love of our God, make intercession for us. Pray for us, O holy Augustine, that we may be made worthy of the promises of Christ. Amen.

died 604: Augustine shares with Pope Saint Gregory the Great the title Apostle of the English, for the pope sent Augustine with a band of forty companions to evangelize England. He had soon converted the king of Kent and thousands of his subjects and, consecrated bishop, established his see at Canterbury.

Saint Mariana Paredes y Flores, the Lily of Quito

Most holy Saint Mariana, beautiful Lily of Quito, you gave yourself selflessly to protect and preserve your people. I ask you now, please pray for *(mention name)* who is ill, that *he/she* may have a complete healing, or if that be impossible, that *he/she* may realize the good that God can make of this illness.

Please intercede also for *(mention location)* and its people, who are experiencing terrible natural calamities, that the floods may recede, the droughts may end, the wildfires may burn out, the earth cease its trembling, the hurricanes and tornadoes calm their terrible roar. Preserve all from hurt and death, and assure them of your prayers so that they may experience the never-ending love of God. I ask this in the name of Jesus, who stilled the winds and calmed the seas. Amen.

1618–1645: When Ecuador was struck by a series of calamities—earthquakes, epidemics, and a volcano eruption—Mariana gave herself as a propitiatory offering. The calamities stopped, and she was stricken at once with an unidentifiable, lingering sickness, from which she died two months later.

Blessed Joseph Gérard

Dear Joseph, sometimes when I find myself among people who are different from me—perhaps on a bus or the subway train—I feel completely isolated. Their manners, their dress, their language are all strange to me; I can't understand them, and I feel, I must admit, afraid. You who were a missionary eager to understand souls, help me in these moments. Lend me some of your understanding, that I may dare to extend my hand in friendship to people who are not like me, that I may risk a close encounter, that I may hope to follow Jesus' example of seeking relationships with all people whomever they might be. Blessed Joseph, encourage my faltering efforts, and bless me in my failures, that I may, like you, not give up but rededicate myself, so that I may find God in the face of all people. I ask this through Christ our Lord. Amen.

1831–1914: Born at Bouxières-aux-Chênes, France, Joseph joined the Oblates of Mary Immaculate and was ordained in Natal, South Africa. Determined to serve the native peoples of the area faithfully, he took up residence in a tent and went from village to village to care for the sick and minister to the people's spiritual needs. When he died in Roma, Lesotho, officials from all the regional tribes gathered to lay him to rest as the "Friend of the Africans."

—MAY 30—

Saint Joan of Arc

PATRON OF FRANCE

Most holy Saint Joan, you bravely obeyed the voices you heard because they were carrying messages to you from God. Intercede for me, that I may clearly hear those voices telling me of God. Clear away all extraneous noise, and quiet those other voices that doubt the authenticity of God's message.

O dearest Joan, bless me also with the desire to pray, that I may commune with God. Teach me to quiet my own internal noise; teach me to listen. As well, give me courage to bring God's word to others, that I may share with them the good news of God's love for all. I implore your blessing through Jesus our Lord, whose voice speaks clearly through the ages. Amen.

1412–1431: The daughter of Domrémy peasants, at the age of seventeen Joan heard supernatural voices commanding her to take up arms and lead the French army against the English invaders. Joan's rapid successes enabled Charles VII to be crowned at Rheims. However, the Burgundians handed her over to the English, who condemned her as a heretic. She was burned at the stake at Rouen.

—MAY 31—

Saint Mechtildis of Edelstetten

Mechtildis, give me the courage to stand up for the rules when I know they are fair and just. Also help me in difficult tasks involving human relations, such as hiring, firing, promoting, and reprimanding those for whom I am responsible. Let me never be vindictive in these decisions, but let me carry them out with grace, good humor, and love.

TOM COWAN

1125–1160: The daughter of nobility, Mechtildis was placed in the convent her parents sponsored at Diessen, where in due time she professed the Benedictine rule and became abbess. Later, the bishop of Augsburg appointed her abbess of the convent of Edelstetten, which was in dire need of reform. In the teeth of fierce opposition—some of the nuns having in fact to be expelled—she carried through the job and was greatly revered by her contemporaries.

June

Saint Justin

PATRON OF PHILOSOPHERS

Saint Justin Martyr, you are known as the first Christian philosopher, the first to combine the best elements of Greek philosophy with the Christian faith. Pray for me, that in my search for Truth, God will open the gates of light for me the way God did for you and give me the wisdom no human being can give. Remind me daily of what you and the other early saints of the Church knew, that I believe in order to understand, and that I understand in order to believe. I pray through Jesus our Lord, who is the Way, the Truth, and the Life. Amen.

c. 100–165: Born in Samaria, Justin first heard of Christianity while on his way to study Platonic philosophy in Alexandria. After his baptism, he traveled extensively, debating nonbelievers, one of whom, Crescens, reported Justin to the civil authorities, who had him executed.

—JUNE 2—

Saint Elmo of Formiae

PATRON OF SAILORS AND WOMEN IN LABOR;
INVOKED AGAINST COLIC, SEASICKNESS,
AND STOMACHACHE

Holy martyr Elmo, who willingly and bravely bore the trials and sufferings of life, and by your charity consoled many fellow-sufferers; I implore you to remember me in my need and to intercede for me with God. Staunch confessor of the faith, victorious vanquisher of all tortures, pray to Jesus for me and ask him to grant me the grace to live and die in the faith through which you obtained your crown of glory. Amen.

TRADITIONAL

died c. 303: A Syrian bishop who fled to a cave on Mount Lebanon to escape persecution, Elmo, also known as Erasmus, was fed by a raven before finally being captured and set afire. He survived and escaped in a boat, crossing the Mediterranean to Italy, where he died of his wounds.

—JUNE 3—

Saint Charles Lwanga and Companions, Martyrs of Uganda

PATRONS OF AFRICAN YOUTH

Holy Martyrs of Uganda, pray for the faith where it is in danger and for Christians who must suffer because of their faith. Give them the same courage, zeal, and joy you showed. And help those of us who live in places where Christianity is accepted to pro-

tect all those who suffer persecution in other parts
of the world.
   Saint Charles Lwanga, pray for us.
   Saint Joseph Mukaso, pray for us.
   Saint Denis Sebuggwawo, pray for us.
   Saint Kizito, pray for us.
   Saint James Buzabaliawo, pray for us.
   Saint Mbaga, pray for us.
   Saint Matthias Murumba, pray for us.
   Saint Andrew Kagwa, pray for us.
   O holy Martyrs of Uganda, pray for us, now and
at the hour of our death. Amen.

1865–1886: Kept in the palace as a sex object for King
Mwanga, Charles, a recent convert to Christianity, sought
to convert his fellows and keep them from participating in
the king's lustful activities. When the king discovered
Charles's proselytizing, he had him and twenty-two Christian companions burned alive.

—JUNE 4—

Saint Francis Caracciolo

O holy Saint Francis, adorer of the Eucharist,
preacher of Divine Love, apostle to the poor, the
sick, and the imprisoned. We implore you, send us
your spirit, that we may imitate your love for Jesus
in the Eucharist. Send us your spirit, that we may
courageously speak to friend and stranger alike of
the wondrous things that God has done for us. Send
us your spirit, that we may spare no effort to ease
the suffering of those who can no longer help themselves. Teach us to heal the sick, to rehabilitate the
imprisoned, to empower the poor. And through all,
inspire us to aim always for the greater glory of the
Risen Lord.

Through your intercession, O holy saint, we ask finally that you inspire many young men and women to follow Christ totally in a spirit of prayer, penance, and zeal for the building of God's kingdom on earth. Amen.

ADORNO FATHERS

1563–1608: A scion of a noble Neapolitan family, Francis suffered from a leprosy-like disease during his youth, but he was cured upon deciding to become a priest. He founded with John Augustine Adorno the order of Minor Clerks Regular. Francis was the first general of the order and spent his life in governing it and in preaching.

—JUNE 5—

Saint Boniface of Mainz

PATRON OF GERMANY, PRUSSIA, AND BREWERS

Dear Saint Boniface, holy martyr, you spread the faith by your teaching and witnessed to it with your blood. By the help of your prayers, keep us loyal to our faith, and give us the courage to profess it in our lives. Grant this through our Lord Jesus Christ, who lives and reigns for ever and ever. Amen.

Saint Boniface, pray for us.

TRADITIONAL

680–754: An Anglo-Saxon, Boniface became a Benedictine monk at Exeter. His first mission to Germany was a complete failure, so he went to Rome to get the pope's blessing before his next endeavor, which was successful, in that he evangelized Bavaria, Hesse, Friesland, Thuringia, and Franconia. Boniface was made bishop over the Germanies and finally archbishop of Mainz. He founded the abbey of Fulda, among many others, as the focus of German missionary activities. He was martyred with fifty-two companions at Dokkum and is known as the "Apostle of Germany."

Saint Norbert

Dear Saint Norbert, when you heard the voice of God telling you to turn from evil and do good, to seek and pursue peace, you did not hesitate but immediately devoted yourself to prayer and penance. When your former friends denounced you as a hypocrite, your response was to give everything you owned to the poor and to set out as an itinerant preacher to spread the Gospel.

O holy Saint Norbert, be my guide when the voices of the world try to divert me from God. Help me to follow wherever God may lead, despite opposition and hardship. And ask God to send the Holy Spirit to me, to strengthen my commitment to the mission the Lord has entrusted to me. I ask this through Christ our Lord. Amen.

c. 1080–1134: A narrow escape from death brought about Norbert's conversion, and he became an itinerant preacher. He founded a community of canons regular under the Rule of Saint Augustine near Laon, and the order, known as Norbertines, spread over western Europe. Norbert was appointed bishop of Magdeburg, where he reformed the clergy, and he was known for his zeal in fostering the cult of the Blessed Sacrament.

Venerable Matt Talbot

O holy Matt, God gave you the wisdom to realize that your addiction was destroying your life and the courage and fortitude to do something about it. Intercede, I implore you, on behalf of all those who suffer from addictions. Help them to see how ruinous their addictions are, to themselves and to those who love them. Bless them with a spirit of humility, that they may seek assistance in overcoming their addictions. Ask the Lord to give them the gift of fortitude, that they may persevere, become free of their addiction, and do what they must to remain free for the rest of their lives, as you did. Dear Matt, I pray especially for *(mention name)*. Bless *her/him* in a special way, and ask the Lord to wrap *her/him* in his protective and healing love. I ask this in the name of Jesus, our great healer. Amen.

1856–1925: An alcoholic, Matt came home drunk from his first job in a wine-bottling store at age twelve and spent little time sober until he was twenty-eight, when he encountered a priest and made a pledge not to drink for three months. He extended that pledge until his death, at age sixty-nine, from heart failure. He was on his way to Mass.

—JUNE 8—

Saint William of York

William, your career as a churchman proves how God can throw obstacles in front of us, testing our resolve and patience. Help me when things always seem to go wrong to stay optimistic and to believe that what happens is God's will. I pray that I will learn from my adversities and grow spiritually even when setbacks and misfortunes challenge my faith.

TOM COWAN

died 1154: William Fitzherbert was appointed archbishop of York, but his powerful enemies, chiefly the White Monks, contested the appointment as an example of simony. Pope Innocent II had to step in, deciding in favor of William; but the pope died, and the next pope, Eugene III, sided with the opposition and had William deposed. He went into retirement, until the next pope reappointed him archbishop. William died one month after his installation.

—JUNE 9—

Blessed Annemarie Taigi

O Blessed Annemarie Taigi, you loved your family and were committed to their needs during your earthly life and to all those who turned to you for spiritual and material help. Open my heart to the hope of receiving your help, even from heaven.

O most worthy servant of God, model and patroness of Christian mothers, obtain for me the grace to imitate you in all those virtues you practiced so perfectly here below in carrying out your noble mission. Grant me the grace to give good example before giving advice and to practice my Christian duties. May I also faithfully love Jesus crucified and Mary most holy, Mother of Mercy. May I listen attentively to their holy words.

Grant me sweetness in correcting, impartiality in loving, fidelity in my duties, order and preciseness in everything. And may I be able to bear, as you did, my [spouse's/partner's] faults.

Obtain for me perfect resignation in my afflictions and perfect submission to the will of God. May I live a holy life, at peace with everyone here on earth, and enjoy the eternal bliss of heaven with my dear ones. Amen.

DAUGHTERS OF SAINT PAUL

1769–1837: Born at Siena, Annemarie worked in Rome as a domestic servant before marrying Dominic Taigi, a butler, living the life of a married working-class woman and raising seven children. She was endowed with the gift of prophecy and could read thoughts, and her home became the rendezvous of cardinals and other dignitaries seeking her counsel.

—JUNE 10—

Saint Margaret of Scotland

PATRON OF SCOTLAND

Dearest Saint Margaret, you had a great love for the poor and helped them as much as you could, yet you knew that your time belonged to your own family, and you gave them your all. Help me to remember, as I go about my busy day, to give my best to my spouse/partner, my children, my parents, and my siblings. Keep them always before me, that in everything I do I will consider them first, doing nothing that will bring them harm in any way. Most of all, help me to express my love for them, that they will know how unconditionally I love them and will always love them. Saint Margaret, please bless my family. Amen.

1046–1093: Granddaughter of King Edmund "Ironside" of England, Margaret married King Malcolm III Canmore of Scotland and used her influence as queen for the good of religion and for the promotion of justice. She had eight children, gave charity to the poor, and founded the Benedictine abbey of Dunfermline.

—JUNE 11—

Blessed Paula Frassinetti

O Blessed Paula, despite your frail health, you took on the difficult labor of educating those children whose families could not afford schooling. You also became leader of a group of women dedicated to the education of the poor. By your example, remind me that I can do more than others expect of me. Indeed, inspire me to rise above the limitations my family members or friends or "those who know best" might place upon my life. Help them to understand me and what I must do. And pray for me, that the Lord may strengthen my resolve to follow wherever he calls me to go. I ask your intercession through our Savior, Jesus Christ. Amen.

1809–1882: Born at Genoa, Paula lived with her brother, a parish priest, in the suburbs and taught poor children. This was the beginning of the Congregation of Saint Dorothy, which Paula lived to see flourish throughout Italy and the Western Hemisphere.

—JUNE 12—

Saint Gaspar Bertoni

Saint Gaspar Bertoni, with generous self-giving, you followed the path of filial abandonment to Divine Providence and came to live for God and [God's] glory alone, dedicating your life for the benefit of others. Intercede for us to have the strength not to be overwhelmed with the cares of our own lives. May we accept with love, faith, and hope God's divine will.

Obtain for us, through the intercession of Mary most holy and Saint Joseph, whom you chose as special patrons, the graces we now need. *(Mention request.)* Help us to reach [the Lord's] house one day, to sing there with you our own hymn of eternal gratitude.

We ask you for one more favor. You, who were a tireless apostle for the youth who lived in difficult times, come now to the assistance of so many young people who are searching for God's love. Intercede for them that they might discover the light of faith and live in the grace and love of Jesus Christ. Amen.

STIGMATINE FATHERS AND BROTHERS

1777–1853: Born in Verona, Gaspar experienced the Napoleonic invasions and their aftermath, establishing Marian Oratories and organizing tuition-free schools to prepare young people to assume the responsibilities of a mature Christian life. He also founded the Stigmatine Fathers and Brothers, in reflection of his own physical suffering (he underwent 300 operations) and the suffering of Jesus in the passion.

—JUNE 13—

Saint Anthony of Padua

Saint Anthony, friend of the scatter-brained,
finder of mislaid surnames, pens, umbrellas,
    Daily Missals,
library books, purses, gloves and
    reading spectacles,
scarves, keys, handkerchiefs, and
    important addresses;
in this noise-wracked, unresting,
    scurrying world,
from your serener state,
bring my paraphernalia to me,
tidy my mind, and create
order, out of my chaos.

PATRICIA SOPER

1195–1231: Born in Lisbon, Anthony left the Augustinians to become a Franciscan. Ill health forced him to abandon his missionary activities among the Moors, and during his return voyage from Morocco a storm brought him to Italy, where he remained. He was a famous preacher, undoubtedly one of the greatest of all times, and was reportedly visited by the child Jesus. He is a Doctor of the Church.

Blessed Castora Gabrielli

Blessed Castora, you returned the abuse of a violent, angry husband with Christian charity. Though I honor your example of patient endurance, I ask your intercession for all those who suffer spousal abuse. Protect them from harm, and ask the Lord, I beseech you, to take them out of danger immediately. Help me to help any victims of family violence who seek my aid, and help me and my own family follow our pledge of nonviolence. I ask this through our Lord, Jesus Christ, who through his own example of nonviolence inspires my own commitment. Amen.

died 1391: A Franciscan tertiary, wife and widow of a lawyer, Castora sanctified herself by the daily practice of the domestic virtues.

—JUNE 15—

Saint Vito

PATRON OF ACTORS, COMEDIANS, DANCERS, AND SICILY; INVOKED AGAINST CHOREA, EPILEPSY, SNAKEBITE, STORMS, WILD ANIMALS, AND OVERSLEEPING

Angelic youth, giant of virtue, our most glorious protector, we venerate you with all the ardor of our souls. We exult in the reflection of your glory and triumphs, as well as those of the other martyrs, surviving the flames, the burning pitch, the liquid lead, and the famished savage beasts. As you were assisted by the Almighty, assist us, your unworthy petitioners, so that we also may overcome the temptations that prevent us from doing good. As you

loved Saints Modesto and Crescenza, your inseparable companions even in your martyrdom, so love
us, your devoted followers, granting us all good for
soul and body. We praise Almighty God, who established you as a powerful protector, and we beseech you—through the ardent flame of love that in
the midst of your extreme torments renewed in you
the desire to be reunited with your and our God—
to protect us in life, and especially at the moment of
our death, from the insidious arts of the devil. Amen.

CHURCH OF ST. VITO

c. fourth century: While still a young boy, Vito was baptized against his father's wishes. Warned by an angel, he
fled his father's wrath. Thereafter, he earned such a reputation for holiness that the emperor Diocletian summoned him
to cure his son. After the cure, the ungrateful emperor tried
to persuade Vito to renounce Christ and subjected him, along
with Modesto and Crescenza, to vile tortures. When they
still remained resolute, they were torn asunder on the rack.

—JUNE 16—

Saint Lutgardis
of Aywières

Holy Saint Lutgardis, the Lord took you, a completely unspiritual person, and wooed you with his
love to make you a saint. Intercede for all those who
lack any spiritual inclinations, that the Lord may
bestow upon them the grace to seek him out and
learn of his love. Pray for them, that they may discover their spiritual natures and find the deeper value
of being loved by the Lord. Bless them, that they
may commit themselves to establishing a relationship with God.

Pray also for all parents who bewail the light-mindedness or frivolity of their children. Reassure them that the Lord has his own time, and that in due time he will make himself known to these children. Urge them as well to continue to pray, so that they themselves may continue to enjoy a fruitful relationship with God. This we ask in Jesus' name. Amen.

died 1246: Lodging in a convent because her family had lost her dowry in a business transaction, Lutgardis lived a frivolous life until the Lord appeared to her and asked for her love. From that moment, Lutgardis communed with our Lord. She also had the gift of visitations from the Blessed Mother and other saints. She eventually went to live with the Cistercians, receiving the gifts of healing, prophecy, and understanding of the Scriptures.

—JUNE 17—

Saint Albert Chmielowski

Albert, you lost a leg in fighting for the freedom of your nation. Remind me that any worthy cause has its price, and sometimes the price can be high. Give me the strength and commitment to fight for freedom wherever I see the need, especially where it will help the poor and the powerless, who may not be able to fight for themselves.

TOM COWAN

1845–1916: Having joined the Polish uprising against the Russian occupation in 1863, Albert was imprisoned and had to have his leg amputated. When the revolt failed, he returned home and became a well-known artist. After an unsuccessful stint with the Jesuits, he became a Franciscan tertiary, working with the poor. He eventually donned the religious habit and committed himself to serve others. To this end he founded the Albertine Order.

—JUNE 18—

Saint Elizabeth of Schönau

Most holy Saint Elizabeth, blessed visionary, God gifted you with visions so that you could warn people to repent and avert disaster. Indeed, your own penances often prevented predicted calamities. Thus I implore you, if you have recourse to visions of trouble headed my way, please send me warning so that I may repent and escape disaster. But if the troubles are unavoidable, then help me to endure all patiently, with God's grace. Pray that I may also be a source of comfort to others in times of sorrow, that I may comfort the afflicted and soothe the troubled, that I may myself be a messenger of God's grace and an agent of Jesus' love. I ask this through Christ our Lord, who is love and peace. Amen.

died 1164: Entering the convent at age twelve, Elizabeth practiced austerities and mortifications despite her illnesses. She was gifted with celestial visions and prophecies, as well as diabolical persecutions. Her brother later published accounts of her visions, *The Book of the Ways of God.*

—JUNE 19—

Saint Romuald

O glorious witness of Christ, Romuald, father and guide of the Camaldolese, intercede for our salvation and that of all, so that with the help of your prayers we may gain the kingdom of heaven.

Glory be to the Father and to the Son and to the Holy Spirit, so that with the help of your prayers we may gain the kingdom of heaven.

Pray for us, holy Father Romuald, that we may be made worthy of the promises of Christ. Amen.

CAMALDOLESE HERMITS OF MONTE CORONA

c. 951–1027: During his youth, Romuald witnessed his father commit murder and vowed to atone for the crime by becoming a monk at the Benedictine abbey of Classe near Ravenna. After three years as abbot, Romuald resigned to lead a wandering life, establishing hermitages and monasteries, the best known of these being that of Camaldoli near Arezzo, Italy.

—JUNE 20—

Blessed Michelina Metelli of Pesaro

O Blessed Michelina, a chance meeting caused you to change your life and follow the Lord. Remind me that I represent Christ to others, in what I say and in how I act. Pray for me, that my chance and casual encounters with other people will be for them occasions of grace. Bless me, that I may always act with charity, so as to show other people how much God loves all of us.

O Blessed Michelina, remind me also of how deeply I am trapped in the vain pursuit of worldly goods and glory. Bless my efforts to live simply, and bless my attempts at humility. I pray for your blessing in Jesus' name. Amen.

died 1356: From Urbino, Italy, Michelina was a wealthy widow and mother who continued her life of pleasure until she met Syriaca, a Third Order Franciscan recluse begging alms. This meeting led to Michelina's conversion, and when her son died she became a Third Order Franciscan, giving all her wealth to the poor. Her family had her committed as mentally ill, but she was released as harmless and began a ministry to lepers and others with terrible illnesses.

Saint Aloysius Gonzaga

PATRON OF YOUTH, SPECIAL
PROTECTOR OF YOUNG STUDENTS

Aloysius, is there a single secret or seed of the kingdom you do not know or bear within? Born in a
most arrogant time, when belief in the self and all
that one could do had tilted minds and faces like
elegant Botticellis to the new gods who peered from
the convex and concave mirrors of the High Re-
naissance. In the painted, sculpted images of you,
however, one can still see the precocious boy who
taught simply, like the Lost Child, from the starched
ruff and collar of your brief childhood. Or in
Guercino's masterpiece, you are a lambent flame,
flickering and burning 'neath a smoke of singing
angels before the Capuchin cross. Or in hospitals
and hospices you are captured as Legros's healing
boy, carrying the sick and dying; youthful midwife
to the second birth, watching souls pass like spirit
birds into the Light of [God's] presence. And then
you are happily home, perched on the clouds, wav-
ing a shaft of lilies, and smiling, from Pozzo's trompe
l'oeil skies. But in the shadows of my night, when I
cannot find your smile or the harbor of your wings,
when I fear my limbs and will are clay, I remember
you also grew from silt and sludge, and then
suddenly...you appear as the flowering lotus, and
this sutra is all I need touch and know and hear of
you for now.

"ALUIGI GONZAGA: THE LOTUS SUTRA,"
WILLIAM HART MCNICHOLS, S.J.

1568–1591: Aloysius served as a page at the courts of Tuscany,
Mantua, and Spain, entering the Society of Jesus when eighteen after overcoming his family's opposition. Within six years
he fell sick while nursing the plague-stricken and died.

—JUNE 22—

Saint Thomas More

O glorious, merry martyr, Saint Thomas More! Your
constant prayer was that your heart should never
grow cold or lukewarm in love for your sweet savior, Jesus! With noble charity for your enemies, you
went to your martyrdom with a kindly jest on your
lips; pray for us, that we may obtain the grace that
was your glory, of cheerful giving both to God and
our neighbors. From your glory on high, intercede
for us that we may join you in the company of the
saints and rejoice with him who won our salvation
through his bitter Passion and death. May your
prayers to Christ the King guide those who work in
the legal profession to learn from you that service
to others is inseparable from the laws of God and
the holy Church. Amen.

LEAFLET MISSAL COMPANY

1478–1535: Thomas More was Lord Chancellor of England
under Henry VIII. Unable to support the king on the question of royal divorce, Thomas resigned his post. On refusing to take an oath affirming the king as supreme head of
the Church in England, Thomas was imprisoned and later
beheaded. He is known as the "martyr of the papacy."

—JUNE 23—

Saint Etheldreda

Most holy Saint Etheldreda, you were fortunate that
the authorities of your day allowed you to follow
the vows you had made to God, no matter the civil
customs of the time. Intercede for all those who find
themselves in unusual domestic situations, that their
positions may be resolved with discernment and love
on the part of all parties. Pray for them, that their

first priority always be the love of God and the love
and well-being of their spouse/partner. Inspire them
to seek and follow Truth, that they may overcome
any conflicts with confident assurance that they are
doing God's will. In Jesus' name. Amen.

died 679: Also known as Audrey, the widow Etheldreda
was remarried to the king of Northumbria while he was but
a boy, and he granted her wish of a continent marriage.
When he came of age and desired a real wife, however,
Church authorities decided it would be best for Etheldreda
to become a nun. She thereafter was founder of a double
abbey at Ely.

—JUNE 24—

Saint John the Baptist

PATRON OF AUTO ROUTES, CANDLEMAKERS,
FARRIERS, HEALTH SPAS, JORDAN, LEATHER
WORKERS, ROAD WORKERS, AND WOOL WORKERS

Saint John the Baptist, precursor of Christ and glorious forerunner of the Sun of Justice, be for us a
burning lamp lighting our way to the Savior.

Saint John the Baptist, voice crying in the wilderness and intrepid preacher of truth, tell us clearly
the true path we each must follow.

Saint John the Baptist, example of profound humility, show us how to put God in the first position
in our daily lives.

Saint John the Baptist, glorious martyr of zeal
for God's holy law, help us to show others by our
own example that God's kingdom is our ultimate goal.

Saint John the Baptist, most of all, pray for us
and all people of faith, that we may rejoice in the
way of eternal salvation, through Jesus Christ our
Lord. Amen.

first century: The four Gospels fully describe John's career
as forerunner of the Messiah. He was the son of Zechariah
and Elizabeth and cousin to Jesus, whom he baptized in the
Jordan River. John was beheaded by Herod.

—JUNE 25—

Saint William of Vercelli

Saint William, in the exuberance of youth you went
to live as a hermit, eager for the opportunity to ex-
plore the Word of God in all its wonder and challenge, and your loving spirit attracted many souls,
whom you formed into a great community. Bless all
young people, that they may joyfully follow the
promptings of their spirits. Encourage them to go
where they hear God calling them, to do what they
hear God asking them, to be what they hear God
suggesting to them. Ask the Lord to remove all im-
pediments from before them; remind us as well to
stay out of their way, that they may with youthful
exuberance, like you, do something wonderful for
God. In Jesus' name we pray. Amen.

1085–1142: A noble orphan, William went to live as a hermit on Monte Virgiliano, where he attracted many disciples
whom he eventually formed into a community known as
the Hermits of Monte Vergine. William established five other
houses and served as adviser to King Roger I of Naples.

—JUNE 26—

Blessed Josemaría
Escrivá de Balaguer

O Blessed Josemaría, God granted you countless
graces, choosing you as a most faithful instrument

to found Opus Dei, a way of sanctification through daily work and the fulfillment of the ordinary duties of a Christian. Pray for me, that I also may learn to turn all the circumstances and events of my life into occasions of loving God and serving the Church and all souls, with joy and simplicity, lighting up the ways of the earth with brightness of faith and love.

Dear Josemaría, through the intercession of your love for Christ, grant me the favor I ask of you here. *(Mention request.)* I ask this in the name of Jesus our Lord, who lives and reigns forever. Amen.

1902–1975: From Spain, Josemaría felt at an early age that God had some special work in store for him. He became a priest, sensing that this would more easily enable him to discern God's plan, and during a retreat he received the answer he sought: he was to found Opus Dei. He dedicated the remainder of his life to spurring the growth of Opus Dei around the world.

—JUNE 27—

Blessed Marguerite Bays

Holy Marguerite, you endured unique trials, including familial misunderstanding, yet you kept your heart open to the vastness of Christ's love for humankind. Pray, bless all those whose families cannot understand their unique gifts. Encourage them to persevere in becoming the wonderful person whom God intended them to be. Reaffirm them in God's loving acceptance. As well, send them, if possible, friends or companions who can offer support and guidance. I pray especially for your intercession on behalf of *(mention name)*, for *she/he* is having a difficult time in finding acceptance just now. O Blessed Marguerite, pray for us. Amen.

1815–1879: Spending her life in Siviriez, Switzerland, Marguerite was a Third Order Franciscan who recovered miraculously from intestinal cancer. A true mystic, she received the stigmata and agreed to become a victim soul, inspiring many people by her devotion and sufferings.

—JUNE 28—

Saint Irenaeus

Saint Irenaeus, champion of truth, through your preaching and writing you taught people that God's love and truth are not reserved for a select few but are available to all. When, then, I am inclined to hoard knowledge, to store up secrets, to keep things from colleagues or friends so that I might enjoy power over them, remind me that knowledge is not something to be hoarded; rather, it should be spread about, so that all may enjoy its fruits and contribute to its increase. And when I am faced with someone who keeps secrets, increase my patience, that I may be a diplomat and a peacemaker in a difficult situation. Help me to be open myself, to be an example that others, even the hoarders and secret-keepers, may begin to follow in this respect. I ask this through Christ our Lord. Amen.

c. 125–c. 202: A native of Asia Minor and a disciple of Saint Polycarp, Irenaeus studied in Rome, migrated to Gaul, and became bishop of Lyons. Through his preaching he converted many, and his writings did much to combat the heresies of the time, especially those of the Gnostics and Valentinians. His principal works are *Against Heresies* and *The Proof of the Apostolic Preaching,* and he is a Doctor of the Church. Irenaeus died as a martyr during the persecution of Septimus Severus.

—JUNE 29—

Saint Peter

PATRON OF ANGLERS, BOATWRIGHTS,
CLOCK MAKERS, AND NET MAKERS;
INVOKED AGAINST FEVER AND FOOT TROUBLE

O holy Apostle, because you are the Rock upon which almighty God has built the Church, obtain for me, I pray you, lively faith, firm hope, and burning love; complete detachment from myself, contempt of the world, patience in adversity, humility in prosperity, recollection in prayer, purity of heart, a right intention in all my works, diligence in fulfilling the duties of my state of life, constancy in my resolutions, resignation to the will of God, and perseverance in the grace of God even unto death; that by means of your intercession and your glorious merits, I may be made worthy to appear before the chief and eternal Shepherd of souls, Jesus Christ, who with God and the Holy Spirit lives and reigns forever. Amen.

TRADITIONAL

died c. 67: Peter was a Galilean fisherman who lived with his wife at Bethsaida. He was a disciple of John the Baptist before being called by Jesus, who made Peter the "rock" upon whom the Church was built. Peter preached at Jerusalem and Samaria before making his way to Rome, where he was crucified, upside down.

—JUNE 30—

Blessed Gennaro Sarnelli

Blessed Gennaro, you showered the Lord's wonderful mercy and loving care upon those most terribly oppressed members of your society, the young, impoverished prostitutes. By your example and prayers, inspire me to serve my outcast neighbors in like manner, and serve the Lord by bringing his loving care to those who are in the greatest need. I pray for your intercession through Christ our Lord. Amen.

1702–1744: A friend of Saint Alphonsus, Gennaro was another social reformer. His special ministry was to remove the scandal of Neapolitan youngsters whose poverty forced them into prostitution. He was the author of many books on spirituality.

July

—JULY 1—

Blessed Junípero Serra

Most Blessed Junípero, you sowed the seeds of faith amid the mountainous changes brought by new settlers to your adopted land. Under your leadership, people learned to live communally, as the first Christians did, in mutual love and cooperation. Inspired by your zeal, I pray for a return to the spirit that you brought to this land. Help me and my neighbors learn to cooperate with one another; teach us the way of living communally, for the greater good of all. Bless my community's leaders with insight, that they may know how to bring out the best in all of us, how to get us to work together, how to get along. Remind us, when our thoughts turn selfish, that self-serving actions bring harm to ourselves as well as to our community. Show us the way of love.

Blessed Junípero, pray for us. Amen.

1713–1784: Miguel José, born on the island of Mallorca, took the name Junípero when he became a Franciscan. After teaching philosophy and theology at the University of Padua, he went to Mexico City and spent the rest of his life in the Americas. Junípero was largely responsible for the foundation and spread of the Church on the coast of California, founding twenty-one missions—among which were San Luís Obispo, San Juan Capistrano, Santa Clara, Santa Barbara, and San Francisco de Asís—and converting thousands.

—JULY 2—

Blessed Eugénie Joubert

O Eugénie, you expressed the hope of all hearts with these words: "I want to be just like a tiny child carried in her mother's arms." And your care in preparing the little ones for their first confession and Communion gave them the experience that you craved. You knew that no human child, no matter how poor or humble, is indifferent to God. Each is called to enter the kingdom, and we are all called to help them on their way. So I ask you to bless all those who care for small children. Bless their parents, that they may model themselves on God, our loving parent. Bless their teachers, that they may model themselves on Jesus, our loving rabbi. Bless their siblings and grandparents and relatives and friends, that they may bear the love of the Holy Spirit in their hearts at all times. And bless the children, that they may enjoy God's love through everyone they encounter in their lives. I pray in the name of Jesus' Love, which surpasses all understanding. Amen.

1876–1904: Eugénie, from Isingeaux, France, entered the Congregation of the Holy Family of the Sacred Heart, serving as a catechist for the poor and devoting her service to the Sacred Heart of Jesus. She practiced the "little way" of total reliance upon God, dying from a severe illness at a young age.

—JULY 3—

Saint Thomas the Apostle

PATRON OF ARCHITECTS, BUILDERS,
CONSTRUCTION WORKERS, CARPENTERS,
GEOMETRICIANS, MASONS, SURVEYORS,
THE EAST INDIES, INDIA, AND PAKISTAN;
INVOKED AGAINST BLINDNESS AND DOUBT

Holy Saint Thomas, the Risen Lord appeared to you to dispel your doubts, and you were able to believe so fully in the Resurrection that you became a martyr for the faith. I beg you to help me deal with my doubts, for they are many.

When I find myself doubting the presence and love of God in my life, help my unbelief.

When I find myself doubting the love of my spouse/partner, help my unbelief.

When I find myself doubting the love of my children, my siblings, my parents, help my unbelief.

When I find myself doubting the loyalty and love of my friends, help my unbelief.

O Saint Thomas, your story gives me inspiration to press ahead, despite my doubts and fears. Pray for me, I implore you, that I may take the long view and not become upset with perceived rejections or insults. Pray for me, that I may remain faithful and loving even when assailed by doubts and unbelief. Pray for me, that the Spirit of the Lord will come to me, to calm my anxieties, to soothe my fears, to smooth my spirit, so that I may be the loving *spouse/ partner, parent, son/daughter, brother/sister, friend* God intends for me to be. I ask this with all my heart and soul, in the name of Jesus our Lord, who is undoubted Love. Amen.

first century: Surnamed Didymus—the Twin—Thomas was the apostle who doubted the accounts of the Resurrection and expressed his need to see the wounds in Jesus' hands, feet, and side before believing (John 20). According to ancient tradition, Thomas is said to have preached in India and there to have suffered martyrdom.

—JULY 4—

Saint Elizabeth of Portugal

PATRON OF PORTUGAL AND OF THE THIRD ORDER OF SAINT FRANCIS

O most generous Saint Elizabeth, you demonstrated so clearly that Christian love has no boundaries. Though your position might have caused you to be imperious and arrogant, instead you tended the poor and even raised the children of your husband's adulterous relationships. Pray for us, that we, like you, may overcome all anger and resentment, however justified, especially against family members who have wronged us. Send us your spirit, so that we may become as forgiving as you were. And teach us how to be motherly toward anyone who needs us. This I pray through Christ our Lord. Amen.

1271–1336: Elizabeth was the daughter of King Peter III of Aragon and was married at the age of twelve to King Denis of Portugal. She distinguished herself as a peacemaker between the kings of Portugal, Castile, and Aragon. After the death of her husband she retired to a Poor Clare convent as a tertiary.

Saint Athanasius of Athos

Athanasius, when I feel like running away from my duties, help me to understand that if God wants me to do something, [God] will find me. Pray that I find the grace to live up to the commitments and responsibilities of my life. And may I perform them with enthusiasm, humor, and goodwill.

TOM COWAN

c. 920–1003: Athanasius embraced the monastic life in Bithynia but soon fled to Mount Athos, to live in isolation with the hermits there. The future emperor Nicephorus Phocas brought Athanasius to Crete, then gave him money to build a laura (monastery) at Mount Athos. When Phocas became emperor, Athanasius fled to Crete but was convinced to return to Mount Athos, build a harbor, and establish the place as a wholly monastic republic. Though the hermits did not appreciate Athanasius's efforts, they, as Athanasius, resigned themselves to the emperor's plan. At his death, Athanasius ruled as abbot-general over some sixty communities of hermits and monks. The monastic tradition of Mount Athos is still an example of retreating from the world and living in religious community.

Saint Maria Goretti

PATRON OF TEENAGE GIRLS

Heroic and angelic Saint Maria Goretti, we kneel before you to honor your persevering fortitude and to beg your gracious aid. Teach us a deep love for the precepts of our holy Church; help us to see in them the very voice of God in heaven. May we preserve without stain our white baptismal robe of in-

nocence. May we who have lost this innocence kneel
humbly in holy penance; and with the absolution
of the priest may the torrent of Christ's precious
blood flow into our souls and give us new courage
to carry the burning light of God's love through the
dangerous highways of this life until Christ our King
shall call us to the courts of heaven. Amen.

TRADITIONAL

1890–1902: When she was twelve, Maria was attacked by
her next-door neighbor Alexander Sernelli. Maria repulsed
his attempts at rape, and he fatally stabbed her. She forgave
him from her deathbed, and he went to prison, where he
remained unrepentant until Maria appeared to him in a vision. Alexander became a Capuchin lay brother and attended
Maria's canonization ceremony.

—JULY 7—

Saint Ethelburga
of Faremoutier

Holy Saint Ethelburga, you discerned your vocation at a young age and were able to pursue it without hindrance. Intercede on behalf of all those young
people who similarly perceive their vocations but
who encounter resistance. Help them to persevere,
and ask the Lord to remove all obstacles from their
path. As well, bless all those who perceive their vocations at later stages of their lives. The obstacles
standing in the way of their callings may be even
more mountainous, so ask the Lord to smooth their
way. And bless all those people who never discern a
vocation, who never hear a calling. Encourage them
to look deeply at their own lives, so that they may
see the calling to serve the Lord in the very routine

that they follow on a daily basis. O Saint Ethelburga, pray for us. Amen.

died c. 664: The daughter of Anna, king of the East Angles, Ethelburga became a nun at Faremoutier, France, and, eventually, abbess. In France she is known as Aubierge, and she is among the incorruptibles.

—JULY 8—

Saint Sunniva

Saint Sunniva, your life is testament to the saying that the truth will out. You were unjustly accused, but the truth revealed supernaturally vindicated your holiness. Remind me, then, of the necessity of not judging others. What I perceive can be only a small view of a much larger picture, and it is unfair to base a judgment on such a limited perspective. Teach me to give others the benefit of the doubt, and to forgive them for slights or mistakes. Help me to put all perceived wrongs in God's hands and then to leave them alone.

As well, teach me not to judge myself too harshly, for even with myself I cannot be aware of all the factors that bear on a situation. Help me to accept God's forgiveness and to forgive myself for the times when I fall short of the mark, and then to let go of the situation and move on. I ask your blessing through Christ our Lord. Amen.

tenth century: An Irish princess, Sunniva and her brother Alban, along with several women companions, fled from home so that she could avoid an arranged marriage. According to legend, they landed on the island of Selje, off Norway, and settled in a cave. Neighbors accused them of stealing cattle, but an armed band arriving to punish

Sunniva's group found that a landslide had sealed the cave
where they were living. A few years later strange lights were
reported in the area, and when the king had the cave opened,
Sunniva's body was found, incorrupt. The king built a church
there in her honor.

—JULY 9—

Blessed Pauline
Amabilis Visenteiner

Blessed Pauline, you are the "first saint who grew
up in Brazil." Your special gift, in converting all
your words and actions into continual praise to God,
was to think of "what is above." Your being-for-
others was simply your acknowledgment that every
person is a reflection of the Divine.

Remind me, I pray, to seek the face of Christ in
all persons I encounter this day. Remove the blind-
ers from my heart's eye, that I may see with the eyes
of God and greet each person as a sister or brother
in God's kingdom. Help me to forge eternal relationships, that when I finally enter heaven I may
find there untold numbers of good friends and old
acquaintances. Ask the Lord especially to surround
me with holy friends and good people, that we may
mutually support one another in our journey of faith.
This I pray through Christ our Lord. Amen.

1865–1942: Raised in Brazil, at the age of fifteen Pauline
and a companion moved into a shack to care for a woman
with cancer. From this humble act grew the Daughters of
the Immaculate Conception, and Pauline became Sister
Pauline of the Heart of Jesus in Agony. In time, Pauline herself became invalided with diabetes and lived her final years
in seclusion and prayer in the motherhouse.

Saint Rufina

Saint Rufina, like Jesus, you suffered cruel betrayal, for those closest to you denied what you held most important and turned against you. I pray you, be with all those who similarly suffer betrayal at the hands of their loved ones. Protect them from further harm. And help to heal their hurts, that they may soon be able to trust and love again. I pray for your intercession through Christ our Lord. Amen.

died 257: Rufina and her sister Secunda were engaged to be married when, under Emperor Valerian's persecution, their fiancés denied the Christian faith. Because the young women refused to deny Christ, they were tortured and beheaded.

Saint Benedict of Nursia

PATRON OF ARCHITECTS, COPPERSMITHS, THE DYING, EUROPE, FARM WORKERS, MONKS, SERVANTS, SPELUNKERS; INVOKED AGAINST GALLSTONES, POISON, AND WITCHCRAFT

O holy Father blessed by God both in grace and in name, who while standing in prayer with your hands raised to heaven did most happily yield your angelic spirit into the hands of your Creator, and who has promised zealously to defend against all the snares of the enemy, in the last struggle of death, those who should daily remind you of your glorious departure and your heavenly joys, protect me, I beseech you, O glorious Father, this day and every day, by your holy blessing, that I may never be separated from our blessed Lord, from your company,

and from that of all the blessed, through the same
Christ Our Lord. Amen.

Saint Gregory the Great

c. 480–c. 547: Born in Umbria, Italy, Benedict fled from the
license of Rome and lived as a hermit at Subiaco, where he
attracted a number of disciples. He founded the monastery
of Monte Cassino, for whose monks he wrote the rule that
bears his name. That rule spread throughout Europe and
became the norm for all Western monasteries.

—July 12—

Saint Veronica

Patron of Laundresses

Most holy Saint Veronica, I praise you for the compassion you showed to our Lord during the very
time it was most dangerous even to acknowledge
his acquaintance. Help me carry the image of Jesus
in my daily life so that I may recognize him in the
faces of those people in need who may cross my
path. Teach me the way to calm my fears, so that I
may show others compassion like unto yours, when
on his way to Calvary you wiped Jesus' face with a
cloth. Remind me that I am my brothers' and sisters' keeper, that I am called to be like the Good
Samaritan, that God's love asks me to wash the feet
of my companions. Pray for me, dear saint, that I
may learn this lesson of love. I ask this in the name
of Jesus, who called himself servant of all. Amen.

first century: According to tradition, when our Lord fell
beneath his cross on the road to Calvary, a compassionate
woman wiped his face with a towel, on which an image of
the holy face remained imprinted. The name given her by
tradition is from the Graeco-Latin *vera ikon*, which means
"true image."

—JULY 13—

Saint Clelia Barbieri

Dear Saint Clelia, your devotion to the Eucharist brought forth multiple charitable activities. Lead me by your example, then, to devote more of my riches to those in need. Open my eyes especially to those who need immediate assistance and intervention, that I may take to heart the lesson our Lord intended with the story of the Good Samaritan. O Mother Clelia, remind me not to be stingy—neither with my resources nor with my love. And help me to trust in the Lord's providence, that he will provide for all my needs too. With trust that the Lord will never abandon me, I pray in Jesus' name. Amen.

1847–1870: The founder of the Little Sisters of Our Lady of Sorrows, Clelia designed the congregation as both an active and a contemplative apostolate. She herself received many mystical graces, and she demonstrated her love for God through her fidelity to everyday, parish-level activities.

—JULY 14—

Blessed Kateri Tekakwitha

Kateri, favored child and Lily of the Mohawks, I come to seek your intercession in my present need. *(Mention request.)*

I admire the virtues that adorned your soul: love of God and neighbor, humility, obedience, patience, purity, and the spirit of sacrifice. Help me to imitate your example in my state of life.

Through the goodness and mercy of God, who has blessed you with so many graces that led you to the true faith and to a high degree of holiness, pray to God for me and help me. Obtain for me a very fervent devotion to the Holy Eucharist so that I may love holy Mass as you did and receive holy Communion as often as I can.

Teach me also to be devoted to my crucified Savior as you were, that I may cheerfully bear my daily crosses for love of him who suffered so much for love of me. Most of all, I beg you to pray for me that I may avoid sin, lead a holy life, and save my soul. Amen.

Kateri, Lily of the Mohawks, pray for me.

PAULY FONGEMIE

1656–1680: Daughter of a Mohawk chief and an Algonquin mother, Kateri defied tradition by converting to Christianity and dedicating her entire life to God. Because of her unorthodox lifestyle of prayer, charity, and penance, her life was in danger, and the Jesuit father ministering to her community advised her to go to live in Sault St. Louis, 200 miles away through the wilderness. She made the journey, took a private vow of virginity—unheard of for a Native American woman—and led an exemplary Christian life. She was revered as a saint in her own community.

—JULY 15—

Blessed Anne-Marie Javouhey

O Blessed Anne-Marie, I thank God for your service to children, the poor, and the sick. Give courage to all those who minister to others, especially those who endanger their lives to do so. Support those who uproot themselves to serve others in times of trouble or in distressed areas of the world. Pray the Lord to free all who are bound by sins of prejudice, blindness, and indifference to the plight of others. Ask the Spirit to comfort all who are wrongly sanctioned by ecclesiastical authority and to give them inner peace. And pray that I may recognize my gifts and talents as God's gifts to be used for the service of others. I ask this in the name of Jesus, whose Gospel you so faithfully followed. Amen.

1779–1851: From Jallanges, France, Anne-Marie founded the Sisters of Saint Joseph of Cluny, who dedicated themselves to the care of the sick and to teaching. She also devoted herself to the emancipation of the slaves in the French colonies.

—JULY 16—

Saint Marie-Madeleine Postel

Dear Marie-Madeleine, you sought to embrace the blessed cross, asking the Lord for more, and yet more to bear and to do. And indeed, you accomplished much in Roman Catholic education during a time of great opposition. Shining still as a beacon for new generations of the faith, you illuminate the path for young people so that they can be intellectually and morally prepared for their Christian vocations. Bless all students, that they may come to love learning and enjoy an education that continues throughout their lifetime. Bless in particular *(mention names)*, that they may learn well and joyfully.

Bless as well all teachers, especially those who are charged with teaching faith and morals. Inspire them to continue to seek Truth, and to challenge their students to seek Truth as well. Bless in particular *(mention names)*, my *child's/children's/ grandchildren's* teacher, that *he/she* may always teach with compassion and sensitivity. This I pray through our great rabbi, Jesus Christ our Lord. Amen.

1756–1846: Born in Barfleur, France, Marie-Madeleine sheltered fugitive priests in her home during the French Revolution. Afterward, she founded the Sisters of the Christian Schools of Mercy.

—JULY 17—

Saint Hedwig of Lithuania

Saint Hedwig, your life was a reflection of the love of Christ and of surrender to God's will for the greater good of God's people. Although I may not wish to make the sacrifices that you made, help me to take the long view, so that I may see the events of my life through God's eyes. Remind me that all things work together for good for those who love the Lord, and bless the events over which I have no control, that they may serve the Lord's intentions. Bless also my decisions, that I may make wise choices and lay down Christ-centered plans.

As well, intercede on behalf of young lovers, that they may come to know the joy of mature and mutual self-giving. I pray especially for *(mention names)*, who are embarking upon a new life together. Bless them with love and joy today and always. Amen.

1374–1399: The daughter of King Louis of Poland, Hedwig was betrothed to William, the Duke of Austria, but the Polish Diet ruled against the marriage. When she was crowned queen of Poland at the age of ten, she gave up her betrothal to William. Instead, she married Grand Duke Ladislas Jagiello of Lithuania, forming a mutually beneficial alliance. Part of the marriage agreement included the baptism of the entire population of Lithuania, and the kingdom became one of the truly devout Christian regions in Europe. Hedwig died in giving birth to her first child.

Saint Bruno of Segni

Saint Bruno, sometimes we face irreconcilable conflicts in life. You wanted to resign your post to live
as a monk, but you had also pledged yourself to
obedience to the pope, who thought your talents
more useful as a bishop. Somehow, you were able
to forge a working compromise. I ask you, pray for
me, that I may find a working compromise between
all the pressures and forces that want a part of me
today. Between my boss and my spouse/partner and
my children and my friends and even my pets, I can't
seem to satisfy anyone because there's not enough
of me to go around. And besides, like you, I just
want to go off by myself to the mountaintop to commune with the Lord. Ask the Lord to send me a
supple spirit, that I may be able to meet all these
conflicting demands. And bless me with the peace
that you found, that I may somehow accept what's
necessary while working at that which I most desire. This I ask through Christ our Lord. Amen.

1049–1123: Born of a noble family in the Piedmont, Bruno
first became known as the opponent of Berengarius and was
appointed bishop of Segni. But he left the episcopacy and
became a monk, and then abbot, of Monte Cassino. Eventually, Bruno had to return to his see. He was a profound
theologian whose writings on the holy Eucharist are still
revered.

—JULY 19—

Saint Macrina

Saint Macrina, there are today many theologians who lack the holiness of life and vision of the great Fathers and Mothers of the Church whom you led to sanctity. Pray for them, that God will send them Wisdom and Truth, to become good leaders and teachers of the people of God. Pray for us also, that we ourselves may become so holy that the truths of the Holy Spirit may reach others through our ministry. We implore your help in the name of Jesus our Lord. Amen.

fourth century: Born in Cappadocia, Macrina was the daughter of Saints Basil and Emmelia and the eldest of ten children, among whom were Saints Gregory of Nyssa, Basil the Great, and Peter of Sebastea. When her fiancé died, she dedicated herself to the education of her siblings and to the spiritual inspiration of many of the most renowned theologians and saints of her time.

—JULY 20—

Saint Margaret

PATRON OF CHILDBIRTH, NURSES, AND PEASANTS

Saint Margaret, holy virgin and martyr, you faithfully preserved the robe of holy innocence and purity, valiantly resisting all the blandishments and allurements of the world for the love of your divine spouse, Jesus Christ; help me to overcome all temptations against the choicest of all virtues, holy purity, and to remain steadfast in the love of Christ, in order to preserve this great gift of God. Implore for me the grace of perseverance in prayer, distrust of myself, and flight from the occasions of sin, and finally the grace of a good death, so that in heaven I may "follow the Lamb whithersoever he goes." Amen.

TRADITIONAL

died c. 304: A maiden of Antioch, Margaret was martyred under the Diocletian persecutions. Most of what is believed about her is legend, yet she is one of the most popular of the maiden-martyr saints, and her cult is ancient.

—JULY 21—

Saints Symeon of Emesa and John

Holy Symeon and John, you took literally the Lord's command to leave family and friends in order to follow him. Bless all those who are called similarly, for the decision to leave loved ones is difficult, even when the Lord calls and the destination is the kingdom of God. Bless as well all those who are called to the type of intimate friendship that you shared, that they may be mutually supportive and may help each other along the way to the kingdom. And bless all those who are called to be "holy fools," people, like Saint Francis and yourselves, who do what seems foolish in the eyes of most in order to accomplish what the Lord desires. Encourage them for the trials and difficulties they will encounter, and reassure them that the call they hear is authentic and holy. O Saints Symeon and John, pray for me. Amen.

sixth century: Symeon, with his mother, and John, with his new wife, met on a pilgrimage to Jerusalem. They became friends and decided to dedicate their lives to God, joining a monastery and afterward living together as hermits in the desert of Sinai. Toward the end of his life, Symeon left John to go to Emesa, in Syria, where he earned the nickname "Salus," or holy fool.

—JULY 22—

Saint Mary Magdalene

PATRON OF CONTEMPLATIVES, GLOVERS, HAIRDRESSERS, PERFUMERS, AND PROSTITUTES

Dear Saint [Mary] Magdalene, from your honored place in paradise as Penitent Extraordinary, help us to see that all holiness consists in a personal love of God. When you found that Love, it forestalled and included all other loves. Your personal relations to Christ were most tender and intimate. Help us to know that the sacraments and graces are to infuse or to elicit that love, and the more they infuse, the more do they contribute to the facility of our triumphant sanctity. Help us to give up, as you did, the garish, false beauty of the world, and make us secretly and sweetly discontented with its natural loveliness. Make us see the mutability of all transitory things, and the immutability of the dear intimacy to which God will admit us one day in heaven.

MARIE C. COMMINS

first century: Mentioned in the four Gospels as one of the most devoted followers of Jesus, Mary Magdalene has been identified with Mary the Sinner (the reformed prostitute). She stood by the cross during the crucifixion of Jesus and was granted an appearance of the Risen Christ on Easter morning.

—JULY 23—

Saint Romula and Companions

Holy Saint Romula, you desired quiet and recollection so as to be open to receive the graces of God, free from any distraction. Through your intercession, may I come to love contemplation and silence. Pray that I may learn how to quiet myself so that I may be attentive to the voice of our Lord.

Pray also, dear saint, that I may discern how to control my tongue. When I speak, help me to do so in a manner pleasing to God. Inspire me to follow your spirit, that all my words may be kind and loving and full of compassion for my companions.

As well, I implore you and your companions to intercede for all people who share living space, that they may coexist in harmony. Moreover, help them all to take an active interest in the welfare of their companions, so that each may be a helpmate and support for the others. I ask this in Jesus' name. Amen.

sixth century: Romula and her companions, Redempta and Herundo, lived in a hermitage near the Church of Santa Maria Maggiore in Rome. They lived in perfect silence, never speaking except to pray.

—JULY 24—

Blessed Mercedes Prat

O Blessed Mercedes, you displayed a great love for your sisters and neighbors, but most of all you displayed a great love for our Lord, giving up your life in martyrdom as a witness of your devotion and faith. Grant that, like you, we may joyfully and lovingly do all that God asks of us in our daily lives.

Inspire us to prudence and truthfulness in thought, word, and deed. Help us to be calm and gentle with ourselves and with others. Most of all, send us courage so that, if persecuted or reviled, we shall not abandon our faith but shall proclaim to all the world how God loves us—and how we love God! In Jesus' name we pray. Amen.

SOCIETY OF SAINT TERESA OF JESUS

1880–1936: Mercedes made her temporary profession in the Society of Saint Teresa of Jesus and was eventually assigned to the motherhouse in Barcelona. In 1936 the community was forced to give up the school and flee because of the Spanish Civil War, and Mercedes was arrested and shot because she was a religious.

—JULY 25—

Saint James the Greater

PATRON OF GUATEMALA, SPAIN, NICARAGUA, VETERINARIANS, EQUESTRIANS, LABORERS, FURRIERS, AND SOLDIERS; INVOKED AGAINST ARTHRITIS AND RHEUMATISM

O glorious apostle Saint James, you were chosen by Jesus to be a witness of his glory on Mount Tabor. You were also present during his agony in Gethsemane because of your fervent and generous heart. You, whose very name is a symbol of struggle and victory, obtain for us strength and consolation in the pilgrimage of this life. May we constantly and generously follow Jesus so that we may be victorious over evil and receive the heavenly reward.

DAUGHTERS OF SAINT PAUL

died 43: Son of Zebedee and brother to Saint John the Evangelist, James was one of the first disciples called by Jesus. He was also the first of the Twelve to be martyred. Legend has it, however, that James was the first missionary to Spain, and he is venerated at Compostella.

—JULY 26—

Saint Jacob Netsvetov

O righteous Father Jacob,
Adornment of Atka and the Yukon Delta,
You offered yourself as a living sacrifice,
To bring light to a searching people.
Offspring of Russian America,
Flower of brotherly unity,
Healer of sickness and terror of demons,
O Holy Father Jacob,
Pray to Christ God that our souls may be saved.

HOLY TRINITY CATHEDRAL

1802–1864: Born at Atka Island when Alaska belonged to Russia, of a Russian father and an Aleut mother, Jacob entered the theological seminary when his family moved to Irkutsk. Like Saint Patrick, however, Jacob yearned to return to the land of his youth, so upon his ordination he returned to Atka. His parish covered two thousand miles of island territory, and he endured tortures of cold, wet, wind, illness, hunger, and exhaustion to minister to his flock. As well as his pastoral duties, he undertook to record the alphabet of the Unangan-Aleut language and to translate the Scriptures. After the death of his wife, Jacob was assigned to minister in the Yukon, devising another alphabet, building yet another church, and distinguishing himself as the evangelizer of the Yup'ik and Athabascan peoples.

—JULY 27—

Saint Pantaleon

PATRON OF DOCTORS AND VENICE;
INVOKED AGAINST CONSUMPTION

Saint Pantaleon, who during life had great pity for the sick and with the help of God often relieved and cured them; I invoke your intercession with God, that I may obtain the grace to serve the Lord in good health by cheerfully fulfilling the duties of my state of life. But if it be God's holy will to visit me with illness, pain, and suffering, aid me with your powerful prayer to submit humbly to these chastisements, to accept sickness in the spirit of penance, and to bear it patiently according to the Lord's holy will. Amen.

TRADITIONAL

died c. 305: A physician by profession, Pantaleon practiced his art without taking any fees. He was martyred under the Diocletian persecutions. His name, from the Greek, means "the All-compassionate."

—JULY 28—

Blessed Alphonsa Muttathupandatu

Most Blessed Alphonsa, victim of love, you achieved greatness through humility, and your spiritual journey is a model for all who love God. You knew that only love counts, that only love unites us perfectly with God and aligns our will with the Lord's. So we pray: use your power in heaven to help us love God. If only we love Jesus, we shall want others to love him, and we shall dedicate our prayers to other souls.

We shall no longer fear death either, because it will bring us to him. Obtain for us, dear Alphonsa, the grace to do all for the love of God, to bring God pleasure in our love, to love Jesus so well that we may please him as much as you did.

Intercede for us all the days of our life, and obtain for us from God the graces and favors we ask through your intercession. Amen.

1910–1946: Born in Arpukara, India, Alphonsa refused all offers of marriage, believing Christ had called her to the religious life. To discourage suitors, she went to the local fire pit to burn her feet; however, her accidental fall into the pit and the severe burns over her entire body convinced her family of her conviction, so she was permitted to join the Clarist Sisters, a Franciscan tertiary congregation in the Syro-Malabar rite. Alphonsa offered herself as a victim for others and displayed amazing spiritual gifts, including prophecy. People of all faiths attended her funeral, and her grave became an ecumenical pilgrimage destination. She is known as "Sister Alphonsa of India."

—JULY 29—

Saint Martha

PATRON OF COOKS, DIETITIANS, HOMEMAKERS, AND WAITERS

O glorious Saint Martha, I have recourse to your protection, and as proof of my affection and faith, I promise to complete this novena faithfully. Comfort me in my difficulties and intercede for my family with your intimate friend, our Savior. Ask that we may always hold God in our hearts and be provided for in our necessities. I beg your supplications, especially on behalf of the favor I ask of you. *(Mention favor.)* I ask you, Saint Martha, by your inter-

cession, to help me overcome all my difficulties.
Teach me to become great in the kingdom of heaven
by becoming as humble as you in this world. Amen.

DAUGHTERS OF SAINT PAUL

died c. 80: Sister of Saints Lazarus and Mary of Bethany,
Martha was the hostess of Jesus during his numerous visits
to her house. She is mentioned in the Gospels of Luke and
John.

—JULY 30—

Blessed María Vicenta of Saint Dorothy Chávez Orozco

Dear María Vicenta, the threat of punishment or
death would make most of us flee our posts and
abandon the sick or helpless under our care, yet you
courageously stood your ground, knowing that the
Lord wanted you to take care of the least of his
people and would not abandon you either. So I ask
for your prayers, María Vicenta, for those caregivers
in places where military violence is a daily occur-
rence. Intercede for their protection, and ask the
Lord to encourage and strengthen them in their
work. Protect as well the sick or wounded under
their care, that they may grow strong and get well
quickly. I pray especially for caregivers and relief
workers in *(mention place)*, that the Lord will protect them as they go about helping those in need.
Amen.

1867–1949: Born in Catija, Mexico, María Vicenta, while recovering from an illness, received the special calling to aid the sick. She founded the Servants of the Holy Trinity and the Poor to help patients in hospitals. During the Mexican Revolution, María Vicenta and her sisters endured death threats when they refused to leave St. Vincent's Hospital in Zapotlán. The commanding officer of the anti-Catholic troops eventually praised María Vicenta as a courageous model of charity.

—JULY 31—

Saint Ignatius of Loyola

PATRON OF THE MILITARY AND RELIGIOUS
RETREATS; INVOKED AGAINST BEING
OVERLY CONSCIENTIOUS

O glorious patriarch, Saint Ignatius, we humbly beseech you to obtain for us from God, above all things, freedom from sin, the greatest of evils. May your example inflame our hearts with an efficacious glory to God and the good of our neighbor; and obtain from the loving heart of Jesus our Lord the crown of all other graces, the gift of final perseverance, and eternal beatitude. Amen.

TRADITIONAL

1491–1556: A nobleman of Spain, Ignatius heard the call of God after being wounded in battle against the French. He founded the Society of Jesus, whose members are to be spiritual soldiers. His *Spiritual Exercises* continues to be a religious work of vast influence.

August

Saint Alphonsus
Maria dei Liguori

INVOKED AGAINST ARTHRITIS
AND SCRUPULOSITY

Glorious Saint Alphonsus, my most beloved protector, who has labored and suffered so much to secure for us the fruits of the Redemption, behold the miseries of my poor soul, and have pity on me. Through your powerful intercession with Jesus and Mary, obtain for me true repentance, together with the pardon of my past faults, a great horror of sin, and strength always to resist temptation. Impart to me, I pray, a spark of that ardent charity with which your heart was ever inflamed; and grant that, imitating you, I may make the good pleasure of God the only rule of my life. Obtain for me, moreover, a fervent and constant love for Jesus Christ and a tender and filial devotion to his mother, Mary, together with the grace to pray always and to persevere in the service of God until death, so that I may at length join with you in praising God, and the most Blessed Virgin Mary, for all eternity. Amen.

THE REDEMPTORISTS

1696–1787: Born in Naples, Alphonsus gave up a successful career as a lawyer to become a priest and minister to the outcasts of Neapolitan society. He founded the Congregation of the Most Holy Redeemer, known as the Redemptorists. Named a Doctor of the Church for his prolific theological and devotional writings, he suffered from scrupulosity and severe arthritis.

—AUGUST 2—

Blessed Ceferino Gimenez Malla

Most Blessed Ceferino, glory of the Church and glory of your people, though you and your people have been scorned and reviled through the centuries, you returned love for hatred, serving as a perfect example of Christian charity. You proved that a death for the faith is always rooted deeply in a life of faith. As I try to lead a life of true faith, encourage and support me, for, as you well know, sometimes it is not easy to respond with Christian love to those who hate or torment or even merely annoy. And when I fall short, remind me of your great example of devotion to our Lady, and teach me to run to her loving arms when I feel myself losing my grip, that I may find rejuvenation in her great faith and love. Intercede for me in times of trial, that I may remember to cast my cares upon the Lord and do what a life of faith requires. I pray in the name of Jesus our Savior, who showed us how to live and how to accept the consequences of a life of faith. Amen.

1861–1936: Born in Spain, Ceferino was a Gypsy who became a respected horse dealer. Both the poor and the politically powerful sought his wise counsel, and he, his wife, and their adopted niece were known as devout Catholics. When he protested the arrest of a priest by Spanish revolutionary soldiers, Ceferino was imprisoned. Though knowing that it would incite the guards, he refused to stop reciting the rosary. He was shot to death because of his religious fervor.

—AUGUST 3—

Saint Nicodemus

O holy Saint Nicodemus, though you were a learned scholar, God led you to seek wisdom from the mouth of God's very Son, Jesus. Pray then to Jesus, that he may give to all persons, both scholars and others, minds that are open and hearts that are ready to hear the Good News of salvation, not rejecting out of hand what seems strange or unfamiliar in it, but carefully studying to understand it. I make this prayer in the name of Jesus Christ our Lord, the rabbi whom you questioned and from whom you learned the essence of the life of the spirit. Amen.

first century: Mentioned in the Gospel of John (chapter 3), Nicodemus came to Jesus in the night, seeking the truth of faith. According to legend, he shared with Saint Joseph of Arimathea the privilege of laying Jesus in the tomb. Nicodemus is venerated as a martyr, though nothing for certain is known of his fate.

—AUGUST 4—

Saint John-Baptist-Marie Vianney

PATRON OF PARISH PRIESTS

O holy priest of Ars, you lived in an age of much upheaval, in a time when [people] turned their backs on God. Your bishop told you of a parish to which he wished to send you where there was no love. He assigned you to Ars and said that you would be the priest who would enable the people to know the love of God. Not only did you draw these people back to God, but your saintly reputation soon spread and many people were converted to a life of holiness. You said that a good priest, a priest after Christ's own heart, is the greatest treasure that God can give a parish. Give us such priests!

O great Saint John Vianney, once again we are living in days of upheaval. There is much evil in the world. Obtain for me the grace to persevere in my faith and never to despair. May I walk with the Lord and trust in him all the days of my life. Obtain through your heavenly intercession, for all priests, religious, and seminarians, the grace of modeling their lives after that of Jesus Christ. We need, more than ever, priests full of the love of God, able to bring the world to Christ. Pray for good priests, O great priest of Ars.

ANTHONY MANUPPELLA

1786–1859: Known as the Curé of Ars, John-Baptist-Marie had the gifts of healing and hidden knowledge; and hundreds of thousands of pilgrims flocked to his small village near Lyons, France, just to receive the sacrament of reconciliation from him.

—AUGUST 5—

Blessed Mary MacKillop

Oh, MacKillop's the name of a fine Scottish clan.
Alexander and Flora were part of God's plan
To come to Australia, the land of New Dawn,
Where they met and they married and Mary was
    born.
As the place of your birth 'tis Fitzroy wears the
    crown.
Baptised at St. Francis', in new Melbourne Town,
You learnt from your parents to sing and to pray,
To trust and be faithful in work and at play.
"Little Mother" of children, your family came first,
As the call of your Saviour became a great thirst.
You worked on the farm, in the shop in the school,
In a re-modelled stable, established your Rule.
Now, the Church in Australia pays homage as due,
While the Pope, for the world, calls you "Blessed,"
    for you
Showed your love for the needy, the weak and the
    young.
You inspire us to follow the path you've begun.
Now, the breadth of the land is encompassed by
    you,
Overseas shares your knowledge and holiness, too.
Australia's own Patrons, with Mary, we praise:
Mary, Help of all Christians, Francis and Therese!
Give praise to the Lord for our gladness this day;
Give thanks, for our Mary has shown us the way.

KATHLEEN T. BOSCHETTI, M.S.C.

1842–1909: Born at Fitzroy, Australia, Maria Ellen took
the name Mary of the Cross upon her religious profession.
She founded the Sisters of Saint Joseph to provide a Roman
Catholic education to children in Australia, but Bishop Sheil

excommunicated her because of her unorthodox procedures (such as having her sisters ride horseback throughout the vast country). The bishop lifted the excommunication shortly before his death. Mary went on to open a home for destitute women in a seedy section of Melbourne, continuing to adapt the methods of the Church to fit the times.

—AUGUST 6—

Blessed María Francesca of Jesus Rubatto

Blessed María, how well you remind me of the meaning of the parable of the Good Samaritan. And how easily and naturally you cared for someone you had never met before. Your story brings tears of bitterness to my eyes, for it brings to mind the numberless times I have averted my eyes from the beggar in the subway or from the homeless person standing in the middle of traffic with a sign begging for the price of a sandwich. And even when I do take on a charitable work, how often do I really see the person to whom I am handing a bag of food—how often do I perceive the precious soul behind the rough and sometimes hostile facade? And how often do I feel anything like love for that rough neighbor? I'm afraid, dear María, not very often. My charity is like an item on a list—get it done, and move on to the next item—and quickly now, because I have so much to accomplish. But you saw the soul beneath the bleeding wound and gave that soul your time and your trouble and your resources. Teach me, then, how to meet a need without fear— how to give without expectation—how to treat the soul as well as the body. Teach me the true meaning of the parable of the Good Samaritan. Amen.

1844–1904: Though she had made a vow of virginity at an early age, María led a relatively routine life in Turin. During a vacation to the Ligurian coast, she saw a stone from a convent under construction strike a young worker on the head. She cleaned his wound, gave him two day's wages so that he could rest, and went on her way. Her charitable act became so well known that the sisters from the new convent asked her to join their community. María eventually became superior of the group, which is now called the Capuchin Sisters of the Third Order of Loano. María also founded missions in Uruguay and Argentina.

—AUGUST 7—

Pope Saint Sixtus II and Companions

O blessed saints, martyrs for the faith, pray for me, that I may have the faith to follow Jesus and the courage to profess Christ always.

Saint Sixtus II, pray for me.
Saint Felicissimus, pray for me.
Saint Agapitus, pray for me.
Saint Januarius, pray for me.
Saint Magnus, pray for me.
Saint Vincent, pray for me.
Saint Stephen, pray for me.
Saint Quartus, pray for me.
O holy saints, martyrs for Jesus, pray for me, now and at the hour of my death. Amen.

died 258: Pope Sixtus II reigned for one year. While he was preaching in the catacombs, he and his clergy were discovered, and they were taken away and beheaded.

—AUGUST 8—

Saint Dominic de Guzmán

PATRON OF ASTRONOMERS AND
THE DOMINICAN REPUBLIC

O Holy Father, I call upon you as my patron. Earnestly I pray to you, devoutly I commend myself to you. Receive me graciously, I beseech you. Keep, protect, help me, that through your care I may be made worthy to obtain the grace of God that I desire, to receive mercy, and all remedies necessary for the health of my soul in this world and in the next. Obtain this for me, O my master. Do this for me, O blessed Dominic, our father and leader. Assist me, I pray you, and all who call upon your name. Be unto us a Dominic, that is, a man of the Lord. Be a careful keeper of the Lord's flock. Keep and rule us, who have been committed to your care. Correct our lives, and reconcile us to God. After this exile is ended, present us joyfully to the beloved and exalted Son of God, our Lord and Savior, Jesus Christ, who, with the glorious Virgin Mary and all the court of heaven, dwells in honor, praise, glory, ineffable joy, and everlasting happiness, world without end. Amen.

BLESSED JORDAN OF SAXONY

1170–1221: An Augustinian, Dominic left his native Castile to accompany his bishop to Languedoc, to minister among the Albigenses. The convent he opened at Prouille became the nucleus of his order of friars known as the Friars Preachers, or Order of Preachers, also known as the Dominicans, whom he sent everywhere to preach and teach.

—AUGUST 9—

Saint Edith Stein

Saint Edith, through your love for truth, God led you to the very core of Divine Wisdom. Your life of prayer and simplicity prepared you for the martyrdom that would bear witness to your complete acceptance of the mystery of faith. You were an angel of mercy to those imprisoned with you, light and love in the midst of darkness and evil.

We implore you, beseech God for the grace to do our part to banish evil from the world, especially the evil that hates particular groups or categories of people. Help us to see that we are one human family. Remind us that we are each of us God's holy temple. Show us the way of transformation, the way of taking God's love into the vilest of circumstances, of awakening the kingdom of heaven among us.

O Saint Edith, beseech Jesus to forgive us our sins against one another, and ask the Lord to grant us the love and courage to die for one another, if necessary. We ask this in Jesus' name. Amen.

1891–1942: A brilliant scholar, Edith converted from Judaism to Roman Catholicism and later became a Carmelite nun in Cologne. She escaped to Holland when German persecution of the Jews began in 1938, but in 1942 she was deported to Auschwitz, where she died in the gas chamber.

—AUGUST 10—

Saint Lawrence

PATRON OF COOKS, LIBRARIANS,
THE POOR, AND SRI LANKA; INVOKED
AGAINST FIRE AND LUMBAGO

O glorious Saint Lawrence, martyr and deacon, who, being subjected to the most bitter torments, did not lose your faith nor your constancy in confessing Jesus Christ, obtain in like manner for us such an active and solid faith, that we shall never be ashamed to be true followers of Jesus Christ, and fervent Christians in word and in deed.

THE RACCOLTA

died 258: During the unholy reign of Emperor Valerian, Roman authorities commanded Lawrence to gather together and turn over all the Church's wealth. When Lawrence presented thousands of orphans, widows, blind people, and people with leprosy, he was arrested, tortured, and roasted over a gridiron.

—AUGUST 11—

Saint Philomena

Illustrious virgin and martyr, Saint Philomena, behold me prostrate before the throne whereon it has pleased the Most Holy Trinity to set you! Full of confidence in your protection, I entreat you to intercede for me with God. Ah! from the heights of heaven, deign to cast a glance upon your humble client. Spouse of Christ, sustain me in suffering, fortify me in temptation, protect me in the dangers surrounding me, obtain for me the graces necessary to me, and in particular (*mention request*). Above all, assist me at the hour of my death. Amen.

SAINT JEAN-BAPTIST-MARIE VIANNEY

In 1802 a tomb marked with the words "Peace be with you, Philomena" and containing the bones, skull, and a vial of blood from a young girl was discovered in the catacombs of Saint Priscilla in Rome. When the relics were placed in a shrine in Mugnano, Italy, visiting pilgrims began receiving miraculous blessings and favors. Philomena is known to grant requests for conversions, cures, and the resolution of marriage difficulties.

—AUGUST 12—

Blessed Karl Leisner

When many people had lost their way or gone astray, you, Blessed Karl, continued to bear witness to the truth, pointing to Christ as the true way. During your studies you wrote, "Christ, you have called me. I say decisively and with conviction: here I am, send me." And in following Christ, you made no concessions to the popular world view. Your martyrdom was but an inevitable consequence of a life lived in following Christ.

So I call upon you, dear Karl, to lead me in the way of truth, to lead me to Christ. Be with me, particularly during my crises of conscience, and help me to stay on that way that leads directly to God. Encourage me to speak the truth, no matter the consequences, and entrust my safety and my life to God's loving providence. I pray in the name of Jesus, who is our Way, our Truth, and our Life. Amen.

1915–1945: While a seminarian in Munster, Germany, Karl was forced into compulsive agricultural labor for teaching catechism to the young. Released after six months, he was confined again for criticizing Hitler. Eventually sent to Dachau, Karl was ordained in secret, and one week later he celebrated his first Mass. He was liberated by Allied forces, but he was so ill from tuberculosis that he died just three months later.

—AUGUST 13—

Blessed Jacob Gapp

Blessed Jacob, though you received a medal for wounds received in a military struggle, the metal and ribbon of that honor have long since tarnished and faded, while the honor you gained as a martyr for the faith will never tarnish or fade. When I am tempted to seek worldly honors, remind me of that truth, just as you reminded your congregations of the truth you perceived around you. Help me be unafraid to speak the truth when I perceive political injustice, intolerance, or policies of hate; protect me from dire consequences, if possible, yet prepare me to accept whatever may come my way as a result.

O Jacob, I ask you to intercede especially on behalf of prisoners of conscience everywhere, but particularly in *(mention place)*; please protect them, especially *(mention name[s])*. You were not famous in your lifetime, and few know your name now, but keep their names before the world, that we might never forget their sacrifice of love. Amen.

1897–1943: An Austrian, Jacob became a Marianist after serving heroically in World War I. When the Nazis began to come to power, Jacob warned the faithful about the incompatibility between Nazism and Christianity. The Gestapo eventually forbid him to teach religion. In 1938, after denouncing the Nazis from the pulpit, he fled the country. The Gestapo lured him to France, where he was arrested in 1942. He was executed in Berlin, and his remains were handed over to the University of Berlin for anatomical racial purity "studies" by Nazi scientists.

—AUGUST 14—

Saint Maximilian Kolbe

PATRON OF DRUG ADDICTS;
INVOKED AGAINST DRUG ADDICTION

Crown my soul with a share in your charity and purity, Saint Maximilian. The ardent fire of your love ennobled the white purity of your life. Your red martyrdom of self-sacrifice put the finishing touch on the white martyrdom of your lifelong virtue. It was the Virgin Mary who first offered you these crowns of red and white. Implore her to obtain from God the graces that I need to walk my earthly pilgrimage in charity and purity of heart.

On the Vigil of Our Lady's Assumption, you became a living holocaust at Auschwitz fifty years ago. Now, crowned with glory in heaven, united with Mary to our Triune God, please intercede for my intentions and for all people. May this world be transformed, through charity and purity, into the Kingdom where God lives and reigns in peace forever. Amen.

Saint Maximilian Kolbe, pray for us.

TRADITIONAL

1894–1941: Born near Lodz, Poland, Maximilian had a vision in which the Blessed Mother offered him a life of purity or a life of martyrdom; without fear, he chose both. He became a Conventual Franciscan and supported the Knights of the Immaculata in Poland, Japan, and India. Back in Poland, he was arrested by the Nazis and sent to Auschwitz. When a Polish soldier, Francis Gajowniczek, was chosen for execution in retaliation for another's escape, Maximilian volunteered to take his place because the man had a wife and children. Along with nine other prisoners, Maximilian was placed in a starvation box, and he eased the deaths of his fellows before he was finally killed by lethal injection.

—AUGUST 15—

Saint Tarcisius

PATRON OF ALTAR SERVERS AND FIRST COMMUNICANTS

O unvanquished martyr of the faith, Saint Tarcisius, who was inflamed with the most intense affection for the holy Eucharist and enjoyed the happiness of dying united to Jesus in the eucharistic species, we beseech you to obtain for us from our Lord that our hearts also may be filled with a like love in receiving him frequently into our breast and above all in the final moments of our lives, and so united with him we may enter into a blessed eternity. Amen.

THE RACCOLTA

died c. 255: While carrying the Blessed Sacrament to some Christians in prison, Tarcisius was seized by a heathen mob and preferred to die rather than expose the Sacred Mysteries to profanation.

—AUGUST 16—

Saint Stephen of Hungary

PATRON OF HUNGARY

Good Saint Stephen, who fostered the growth of the Church on earth and provided Christian leadership during fearful and violent times, continue to be our powerful helper in heaven. Pray that we rest tranquilly in the Spirit and abandon to the Lord all worries about the future, for he holds us all in perfect care. We ask this through our Lord Jesus Christ, who reigns with God and the Holy Spirit, for ever and ever. Amen.

Saint Stephen, pray for us.

975–1038: When Stephen, the sovereign of the Magyars of Hungary, married Gisela, a sister of the emperor Saint Henry II, they set their hands to the common task of Christianizing their people. Stephen gradually welded the Magyars into national unity, organized dioceses, and founded abbeys, among them the famous Benedictine abbey of Pannonhalma. His son, Saint Emeric, predeceased Stephen, and his later years were dark with many difficulties; nevertheless, he is considered a national saint and hero.

—AUGUST 17—

Saint Roch
(Rock, Rocco, Roque)

PATRON OF CATTLE, DOCTORS, DOG LOVERS,
AND PRISONERS; INVOKED AGAINST CHOLERA,
CONTAGIOUS DISEASES, SKIN DISEASES,
TUMORS, AND THE PLAGUE

O great Saint Rocco, deliver us, we beseech you, from the scourges of illness; through your intercession, preserve our bodies from contagious diseases and our souls from the contagion of sin.

Obtain for us salubrious air; but above all, purity of heart.

Assist us to make good use of health, to bear sufferings with patience, and, after your example, to live in the practice of penance and charity, that we may one day enjoy the happiness that you have merited by your virtues.

Saint Rocco, pray for us.

TRADITIONAL

1293–1337: French-born, Roch devoted his life to the service of the plague-stricken, and his therapeutic technique consisted of making the Sign of the Cross over the sick, often with miraculous results. When he became infected himself, he went off into the forest to die so as not to spread the disease. Legend has it that a dog brought him food and that Roch recovered, made his way home, was imprisoned as a spy, and was ministered to by an angel until his death.

—AUGUST 18—

Saint Helena

PATRON OF ARCHAEOLOGISTS

Holy Saint Helena, your zeal for our Lord has inspired countless millions through the ages. Remind me of the cross, that it may be before me as a constant symbol of how much Jesus loves me and of how much he endured on my behalf. Inspire me to run to the cross as you did, that I may find my Lord there, waiting for me, caring for me, loving me. Pray for me, that God may increase my faith in the saving power of the Son's Redemption.

Dear saint, implore Jesus to reveal himself to me, especially in my desperate times, those dark nights of the soul when I feel so alone. I pray this through Jesus our Lord and Savior. Amen.

died 328: The mother of Emperor Constantine, Helena made a pilgrimage to Jerusalem, during which she found the site where reputed pieces of our Lord's cross were unearthed. Her discovery of the true cross is believed to be miraculous.

—AUGUST 19—

Saint Ezekiel Moreno y Diaz

Saint Ezekiel, throughout your life you sacrificed yourself for others, putting their needs ahead of your own. Let me be mindful, dear saint, of those who have less than I, of those who are in greater need than I. Lend me your spirit of generosity, that I may use of my plenty to help them. Lend me your spirit of charity, that in helping others I may do so with love and joy, without any spirit of begrudgment. Lend me your spirit of leadership, that when I am given responsibility I may use my position to serve others and attend to their needs before my own.

O Saint Ezekiel, be mindful of those in *(mention place)*, who find themselves in great need at this time. Infuse me with your spirit, that I may come to their aid without delay. This I pray through Christ our Lord. Amen.

1848–1906: Born in Alfaro Tarazona, Colombia, Ezekiel entered the Augustinian Recollects. He was elevated to the episcopacy, first of Pinara and later of Pasto. He distinguished himself through his care for the needs of his flock, his charity, and his generosity.

—AUGUST 20—

Saint Bernard of Clairvaux

PATRON OF GIBRALTAR, BEES, BEEKEEPERS, CANDLEMAKERS, AND WAX MELTERS

O holy Saint Bernard, you burned with zeal for the glory of God. O pray for me, that truly despising all worldly goods, I may learn to live for God alone. Reveal to me as well the holy mysteries of our Blessed Mother, to whom you were so devoted, that I may understand and honor her role in the redemption brought by Jesus.

I implore you, despise not my petitions, but in your mercy bring them before the Lord. I beseech your intercession particularly for my most pressing needs. *(Mention request.)* I pray in Jesus' name. Amen.

1090–1153: Born in Dijon, France, Bernard formed and became abbot of Clairvaux, the fourth house of the order of Cîteaux. During his lifetime he established sixty-eight Cistercian monasteries, counseled popes, and preached against heresy. He is a Doctor of the Church.

—AUGUST 21—

Pope Saint Pius X

Saint Pius X, you are the glory of the priesthood and the honor of the Christian people. In your life, lowliness seemed blended with greatness, firmness with mildness, simple piety with profound learning. You are the Pope of the Holy Eucharist and of the catechism. You are the Pope of unsullied faith and fearless strength. We ask you now to turn your gaze on the Church that you so loved and to which you consecrated the choicest treasures of your soul. Obtain for the Church safety and steadfastness amid the difficulties and persecutions of our times. Sustain the human race. May this troubled world witness the triumph of peace. We ask you to intercede for harmony among nations, sincere collaboration among classes of society, love and charity among individuals.

Grant our prayer so that those ardent desires that consumed your apostolic life may become by your intercession a blessed reality. We entrust our prayer to the glory of our Lord Jesus Christ, who, with [God] and the Holy Spirit, lives and reigns for ever and ever. Amen.

DAUGHTERS OF SAINT PAUL

1835–1914: Born Giuseppe Sarto, Pius was the 259th pope. His most outstanding accomplishments were the inauguration of liturgical renewal and the restoration of frequent Communion from childhood. He is also known for warning people about the evils of modernism and for giving great impetus to biblical studies.

—AUGUST 22—

Blessed Bernard Tolomei

Most Blessed Bernard, few have been called for the service you performed, the care of those afflicted with a dread and highly contagious disease, yet you and your monks faced mortality lightly because, Good Samaritans all, you realized the necessity of caring for your neighbors in their desperation. Help me to face my mortality, to accept the inevitability of my death, and then to embark upon the wonderful adventure that is my life. Teach me not to fear death, neither my own nor that of my loved ones; remind me that death is only a horizon and that beyond the horizon are wonders and beauties I've never dreamed of. Help me to live each day well, putting aside lesser things and concentrating on what is important—my relationship with God and my relationships with others. The world values power, prestige, and possessions, but you inspire me to abandon those in order to seek the kingdom, as you did.

Dear Bernard, intercede, I beseech you, on behalf of *(mention name)*, who is very ill. Ask the Lord to bring *her/him* healing, or if healing is impossible, to bring peace. This I pray in Jesus' name. Amen.

1272–1348: Bernard studied law in Siena, then filled several municipal posts, including mayor. However, he left the city and began to live in solitude in the wilderness. Others joined him as he formed the Congregation of Monteliveto (Olivetans). After years spent in wonderful deeds of charity, he and eighty of his monks died from the Black Death, having become the saviors of Siena on account of their devotion to the sick and suffering and to the burial of the dead.

—AUGUST 23—

Saint Rose of Lima

PATRON OF CENTRAL AND SOUTH AMERICA, FLORISTS, GARDENERS, PERU, AND THE PHILIPPINES

O most holy Saint Rose, the child Jesus loved to visit you in your garden and romp as your playmate. Please pray for me, that I may sometimes cast off my too-serious adult ways and express my true nature, that of a little child who loves to play and run with the Lord. Intercede on my behalf, that God may send me the grace to dare to be simple. And ask the Lord as well, dear saint, to visit me often in spirit.

O Saint Rose, pray for me now and at the hour of my death. Amen.

1586–1617: Born of mixed Spanish and Native American blood, Rose received visits from the child Jesus and the Blessed Mother at a very young age. Indeed, people of the town often remarked upon her beautiful supernatural playmate who left silver footprints on the road. Rose became concerned for the native peoples who were outcast in her society and dedicated her life to bringing them the Good News. In time, they began to visit the maiden who spent so much time in prayer at church. Upon her death at age thirty-one, Lima experienced miraculous healings and an incredible number of conversions, all attributed to the penances of this native saint.

—AUGUST 24—

Blessed María Encarnación Rosal

Mother María, you gave up many things in order to save what was essential. And you told us, "May all be lost, except charity." May your words remind me not to place my faith in things that rust or fade, in what might be lost to thieves or wasted by profligacy. Inspire me to place my trust in the Lord and his loving providence, for he will never fail me. And pray that I may use the possessions or resources at my disposal not for my own ease or glorification but for the good of God's children, particularly the needy.

As well, I ask your intercession on behalf of all contemplative communities, that they may enjoy interior peace, and that the peace they experience may spread throughout the world. Encourage all contemplatives in their prayers, that they may bring God's joy to all. Amen.

1815–1886: Born in Quetzaltenango, Guatemala, María entered the Bethlehemites, a cloistered congregation. Elected prioress, she revised the rules of the congregation and, because of those opposed to reform, eventually founded a new Bethlehemite house. She forged a new community dedicated to the Sacred Heart of Jesus.

—AUGUST 25—

Saint Louis IX of France

PATRON OF BUTTON MAKERS, MARBLE WORKERS,
MASONS, SCULPTORS, AND WIG MAKERS

O you, whom Divine Providence has given us for father, under whose auspices our congregation was established, and under whose protection it continues to flourish, great saint, graciously look down upon us, pray for us.

Ask for us that spirit of charity which on earth animated all your actions and made you see the person of Christ in each [person], the spirit of humility in which you received from the hands of God the success with which it pleased him to crown your holy undertakings; the spirit of nobility and of generosity with which you bore adversity, happy thus to have the occasion of proving to God the devotedness and disinterestedness of your soul. Ask for us the spirit of patience and of resignation to God's will, such as you gave to the world by your noble example, in the manifold trials to which it pleased [God] to subject you.

Finally, help us by your merits and your intercession to obtain from God all the graces which we need to acquit ourselves of the task confided to us, with all the perfection Our Lord expects of us.

O blessed Saint Louis, show yourself a father to us! Amen.

MOTHER SAINT LOUIS, S.C.S.L.

1215–1270: Succeeding to the throne under the regency of his mother, Blanche of Castile, Louis reigned for forty-four years. Austere and prayerful in his private life, as king he was energetic but considerate, especially to the poor. He led the French to victory over King Henry III of England and led two Crusades: in the first he was a prisoner in Egypt, and in the second he died of dysentery.

—AUGUST 26—

Blessed Mariam of Jesus Crucified Bouardy

Blessed Mariam, despite the prejudices you suffered in your youth, you continued to love and praise God, knowing that the Divine in humankind was so much greater and more loving than individual people exhibited. I thank you for your example of joyful affection for all people, animals, and nature, and I ask you to help me to follow your lead. Teach me to see the Divine in all people, to love them despite the pain they may cause me—to love, as our Lord taught, even my enemies. Help me bring the Word of God to them, that they may come to know how God asks them to love also. And remind me that the love and peace I bring to my relationships with others, particularly those who are prejudiced against me, may often be the only forces separating war from peace.

Blessed Mariam, I ask your intercession as well for peace in all lands, particularly in *(mention place)*. This I pray through Jesus our Lord. Amen.

1846–1878: Born in Galilee under supernatural circumstances, Mariam entered the Carmel of Pau when she began to receive the stigmata. She established Carmels in Mangalore, India, and Bethlehem and Nazareth, Palestine. Her charisms included levitation, ecstatic trances, prophecy, and bilocation, and she also experienced severe demonic temptations. She has been known as the "Little Arab," though she referred to herself as the "Little Nothing."

—AUGUST 27—

Saint Monica

PATRON OF MARRIED WOMEN
AND MOTHERS

O glorious Saint Monica, greatly challenged among mothers, I feel particularly attracted by you who gave such an enlightened example of motherly love.

Who could understand better than you the anxieties and fears of a mother worrying about the eternal salvation of her children? You endured all, since in the order of nature, Saint Augustine is the fruit of your womb, and in the order of grace, the fruit of your tears. For this reason I am greatly convinced that if you here on earth, with the sanctity of your life and the perseverance of your prayers, were one of the great models of the Christian mother, you must enjoy in heaven the privilege of being their singular protector.

Obtain for me the grace to faithfully imitate your virtues, and furthermore, may my children avoid those errors and failures you disapproved of so strongly in your son. And if it will happen, to my misfortune, that they too fall, grant me the grace to obtain with my prayers, supported by yours, as perfect a conversion as you were able to obtain for your son. Amen.

DAUGHTERS OF SAINT PAUL

332–387: Though a Christian, Monica married a nonbeliever and bore three children. Her husband's example led her oldest son, Saint Augustine, to lapse from the faith, but her patience and gentleness converted her husband, and her prayers and tears drew Augustine back to the Church.

—AUGUST 28—

Saint Augustine

PATRON OF BREWERS AND PRINTERS

Holy Father Augustine,
Saint Augustine, example of contrite souls,
Saint Augustine, son of the tears of thy
    mother Monica,
Saint Augustine, light of teachers,
Saint Augustine, exterminator of heresies,
Saint Augustine, illustrious warrior against
    the foes of the Church,
Saint Augustine, pillar of the True Faith,
Saint Augustine, vessel of Divine Wisdom,
Saint Augustine, rule of conduct for
    apostolic life,
Saint Augustine, whose heart was inflamed
    with the fire of Divine Love,
Saint Augustine, humble and merciful father,
Saint Augustine, zealous preacher of the
    Word of God,
Saint Augustine, precious treasure of confessors,
Saint Augustine, illumined expounder
    of Sacred Scripture,
Saint Augustine, ornament of bishops,
Saint Augustine, light of the True Faith,
Saint Augustine, noble defender of Holy Church,
Saint Augustine, refulgence of the glory of God,
Saint Augustine, blossoming olive tree
    of the House of God,
Saint Augustine, indefatigable adorer of the
    Most Holy Trinity,
Saint Augustine, inexhaustible fountain
    of Christian eloquence,
Saint Augustine, shining mirror of holiness,
Saint Augustine, model of all virtues,
Saint Augustine, consoler of the distressed,

Saint Augustine, comforter of the forsaken,
Saint Augustine, friend and helper of the poor,
Saint Augustine, our father,
Pray for us. Amen.

TRADITIONAL

354–430: Born in Thagaste, in North Africa, Augustine experienced a singular conversion in Milan, famously recounted in his autobiography *Confessions*. As bishop of Hippo, he found himself constantly opposing one heresy or another. This Doctor of the Church and greatest of the Latin Fathers is also known for his *City of God*.

—AUGUST 29—

Blessed Edmund Ignatius Rice

Blessed Edmund, your longing for the contemplative life nearly blinded you to the pressing needs all around you. Remember me when I desire something for myself so strongly that I lose sight of the needs of others, and of my own responsibility to do something about those needs. Remind me that the good I do to others in the name of Jesus will eventually return to me a hundredfold.

O Edmund, I pray as well for your intercession on behalf of children who are abandoned to the streets. Ask the Lord to send someone to care for, love, nurture, and educate them. Ask the Lord to send me, if necessary, to do even something seemingly insignificant on their behalf. Though I may not be able to establish great schools as you did, still I may in some small measure be able to bring joy and hope into the life of some young person. Open my eyes, then, Edmund, to the needs around

me; pray for the removal of my doubts and fears,
and bless me with your spirit of intervention.
Saint Edmund, pray for me. Amen.

1762–1844: A devout man, Edmund owned an import/export business in Waterford, Ireland, during economically and politically troubled times. Widowed with a sickly infant daughter, he longed nevertheless for a religious vocation as a contemplative. The bishop, however, pointed Edmund in another direction, asking him if he planned to abandon the ragged youths of the streets. Edmund sold his business and began opening schools. He eventually took the name Ignatius as a religious in a pontifical institute, and he is known as the founder of the Brothers of the Christian Schools.

—AUGUST 30—

Blessed Jeanne Jugan

O Blessed Jeanne, in you the elderly and the poor, the neglected and the homeless found an advocate and a friend. Pray to the Lord that all who suffer may know God's loving compassion and find meaning in their trials. May they know the fullness of Jesus' peace.

Dear saint, bless all who serve those who are so special to you, those most abandoned of society. Through your intercession, may all who work to ease suffering be strengthened in their tasks of mercy. And fill all Christians with your zeal in service to those who are rejected, despised, and persecuted.

O holy Jeanne, grant as well that any service I perform may always be for others and not for personal recognition. Pray that I may find my self-worth in the love with which I do my work, rather than in prestige of position and power. This I ask through Christ our Lord. Amen.

1792–1879: Jeanne's life was changed forever when she carried a sightless invalid woman to her own bed to die. Known as Sister Mary of the Cross, Jeanne founded the Little Sisters of the Poor in France.

—AUGUST 31—

Saint Raymond Nonnatus

PATRON OF MIDWIVES

O Saint Raymond, to free prisoners and slaves you were willing to give yourself completely to others. But dear Raymond, knowing that I will not be required to endure imprisonment, torture, or the threat of death, as you did, to help my brothers and sisters, why am I so reluctant to become involved on their behalf? Teach me to show the concern you exhibited for other people. Inspire me to take action, to go out and do good deeds for others.

O holy Raymond, I pray for your intercession on behalf of all those who are imprisoned unjustly, as well as all those who still suffer enslavement. Implore the Lord for their freedom. And show me what I may do to help them to be free. This I ask in the name of Jesus our Lord, who set the captives free. Amen.

1205–1240: Called "non-natus" (not born) because he was delivered by Cesarean section after his mother died, Raymond joined the Mercedarians, an order formed to free Christian captives from the Moors. While in Algeria, Raymond was himself captured and enslaved. Sentenced to be impaled, he was spared because of the large ransom he would bring; nevertheless, he suffered severe tortures before his rescue. When Raymond returned to Barcelona, he was made cardinal; he died the following year.

September

—SEPTEMBER 1—

Saint Giles

PATRON OF BEGGARS, BLACKSMITHS, PEOPLE
WITH DISABILITIES, HERMITS, HORSES, AND
NURSING MOTHERS; INVOKED AGAINST
LAMENESS, LEPROSY, AND STERILITY

Zealous follower of Christ, Saint Giles; from early
youth you took to heart the words of our Savior:
"Learn of me, because I am meek and humble of
heart." Therefore, you fled from the praise and honors of the world and were rewarded with the grace
to preserve your heart from all sin and to persevere
in a holy life to a ripe old age. I, on my part, through
pride, self-confidence, and negligence, yielded to my
evil inclinations, and thereby sinned grievously and
often, offending my God and Lord, my Creator and
Redeemer, my most loving Parent. Therefore, I implore you to help me through your mighty intercession to be enlightened by the Holy Spirit, that I may
know the malice, grievousness, and multitude of my
sins, confess them humbly, fully, and contritely, and
receive pardon, tranquility of heart, and peace of
conscience from God. Amen.

TRADITIONAL

died c. 712: Abbot of a monastery on the Rhône, Giles was
one of the most popular saints of the Middle Ages; his shrine

was a much frequented place of pilgrimage, and the many legends about his life testify to his miraculous powers of healing.

—SEPTEMBER 2—

Blessed Margaret of Louvain

Blessed Margaret, look with favor upon those who are exposed to dangers and temptations in crime-infested neighborhoods. Intercede on their behalf, asking the Lord to protect the innocent and keep them in his loving care. As well, inspire all of us with your example, that we may refuse to align ourselves with crime and violence in any way. Teach us that even silent assent on our part makes us guilty accomplices. And send us wisdom, that we may learn how best to restore peace and safety to our world. We ask this through Christ our Lord. Amen.

1207–1225: Margaret worked as a maidservant at an inn in Louvain, Belgium. She witnessed thieves rob and kill her employers, and when she refused to keep silent about the murders, they cut her throat and threw her into a river. Supernatural phenomena accompanied the discovery of her body, and many miracles have been attributed to her intercession.

—SEPTEMBER 3—

Blessed Brigida of Jesus Morello

O Blessed Brigida, you endured tragedy at a young age, but you did not allow it to deter you, following wherever God led and coming at last to offer yourself as a sacrifice. When difficulties or challenges come my way, remind me to take the long view. Teach me that the Lord will bring good out of even the tragedies of my life, if only I allow him to. Help me to trust him so completely that in times of distress I will be able to let go of my anguish and hear where he is calling me to go next.

Dear Brigida, I pray especially for *(mention name)*, who has suffered such a great loss and is falling into despair. Hold *him/her* in your heart at this time, that *he/she* may come to know God's boundless love through your gentle care. I ask this through Christ our Lord. Amen.

1610–1679: Born to a noble family in Italy, Brigida lost her husband because of political upheaval and siege. After a period of mourning, she dedicated herself to a life of penance, displaying the mystical gifts of prophecy and miracle-working. She eventually became director of a school for young girls in Piacenza. Out of this arose the Ursuline Sisters of Mary Immaculate. For the last twenty-five years of her life Brigida offered herself as a victim of love for the salvation of souls.

—SEPTEMBER 4—

Saint Rose of Viterbo

PATRON OF FLORISTS

Saint Rose of Viterbo, valiant saint, intercede for all young people, that they, like you, may lead lives of prayer and witness courageously to the truth. Through Christ our Lord. Amen.

RONDA DE SOLA CHERVIN

1234–1252: Rose used to preach in the streets against the Ghibellines and in favor of the pope. She was repeatedly refused admittance to the Poor Clares, but by order of the pope her body was laid to rest in their convent.

—SEPTEMBER 5—

Mother Teresa
of Calcutta

Holy Mother Teresa, mother of the poor and my mother, God called you to serve the poorest of the poor, the most rejected and outcast citizens of our modern world. Reveal to me the face of Jesus in the homeless man begging for change at the intersection on my way to work. Help me to see God in the eyes of the woman with an emotional disability who disturbs my noon meal. Help me to accept those ill-mannered kids from the "wrong side of town" as beloved children of God.

Dear mother, teach me the Beatitudes. Teach me what it means to live the Beatitudes daily as I encounter that man, that woman, those children. Help me to bring God's love to all these—to all "those people" whom society casts aside as worthless. Implore the Lord to remove my own blindness, so that I may see him in every face I encounter. I ask for your blessing in the name of Jesus, who fed the hungry and comforted the sick and led you to do the same. Amen.

1910–1997: Born in Skopje, Gonxha (Agnes) Bojaxhiu left her family in Albania to join the Sisters of Our Lady of Loreto. She soon found herself in Calcutta, India, where she felt called to leave her order to work among the poorest of the poor. As founder of the Missionaries of Charity, she became known as Mother Teresa and inspired countless people to serve the poor. For her work, she won the Nobel Prize for Peace in 1979.

—SEPTEMBER 6—

Blessed Ramón Lull

Blessed Ramón, you were bold in asking our Lord to "descend among us, complete and perfect this work and bring it to the holy end that you desire," yet you were also practical enough to take up missionary work yourself in order to further your wish to see the kingdom of God in your lifetime. Inspire me to remember, then, the twofold nature of my responsibilities: to pray as if all depends upon God, and to work as if all depends upon me. Help me to persevere in both endeavors, trusting in the Lord to bring my efforts to the holy end that he desires. In Jesus' name I pray. Amen.

1232–1316: From Mallorca, Ramón married young and led a wild life at the court of Aragon. When thirty, he was converted by a series of apparitions, became a Franciscan tertiary, and devoted his life to the conversion of the Moors. He went to Tunis three times; twice he was banished, and the third time he was stoned and died of his wounds. His most notable writing, *The Book of the Lover and the Beloved,* is still a highly regarded work of mysticism.

—SEPTEMBER 7—

Blessed John Baptist Mazzucconi

Blessed John, you traveled fearlessly halfway around the world to bring the Good News to people who had never heard of Jesus, and in so doing you offered your life as a sacrifice toward their eventual salvation. Be with all missionaries this day, to protect them from harm and to encourage them in their important work. As well, inspire others to become missionaries, whether in foreign lands or in their own communities. And teach us all the holy art of evangelization, that our lives may be examples of Christian charity, and that our words and deeds may encourage others to seek to know Jesus more personally. This I pray through Jesus our Lord. Amen.

1826–1855: Born near Milan, John was a charter member of the famed Pontifical Institute for Foreign Missions and, after ordination, set off for Australia. He was assigned to the islands of Woodlark and Rook, whose people greeted all missionaries with anger and hostility. After a few years of strained relationships with the native peoples, John was martyred.

—SEPTEMBER 8—

Blessed Jacques Laval

Blessed Jacques, healer of bodies, you gave up your medical practice to become a healer of souls. Now you are proclaimed "Apostle of Mauritius," having cared for the abandoned African people who were liberated but still lost. By your intercession, strengthen us to work unfailingly to care for those in our world who are abandoned by society: the poor in tenements, children who are abandoned or orphaned, people with AIDS or other illnesses or disabilities, drug addicts, the aged who are no longer independent, the people of the streets. Show us how to treat them with dignity, to care for their physical needs, and to lead them to God. Inspire us to follow your example, giving of ourselves to help those who are less fortunate than we. Help us to persevere, even when the situation seems hopeless and our efforts in vain, so that through our small efforts the kingdom of God may shine through the darkness of this world. We ask this in Jesus' name. Amen.

1803–1864: Giving up his medical practice to become a priest, Jacques served as a country pastor until joining Venerable Francis Libermann's Congregation of the Holy Ghost. Jacques was sent to Mauritius to care for liberated African slaves, and by identifying with these abandoned people he transformed them into fervent Christians.

—SEPTEMBER 9—

Saint Peter Claver

PATRON OF AFRICAN-AMERICANS, COLOMBIA, RACE RELATIONS, AND SLAVES

Holy Saint Peter, you sacrificed yourself to succor the most abandoned of society, those thought to belong to others, those Africans taken into slavery to the Americas. Indeed, you called yourself "the slave of the slaves forever" and dedicated yourself to teaching them about our Lord, the Christ who "sets captives free." O holy Peter, send your spirit to us, that we may never forget the evils of slavery and that we may work to overcome its evil residue. Be with us, that we may remember to reach out to the most abandoned of our society, those enslaved by drugs or alcohol, by poverty, by violence, by ignorance and prejudice. Pray for us, that we may be strong to follow your example, you who were strong enough to follow the perfect example of our Lord.

Saint Peter, implore the Lord to send workers so that the Gospel may reach everyone who needs its aid. And bless us, that we may seek God always, and in so doing love our neighbors in truth and in deed. We ask this through Christ our Lord. Amen.

1581–1654: When Peter became a Jesuit, he was inspired to work among the slaves in the Americas. He worked chiefly at Cartagena, at that time the central slave-mart of the West Indies.

Saint Nicholas of Tolentino

PATRON OF SICK ANIMALS, MARINERS,
HOLY SOULS, BABIES, MOTHERS,
AND THE DYING; INVOKED AGAINST FIRE

Nicholas, I may not be a street preacher, but I can use your example to be willing to go where I am needed, or to where people need help. At home, at work, at play with friends. I pray that I will be sensitive to how I might be of service to others and do whatever I can to make their lives a little better.

TOM COWAN

1245–1305: After joining the hermits of Saint Augustine and being ordained, Nicholas vowed to preach daily to the people in northern Italy. He kept this vow until his death thirty years later. He was also known for his work among the poor and as a peacemaker.

Saint John Gabriel Perboyre

Holy Saint John Gabriel, your self-sacrifice for the Word inspires me to repeat your own words of prayer. And so I pray with you, "O my Divine Savior, transform me into yourself. May my hands be the hands of Jesus. Grant that every faculty of my body may serve only to glorify you. Above all, transform my soul and all its powers so that my memory, will, and affection may be the memory, will, and affection of Jesus."

O glorious saint, God did transform you into the hands of Jesus; ask the Lord to grace me with the same transformation, that I may serve my sisters and brothers as selflessly as you did and, by my own life, bring only glory to God. I implore you, continue to look with love upon the poor, filling me and all people with your zeal in service to those who are rejected, despised, and persecuted.

Holy Saint John Gabriel, pray for me. Amen.

1802–1840: Originally from Montauban, France, this Vincentian Father went to China to replace his murdered brother as a missionary. After but a short time in China, John was incarcerated, tortured, and eventually strangled on a cross.

—SEPTEMBER 12—

Saint Guy of Anderlecht

Guy, may I never become so attached to a certain level of income or standard of living that I could not be happy with less. Everything is relative, especially the relationship of money to happiness. It is an old cliché that money cannot buy happiness, but it is often hard to truly believe that. Help me find happiness in ways that do not require a great deal of money and be ready to accept whatever setbacks God chooses to send me.

TOM COWAN

died c. 1012: A poor native of Brabant (in the Netherlands and Belgium), Guy was the sacristan of Our Lady of Laken when he entered a money-making scheme to help other poor people. He lost both his investment and his job, so he went on a seven-year pilgrimage to Rome, the Holy Land, and other sacred sites. Exhausted, he died shortly after his return.

Saint John Chrysostom

PATRON OF ORATORS

Most mellifluent Saint John, you were acclaimed "golden mouthed" not just because of your oratory skills, but also because you remained unafraid to speak the truth in public. Despite opposition from powerful people, you spoke harsh words against all, including the rich and famous, who refused to follow the ideals of Jesus. Help me, then, when the hour arrives, to speak out and say what I know is true. Inspire me with courage when I feel like retreating silently, and teach me the proper words to use, so that my speech may instruct, reform, and build up as well as correct. Most of all, remind me to seek the Lord's guidance in prayer, so that I know when to speak, when to remain silent, and, most important, how to speak truth with love. I also ask your intercession in this special matter *(mention request)*, that the Lord may bless my efforts. In Jesus' name I pray. Amen.

c. 344–407: Born at Antioch, John tried the monastic life but chose to be ordained, and he then delivered a series of sermons that made him famous throughout the East. Against his will he was made bishop of Constantinople, where his uncompromising morals incurred the imperial wrath, and he was deposed and banished. However, public opinion so strongly supported him that the court had to allow his return. But he was soon exiled again, never to be returned. He is a Doctor of the Church and is famous for his revision of the Greek liturgy.

—SEPTEMBER 14—

Saint Notburga

PATRON OF PEASANTS AND SERVANTS

O most generous Saint Notburga, though your generosity to the poor cost you your employment, you steadfastly refused to close your heart to the needs of others. Pray for me, that I may develop the willingness to accomplish my menial tasks with love and joy. Send your spirit to me, that I may learn to practice generosity by second-nature. And intercede for me, that if difficulties do beset me because of my love for those less fortunate than I, my resolve may be strengthened, so that I may continue to share what I have with those who have less. I pray for your assistance in following your example of generosity, as you followed the example of our Lord Jesus. Amen.

1264–1313: A serving maid, Notburga worked in the kitchen of a German count and gave the leftovers to the poor. When the count's wife objected, Notburga was fired. She then went to work in the fields, where she was known for her piety and miraculous signs. Her relics are the occasion of many miracles on behalf of the poor.

—SEPTEMBER 15—

Saint Catherine of Genoa

PATRON OF NURSES

Noble Saint Catherine, keep us ever mindful that we have a secret sanctuary closed to the world, a place shut off from trials, tempests, and pain, where we can converse freely with God, in a loving friendship that is the beginning of heaven. We are not favored by a scene of the unspeakable agony of purgatory as you were, but we do have your revealed word. May those threatening flames drive us to the mercy of God's arms. Intercede that we may love God ardently for the few years left of life, for [the Lord] is the only One worthy of our heart. He is the perfect, ideally lovable Friend, whom we wish to love for all eternity. And since God loves an audacious asker, intercede for us that we may be found at death in the state of grace, in amity with God, sufficiently mortified to be free of all punishment for sin, and in a state of charity that will set the temperature of our heavenly home high. You worked miracles in Genoa, so you can obtain great graces for us now!

MARIE C. COMMINS

1447–1510: Married at the age of sixteen, Catherine underwent a sudden conversion at the age of twenty-six and gave herself to the care of the hospitalized sick. A remarkable example of complete otherworldliness united with capable practicality, she is the author of *Dialogue between the Soul and the Body* and *Treatise on Purgatory.*

—SEPTEMBER 16—

Saint Ludmila of Bohemia

PATRON OF THE CZECH REPUBLIC AND SLOVAKIA

O holy Saint Ludmila, filled with wisdom and the art of teaching, ask the Lord to bless all grandparents. Ask Jesus to grace grandparents with wisdom and love, that they may exhibit the love of God to their grandchildren. Inspire them to follow your own loving example, that they may learn to love their grandchildren unconditionally.

Saint Ludmila, we pray also for your intercession for those grandparents who face challenges to
their faith. Be with those grandparents whose grandchildren are being raised outside the love of God.
Help them to pass on the best of their own faith to
their grandchildren. Especially pray for grandparents whose grandchildren are being raised in bro-
ken homes or dysfunctional families. Ask God to
grant them wisdom, discernment, and sensitivity as
they minister to their grandchildren, and as they
minister to their own children. We ask this through
Christ our Lord, who loved the little children and
rejoiced when they came to him. Amen.

860–921: Baptized by Saint Methodius, Ludmila and her
husband built the first church north of Prague. When her
husband died, she helped raise her grandson Saint Wenceslas.
But her daughter-in-law, jealous of Ludmila's Christian influence, had her strangled. Ludmila is venerated for her learning and piety.

—SEPTEMBER 17—

Saint Hildegard
of Bingen

Dear Saint Hildegard, though you were shy by nature, you were nevertheless fearless when you recognized the Spirit working through you. Pray for
us that we also may recognize God's work in us,
that we may do the Lord's work on this earth—
using the gifts God has given us. And bless all those
who enrich our worship by sharing their gifts.

Send your spirit to us, so that we may expand
our images of God and come to know the Lord in
the fullness of Divine Possibilities. Send your spirit
to us, to illuminate our minds and our hearts, that

God's Word can become incarnate in us. Send your spirit to us, so that we may, like you, know God from the depths of our personal experience.

O holy saint, we pray especially that all people may recognize their self-worth, that all may know the unconditional love of God. Amen.

1098–1179: The first of the great German mystics, Hildegard was a nun and a prior, a poet and a prophet, a physician and a political moralist. She is called the Sibyl of the Rhine.

—SEPTEMBER 18—

Saint Joseph of Cupertino

PATRON OF ASTRONAUTS, THE AIR FORCE, AND PILOTS

Joseph, you were seldom understood or appreciated. God's manifestations in your life brought as much trouble socially as they brought happiness and consolation spiritually. Help me realize that to be favored by God's grace is not always easy, and that others may not understand or approve of my spiritual needs. Give me strength to live my life productively while I nurture my relationship with the Divine.

TOM COWAN

1602–1663: Dismissed several times because of his "poor" intelligence, Joseph finally found a place with the Conventual Franciscans of Grotella as a stablehand and lay tertiary. He possessed rare spiritual gifts, however, and was made a friar and ordained a priest. His life became an amazing, yet perfectly authenticated, succession of preternatural phenomena, including the power of levitation. Despite his humility, the others of his community resented the notoriety he attracted because of his gifts, and he suffered much under the scrutiny of the Inquisition.

—SEPTEMBER 19—

Saint Emily de Rodat

Emily, when things go wrong, we need great discernment of spirits to see if the signs are from God and what they mean. Too often we can jump to conclusions that are inappropriate. Help me to be aware, as you were, of signs and omens, especially the messages that seem commonplace and come from my own family and circle of friends, for God speaks through them as well as through mysterious occurrences.

TOM COWAN

1787–1852: A woman of privilege from Villefranche, France, Emily became aware of the need for good education for poor children and put her resources behind the establishment of a free school. The women who taught with her soon became the Congregation of the Holy Family. When a series of mysterious deaths befell the community, however, Emily began to consider merging with another congregation; but her sisters refused to have any superior other than she.

—SEPTEMBER 20—

Saint Eustace

PATRON OF HUNTERS AND OF MADRID;
INVOKED IN CASE OF FAMILY TROUBLES

Heroic servant of God, Saint Eustace, cast from the height of earthly glory and power into the deepest misery, you were engaged for a long time as a menial servant, eating the bitter bread of destitution; but never did you murmur against the severe probation to which God subjected you. I implore you to aid me with your powerful intercession, that in all conditions I may resign myself to the holy will of

God, and particularly that I may bear poverty and its consequences with patience, trusting in God's providence, completely resigned to the decrees of the Lord, who humbles and exalts, chastises and heals, sends trials and consolations, and who has promised to those who follow him in the spirit of poverty his beatific vision throughout all eternity. Amen.

TRADITIONAL

died 118: Said to have been a wealthy and powerful Roman general, Eustace, according to legend, once encountered a stag with a luminous crucifix between its antlers. He immediately converted to Christianity, along with his family, and they were martyred under Emperor Hadrian's persecutions.

—SEPTEMBER 21—

Saint Matthew

We thank you, Saint Matthew, apostle and evangelist, for your witness to the Gospel of our Savior, Jesus Christ, and we pray that, after your example, we may with ready wills and hearts obey the calling of our Lord to follow him. Pray for us, that we may be open to hearing the call and, upon hearing, may not be afraid to follow, as you did, into ways that we may be unable to foresee. As well, help us to realize that the Lord calls many who are not exactly like we are, and do not let us hinder them from following. Remind us that the Lord has need of many people of varied skills and dispositions, and teach us how to welcome all to the Lord's table. We ask for your aid in calling others to the table in the name of Jesus our Lord. Amen.

first century: A tax-gatherer at Capernaum, Matthew left his post to follow our Lord. Tradition holds Matthew as the author of the first Gospel.

—SEPTEMBER 22—

Saint Thomas of Villanueva

Thomas, I need to be more accepting of people who do not always live up to their commitments, just as you took compassion on new converts who found it hard to practice the Catholic faith. Not everyone who falls short is a hypocrite. Show me the ways to practice patience and compassion toward those who fail and toward myself as well when I fail to live up to my commitments.

TOM COWAN

1488–1555: Thomas joined the Augustinians and after ordination was appointed prior of the friaries at Salamanca, Burgos, and Valladolíd. He later became provincial of Andalusía and Castile, court chaplain, and archbishop of Valencia. His outstanding characteristic was self-sacrifice, and he was known for his charity toward the poor.

—SEPTEMBER 23—

Blessed Padre Pio

Most holy Pio, victim soul, martyr of suffering, you knew Jesus intimately, for you shared the pain of his passion in your very body. Be with me now and ask Jesus to ease my pain *(mention request)*, for it is more than I feel I can bear. But more than that, be with me now and help me to carry this burden of pain. Even more, inspire me to follow your own example, that I may, like you, learn to offer my sacrifice for souls everywhere, but particularly for those in purgatory.

O Blessed Pio, you understood the greatest need of the human heart. Teach me to pray with you your prayer that expresses the deepest desires of my heart: "Stay with me, Jesus!...Stay with me, Lord!" I implore your aid from the depths of my heart, in Jesus' name. Amen.

1887–1968: Born in Pietrelcina, Italy, from his earliest days Francesco Forgione showed a strong spiritual disposition, received visits from our Lady, and had various mystical experiences. Knowing that he was called to become a priest, he joined the Capuchin Franciscans. He is the only priest to ever bear the stigmata, the bleeding wounds of Christ's passion, in his hands, feet, and side. Padre Pio also had the gifts of prophecy, healing, bilocation, communication with angels, and discernment of souls. Known for the beauty of his Masses, he is often called "the second Saint Francis."

—SEPTEMBER 24—

Saint Gerard Sagredo

PATRON OF HUNGARY

Holy Gerard, Apostle of Hungary, I know nothing of Hungary, and I would be afraid to uproot myself and move to a new country without having a job or friends or family waiting for me. Yet this is exactly what you did, in response to the Lord's call. Pray that the Lord will open my ears to hear his call, and bless me with the courage to heed that call, even if it takes me to foreign lands and unknown spaces. Teach me to trust that the Lord will provide for all my needs, no matter what.

Saint Gerard, pray for me. Amen.

died 1046: Gerard walked to Hungary from Venice, befriended the king, Saint Stephen, and became tutor to his son, Saint Emeric. This Benedictine monk became bishop of Csanad, but during the reaction after Saint Stephen's death Gerard was martyred at Buda.

—SEPTEMBER 25—

Saint Findbarr
(Finbar, Finnbar, Barr)
of Cork

PATRON OF CORK

Most holy Saint Findbarr, you well know the sadness of loneliness, the feeling of abandonment that comes when your friends and acquaintances make themselves unavailable to you. Remind me first to thank God for the friends who are involved in my life and for the goodness they bring to me. Help me to be a good friend in return: show me ways to return goodness and blessings to them, that what I desire from my friends I make sure I provide to them also. Most of all, teach me that God is my best friend. Help me to believe that God will never abandon me. Teach me not to apply human standards to God, for no matter what my human companions may do to me, God will always take my hand and shower me with love.

Saint Findbarr, I pray especially for my friend *(mention name)*, who seems to be distancing *himself/herself* from me just now. Show me how to respond with compassion. Amen.

c. 560–c. 630: When Findbarr was going through a friendless period, he went to Eolang, the head of a monastic community. The two men had a vision in which Eolang put Findbarr's hand into the hand of God, his new soul friend. When God began to lead Findbarr to heaven, Eolang protested, so God released Findbarr's hand, which he kept gloved for the rest of his life because it shone so brightly that people could not look at it. Findbarr is believed to have been the first bishop of Cork.

—SEPTEMBER 26—

Blessed Kaspar Stanggassinger

Blessed Kaspar, God gave you the grace to announce the faith with joy and to educate young men for the sacred ministry. Intercede for us, that we may follow your example and become cooperators of the divine Redeemer, in word and deed. We ask this through our Lord Jesus Christ, who lives and reigns for ever and ever. Amen.

1871–1899: Born at Berchtesgaden, Germany, Kaspar became a Redemptorist priest and served as formation director. His short life was marked by an extraordinary dedication and gift of himself to God and his neighbors.

—SEPTEMBER 27—

Saint Vincent de Paul

PATRON OF CHARITABLE SOCIETIES, HOSPITAL WORKERS, PRISONERS, AND MADAGASCAR

Saint Vincent, patron of all charitable associations and father of those who are in misery, come to our assistance. Obtain from our Lord help for the poor, relief for the infirm, consolation for the afflicted, protection for the abandoned, a spirit of generosity for the rich, grace of conversion for sinners, zeal for priests, peace for the Church, tranquility and order for all nations, and salvation for them all. May we be united in the life to come, by your intercession, and experience joy, gladness, and everlasting happiness. Amen.

TRADITIONAL

1576–1660: Having studied with distinction at Toulouse and Saragossa, Vincent was taken captive to Tunis soon after his ordination, but he managed to escape and make his way to Paris. There he embarked upon his life's work of bringing charity to all: abandoned orphans, sick children, prostitutes, the poor, and people with disabilities. He organized his priest helpers into the Lazarists, known as the Vincentians, and his women helpers into the Sisters of Charity.

—SEPTEMBER 28—

Saint Wenceslaus

PATRON OF THE CZECH REPUBLIC, SLOVAKIA, BOHEMIA, BREWERS, AND SHEEP

Dear Saint Wenceslaus, holy martyr, who preferred the kingdom of heaven to all that the earth has to offer, may your prayers free us from our self-seeking and help us to serve God with all our hearts. We ask this through our Lord Jesus Christ, your Master, who lives and reigns for ever and ever. Amen.
Saint Wenceslaus, pray for us.

died 935: Wenceslaus received a pious upbringing from his grandmother, the martyr Saint Ludmila. When he became duke of Bohemia, he tried to stem his people's slide back to unbelief but met his death as a result of a political conspiracy, being murdered by his own brother at the door of a church.

—SEPTEMBER 29—

Saint Michael the Archangel

PATRON OF POLICE OFFICERS, BANKERS,
GROCERS, RADIOLOGISTS, PARATROOPERS,
THE DYING, CEMETERIES, BRUSSELS, GERMANY,
PAPUA NEW GUINEA, AND THE BASQUES;
INVOKED AGAINST PERIL AT SEA

O victorious Prince, most humble guardian of the
Church of God and of faithful souls, who with such
charity and zeal took part in so many conflicts and
gained such great victories over the enemy for the
conservation and protection of the honor and glory
we all owe to God, as well as for the promotion of
[human] salvation: Come, I pray you, to the assistance of my soul, which continually is besieged with
such great peril by its enemies, the flesh, the world,
and the devil. And as you were a leader for the people
of Israel through the desert, so also be my faithful
leader and companion through the desert of this
world, until you conduct me safely into the happy
land of the living, in that blessed [country] from
which we all are exiles.

SAINT ALOYSIUS GONZAGA

Michael is one of the three angels liturgically venerated by
the Church. He is mentioned in the Book of Daniel, the
Epistle of Jude, and the Book of Revelation.

—September 30—

Saint Jerome

Patron of Librarians and Students

Dear Saint Jerome, you now behold and enjoy the Original of your translation, contemplating face-to-face the Word, of whom you wrote so well all your earthly life; help us to remember that it is possible for us to write our names tipped with love across the ramparts of heaven.... The crown of Faith that you kept and defended through persecution and the errors of your day is now resplendent upon your brow; may we not faint away in our straits and struggles for sanctity. The humility that placed you at the feet of all on earth, even to washing and kissing those feet, will detain your turning from our lowliness and great needs. We are almost stunned by your inexhaustible perfections as we lie steeped in our imperfections, impurity, and egotism; help us to see that God offers each, even the lowliest, [God]self with all [God's] beauty, lovableness, wisdom, power, and infinite happiness. Help us to copy the sampler of sanctity you stitched in various hues; in the red of sorrow for sin, in the gold of great deeds, in the black of expiating penance, and in the blue of God's mercy. Before the sands of time run out for us, help us to write many love letters to God in them—greetings to [God] via prayer, work, and suffering.

Marie C. Commins

c. 342–420: From Dalmatia, Jerome, originally named Hieronymus, led a varied life of study, solitude, activity, and travel. He was at one time secretary to the pope and during his years in Rome befriended Saint Paula, with whom he retired to Bethlehem to found a monastic settlement of celibates. He retranslated and commented on the Latin Bible, known as the Vulgate, for which he was named a Doctor of the Church.

October

Saint Thérèse
of Lisieux
(Thérèse of the Child Jesus)

PATRON OF FLORISTS, FOREIGN MISSIONS,
PILOTS, AND FRANCE; INVOKED
AGAINST TUBERCULOSIS

O glorious Saint Thérèse, whom almighty God has
raised up to aid and inspire the human family, I
implore your miraculous intercession. You are so
powerful in obtaining every need of body and spirit
from the heart of God. Holy Mother Church pro-
claims you "Prodigy of Miracles…the Greatest Saint
of Modern Times." Now I fervently beseech you to
answer my petition (*mention here*) and to carry out
your promises of spending heaven doing good upon
earth…of letting fall from heaven a shower of roses.
Little flower, give me your childlike faith, to see the
face of God in the people and experiences of my
life, and to love God with full confidence. Saint
Thérèse, my Carmelite sister, I will fulfill your plea
"to be made known everywhere," and I will continue to lead others to Jesus through you. Amen.

TRADITIONAL

1873–1897: Born in Alençon, France, Thérèse became a Carmelite at Lisieux at the age of fifteen. She is known for her "little way" of simplicity and perfection in doing small things. She died of tuberculosis at a young age, after a long period of suffering. She is a Doctor of the Church, and her autobiography, *Story of a Soul*, is a classic.

—OCTOBER 2—

Saint Léger

INVOKED AGAINST EYE DISEASES

Holy Saint Léger, your words come down to us to this day, for in reforming the monasteries in your diocese, you counseled monks to follow their rule, so that their prayers would preserve the world from untold disasters. Was your exhortation only for monks in monasteries? I think there's an exhortation in there for all of us. But sometimes, dear saint, I get lost in my prayers, and sometimes I can't pray, and so I ask for your help. Bless my efforts at prayer, that I may learn to open my thoughts and feelings to God, and that I may learn as well to listen to what God has to say to me. And bless my activities, that they too may become as prayers, to help me praise God and communicate with our Lord. I pray, with your help, in Jesus' name. Amen.

c. 616–678: As abbot of the monastery of Saint Maxentius, Léger introduced the Benedictine rule to his community. He assisted Saint Bathildis, the queen regent, during the minority of Clotaire III. When he was appointed bishop of Autun, he reformed Church discipline and imposed the Rule of Saint Benedict on all the monasteries. But he was murdered by Ebroin, mayor of the palace, to whom he gave himself up, during bitter infighting over the crown, to prevent the destruction of the city.

—OCTOBER 3—

Saint Thomas of Cantelupe

Saint Thomas, stand with me as I stand for what I believe. It seems as though all my friends and companions have abandoned me, because they don't want me to make so much noise or don't feel as strongly as I do or just don't believe I'm right. But, Thomas, I feel the Lord wants me to take a stand here. So here I stand. Alone. And afraid. That's why I'm asking for your help today. Stay with me, and give me just a bit of courage to say what I believe. And even if I'm wrong—and I may well be—keep me company anyway while helping me to see what's true. Thanks, dear Thomas, for accompanying me. Amen.

c. 1218–1282: From a noble English family, Thomas studied at Oxford, Orléans, and Paris, eventually serving as chancellor of Oxford and, for a time, chancellor of England. Chosen bishop of Hereford, a much neglected diocese, he took over his duties with a firm hand, excommunicating nobles who tried to interfere with his spiritual administration. When he himself was excommunicated by the archbishop of Canterbury, he was received kindly by Pope Martin IV, to whom he pleaded his case. Thomas was known for his love of children and the poor.

—OCTOBER 4—

Saint Francis of Assisi

PATRON OF ANIMALS, ECOLOGY, ITALY, AND
TAPESTRY MAKERS; INVOKED AGAINST FIRE

Saint Francis, God won your heart and blessed you
with childlike joy. By your intercession, may I be
refreshed and renewed. Help me see the fingerprints
of the Divine Master in all God's creatures, especially in those who are weak and helpless. May I become an instrument of God's peace, and sow seeds of
faith and hope wherever I go. Guide me in my prayers,
and hear the requests I make before you. *(Mention
your petitions here.)* Saint Francis, pray for me. Amen.

THE REDEMPTORISTS

c. 1181–1226: The son of a wealthy merchant, Francis spent
his youth in seeking pleasure but, falling in love with Lady
Poverty and her Lord, Jesus Christ, renounced all worldly
goods and founded the order of Friars Minor. He was the
first to bear the stigmata, the wounds of Christ's passion.

—OCTOBER 5—

Blessed Faustina Kowalska

Blessed Faustina, you told us that your mission
would continue after your death and that you would
not forget us.

Our Lord also granted you a great privilege, telling you to "distribute graces as you will, to whom
you will, and when you will."

Relying on this, I ask your intercession for the
graces I need, especially *(mention request)*.

Help me, above all, to trust in Jesus as you did and
thus to glorify his mercy every moment of my life.

MARIANS OF THE IMMACULATE CONCEPTION

1905–1938: Born in a poor family near Lodz, Poland, Faustina had visions of the Virgin Mary and heard Jesus calling her to the convent when she was a youngster. She eventually found a convent in Warsaw that would accept a peasant girl, and she surprised all by her holiness. When she began having conversations with Jesus, her fellow sisters ridiculed her. But Jesus told her to persevere, and he gave her the image of himself as the Divine Mercy and taught her the Divine Mercy Chaplet. Faustina suffered much from tuberculosis but offered herself as a victim soul to help the souls in purgatory. Her diary, *Divine Mercy in My Soul*, is a modern spiritual classic.

—OCTOBER 6—

Blessed Marie Rose Durocher

O Blessed Marie Rose, you knew the great value of education and worked to ensure that all children have access to schooling. When I am in class, remind me that not all people are able to attend school, and inspire me to take advantage of the opportunities presented to me. Pray, as well, for all children who are in school, that they may recognize the great advantage they have and learn their lessons well. And ask the Lord to send his Holy Spirit to all teachers, that they may love and nurture the students entrusted to their care, helping them to advance in knowledge. This I pray through Christ our Lord. Amen.

1814–1849: Though physically weak, Marie Rose taught the children in the parish where her brother was priest. After many difficulties, she founded a congregation in Quebec called the Sisters of the Holy Names of Jesus and Mary. This congregation, bringing suit to the U.S. Supreme Court in the Oregon School case, proved the constitutional right of children to attend private school.

—OCTOBER 7—

Saint Osith

Holy Saint Osith, you learned the hard way that entering into a relationship in order to please one's parents can lead to terrible hardships and even danger. Give me the courage and wisdom to resist the urgings of my parents and my friends when my heart leads me in a contrary direction. As well, pray that I may be able to put emotions aside in order to listen to my heart, to listen to the Lord.

O Saint Osith, if it be God's will, I implore your assistance in finding a suitable partner. And if it be God's will that I remain single, help me find suitable and godly work to which I may dedicate my life. I ask this in the name of Jesus, who holds what is best for each of us in the palm of his hand. Amen.

died c. 675: Brought up in a Benedictine nunnery, Osith escaped an abusive marriage, received permission from the bishop to adopt the religious habit, and later founded a convent at Chich, now called St. Osyth, where she was murdered by Danish pirates.

—OCTOBER 8—

Saint Thais

Thais, wake me up to the inconsistencies in my life. Especially, show me how my work, friends, entertainments, purchases, and use of time may be at odds with the spiritual values that I say are important to me. Help me to live rightly according to the spirit.

TOM COWAN

died c. 348: A famous prostitute in Alexandria, Thais was returned to the faith by Saint Paphnutius, an elderly hermit. She publicly renounced her former life, then went to the monastery, where she performed three years of penance. She died soon after.

—OCTOBER 9—

Saint Denis

PATRON OF FRANCE; INVOKED AGAINST FRENZY AND HEADACHES

Glorious servant of God, Saint Denis, with intense love you devoted yourself to Christ after learning to know him through the apostle Saint Paul, and you preached his saving name to the nations. You did not shrink from martyrdom to bring them to his knowledge and love. Implore for me a continual growth in the knowledge and love of Jesus, so that my restless heart may experience that peace that he alone can give. Help me by your powerful intercession with God to serve the Lord with a willing heart, to devote myself with abiding love to his service, and thereby to attain the eternal bliss of heaven. Amen.

TRADITIONAL

third century: The first bishop of Paris, Denis was one of the original seven missionaries sent from Rome to the Gauls. He was beheaded at Paris. According to one legend, he carried his own head six miles to the site of the cathedral that now bears his name.

—OCTOBER 10—

Blessed Daniel Comboni

O Blessed Daniel, you heard the Lord call you to "go and teach all nations." Because of your missionary efforts, many have heard the Gospel, particularly in Africa. Yet many more of the world's most abandoned have yet to hear the Good News. With you, we pray for missionaries of great faith and zeal. We pray that your spirit will inspire people across the globe to bring light where there is darkness, hope where there is despair, love where there is suspicion and hate, knowledge where there is ignorance, and health where there is disease. We ask you to watch over all missionaries and to pray to the Lord that they will lead people to Life, helping them to recognize themselves as God's children. We ask also that you pray to the Lord to strengthen those who are called to be missionaries, giving them the courage to accept the call generously. We ask this through Christ our Lord. Amen.

1831–1881: From Italy, Daniel was drawn to missionary work in Africa. The Lord inspired him with a plan for the regeneration of Africa, in which Africans would save Africa, and he received considerable support from the bishops gathered in Rome for Vatican Council I. Consecrated bishop of Central Africa, he founded a missionary family of priests, brothers, and sisters, now known as the Comboni Missionaries.

—OCTOBER 11—

Saint María Soledad Torres Acosta

O blessed Saint María, whose great love of God irradiated in your loving devotion to the sick and poor, dedicating yourself to the relief and consolation of their sufferings, obtain for us from God, help in all our sickness of body and soul, and patience and acceptance of the Lord's holy will in all our tribulations.

Inspire in us all great kindness toward the sick and the poor, in order that by our many works of charity done to them for Christ's sake, we may be worthy to receive with you in the end the reward promised by our Lord. Amen.

THE SISTERS, SERVANTS OF MARY

1826–1887: Dedicating her life to nursing the poor and abandoned sick in their own homes, María founded the Congregation of the Sisters, Servants of Mary in Madrid in 1851.

—OCTOBER 12—

Saint Seraphin of Montegranaro

Saint Seraphin, brother in Christ, your weaknesses became for others in your community a lesson in inclusion. Though ill-suited to any sort of manual work, and though nearly illiterate, you did not allow other people to dictate your worth. Instead, you communed with God and eventually showed others the beauty and wonder and worth of all individuals, no matter their weakness or strength, ability or inability. So I ask you to help me learn the lesson you taught your contemporaries, to move from exclusion to inclusion. Help me to overcome my fear of difference, of weakness, of sickness, of inability. Help me to accept each person for the wonderful creation he or she is. Help me to accept my own imperfections too, and to understand that despite them I am still a beloved child of God. And help me to learn from people whom in the past I have rejected or reviled or despised. I ask for your help in the name of Jesus, who dared to associate with outcast members of his own society. Amen.

c. 1540–1604: Clumsy, inept, and for the most part illiterate, Seraphin was allowed to join the Capuchins because his holiness was easily recognizable. His Capuchin brothers may have ridiculed his inabilities and assigned him as porter, but they recognized his devotion to prayer and eucharistic adoration, and people noted his ability to heal and prophesy. As his canonizer Pope Clement XIII noted, Seraphin "knew how to read and understand the great book of life which is our Savior, Jesus Christ."

—OCTOBER 13—

Saint Edward the Confessor

Edward, let me not be troubled when I cannot keep all the promises I make, both spiritual and nonspiritual. Help me to see that circumstances often prevent us from fulfilling our best-laid plans. But also encourage me to find realistic substitutes for the things I cannot do. May I throw myself into the alternative plans with the same enthusiasm I had for the originals.

TOM COWAN

1004–1066: Son of King Ethelred the Unready, Edward became king of England in 1042. Known as the "good King Edward," he was considerate, just, gentle, and unselfish, and his reign was one of peace, prosperity, and good government. He had made a vow to visit the tomb of Saint Peter but when he became king found himself unable to keep his promise. On the advice of the pope, he used the pilgrimage money to fund the building of Westminster Abbey. He was the first king to be buried there.

—OCTOBER 14—

Blessed Marie Poussepin

Blessed Marie, you proclaimed the knowledge and love of Jesus Christ and founded a community to bring the Word to the world. Help us, that we too may proclaim the Good News of the Lord to all. Help us, that we too may serve others with your spirit of charity. Pray for us, that we may be firm in faith and unwavering in hope. Bless us, that the souls of all the faithful may come together in a living community of love and holiness, so that henceforth we may sing an eternal hymn of praise: Glory to God, glory to the Son, and glory to the Holy Spirit. Amen.

1653–1744: Born into a French family whose trade was the knitting of silk stockings, Marie introduced weaving looms for wool stockings. She abolished apprenticeship fees, rewarded production, and promoted good workers. Her industrial revolution ensured the economic prosperity of her city. However, God called her to Sainville to found the Community of the Third Order of Saint Dominic for the instruction of girls and the service of the sick poor of the countryside. Her congregation is now known as the Dominican Sisters of Charity of the Presentation, and members work in thirty-three countries on four continents.

—OCTOBER 15—

Saint Teresa of Ávila

PATRON OF SPAIN; INVOKED AGAINST
HEADACHES AND HEART DISEASE

O holy Saint Teresa, you are a model—a woman
who was faithful to prayer, to your sisters and
friends, and to the work you were called to do. Help
us to be so committed to God that our daily work
fosters our life of prayer and our life of prayer en-
ables us to live fully in the world around us—aware
of its needs and concerns.

Dearest saint, bless all those who seek to reform
institutions; help them to walk before God in sin-
cerity and truth. Console them when the journey
seems dark and the prayers are dry. Free them from
hidden expectations. And grant that they may be
true to the Lord's calling and faithful to a life of
prayer. We ask this through Jesus, who was ever
your friend. Amen.

1515–1582: Born of Jewish descent in Ávila, Spain, Teresa
became seriously ill soon after entering the Carmelite monastery of the Incarnation and was invalided for several years.
With the help of Saint John of the Cross, she worked to
reform the Carmelites. Her three major works on prayer
and the mystical life are *The Life, The Way of Perfection,*
and *The Interior Castle.* She is a Doctor of the Church.

—OCTOBER 16—

Saint Gerard Majella

PATRON OF CHILDBIRTH AND MOTHERS

Saint Gerard, who, like the Savior, loved children so tenderly and by your prayers freed many from disease and even death, listen to us who are pleading for our sick child. We thank God for the great gift of our *son/daughter* and ask God to restore our child to health if such be the holy will. This favor we beg of you through your love for all children and mothers. Amen.

THOMAS E. TOBIN, C.SS.R.

Saint Gerard Majella, women the world over have adopted you as their patron in the joys and fears of childbearing. Today, we invoke your intercession for the pro-life movement. Pray that all will look upon human life as a gift from God, not as an unwanted burden to be destroyed. Assist the efforts of those on earth who are enlisted in the crusade of promoting the dignity and value of all human life, particularly the unborn. This we ask through Christ our Lord. Amen.

THOMAS E. TOBIN, C.SS.R.

1725–1755: Apprenticed as a tailor, Gerard was received as a lay brother by the Redemptorists. He continued his trade in the monastery, where he attracted the attention of Saint Alphonsus. Gerard's wonderful and well-authenticated life was a series of supernatural phenomena—bilocations, reading of consciences, prophecies, and so forth.

—OCTOBER 17—

Saint Ignatius
of Antioch

Holy Saint Ignatius, you were one of the first Christian heroes, for your fame guaranteed a big crowd at the amphitheater, and your dignity in the face of death proved inspirational to your brothers and sisters in Christ. Help me now that I am facing death—not that I expect to be thrown to the lions on account of my faith, but sometimes it feels as if I am being tossed off to the wild beasts of disease or the tortures of aging or simply the chilling indifference of an unfeeling healthcare system. Help me to greet death with dignity, for it is something we all must greet sometime. And teach me to use the short time left to me wisely, as you did when you composed your famous letters. You did not waste a moment in feeling sorry for yourself; so inspire me not to waste any time either, but to spend my final years or months or moments at something worthwhile—something I've always wanted to do—something I feel passionate about—something worth sharing. Bless me as I approach the horizon of this life, that I may enjoy my final glimpse of this beautiful valley. I ask this in Jesus' name. Amen.

died c. 107: Ignatius was bishop of Antioch in Syria for forty years before he was carried to Rome to be thrown to the wild beasts in the amphitheater. On his way to Rome he wrote seven epistles, encouraging and exhorting other Christians not to lose their faith despite persecution.

—OCTOBER 18—

Saint Luke

PATRON OF BUTCHERS, DOCTORS,
GLASS-INDUSTRY WORKERS, GOLDSMITHS,
LACE MAKERS, NOTARIES, PAINTERS,
AND SCULPTORS

Most holy Saint Luke, favored physician, inspired by Almighty God, you declared in your Gospel the love and healing power of God's Son. Pray for the Church, that the same love and power to heal that Jesus shared may continue to work through God's people. Pray for all physicians, surgeons, nurses, and doctors, that their healing efforts may be efficacious—and that they may bear compassion to their patients. And pray for those who are sick and in need of healing, especially *(mention name)*; bring the healing Spirit of Jesus to *her/him*, that *she/he* may be well again.

As well, I ask you to bring the faith to all people of science, that they may understand that behind all scientific explanations is our Creator God, whose Spirit moves the universe.

In Jesus' name I pray. Amen.

first century: A Greek of Antioch and a physician by profession, Luke became the fellow worker of Saint Paul and remained with him until his martyrdom. Luke is considered the author of the third Gospel and the Acts of the Apostles.

—OCTOBER 19—

Saint Isaac Jogues

Holy Saint Isaac, you encountered incredible opposition among the Native Americans to whom you sought to bring the love of Christ, yet you persevered, even to your death. Inspire in me the will to follow Jesus always, in all circumstances, even through danger, and even to death. As Jesus loved me to the death, so help me to be worthy and return that love.

O dear saint, pray for me, that I may do the best I can in whatever situation I find myself. Bless my efforts, even if they fall short of the mark, and pray to Jesus that he will honor even my most dismal attempts to treat others with the same love with which he treats me. I implore your intercession in Jesus' name, for he blessed the woman who gave her all, though it was only a mite. Amen.

1607–1646: A Jesuit missionary who arrived in Canada in 1636, Isaac was involved in several heroic adventures, after which he was tomahawked by the Mohawks in an Iroquois village.

—OCTOBER 20—

Blessed James Kern

O Blessed James, God gave you a share in the sufferings of our Lord, for your war wounds bled and caused you excruciating pain for eight years, yet you bore all with patient cheer and persevered in serving the Lord. Bless all who are wounded or injured, that they may be made well.

Pray also for all people who suffer from incurable illness, that God may ease their suffering. Pray for all those who live with chronic pain, that God's angels may bring them reprieve from their pain. Inspire them with your example, that they may offer their sacrifice to the Lord, for his glory and for the salvation of souls.

Through your prayers, O Blessed James, keep me well, and when suffering comes, help me take up my cross daily with joy, so that I may share in the eternal glory of Jesus, who is Lord for ever and ever. Amen.

1897–1924: From Vienna, James began his studies for the priesthood while but a boy. Called to military service during World War I, he came to be called "guardian angel" and "intercessor with God" by his fellow soldiers. Inspired by his love for God, he asked to suffer for his Savior. He was wounded, and despite the doctors' predictions and his continued bleeding, he returned to seminary to continue his studies. His hemorrhages continued until his death a few years later, but he was ordained and spent as much time as he could in preaching, hearing confessions, teaching, and praying.

—OCTOBER 21—

Saint Gaspar del Bufalo

Saint Gaspar, missionary of the Precious Blood, you continually sought the consolation of prayer and adoration. Keep us faithful when we are overwhelmed by the demands and sorrows of daily life, so that we may be deeply rooted in prayer, living branches on the vine through which Jesus' life-blood flowed.

O Saint Gaspar, ardent preacher of the love of God, you journeyed far and wide, seeking out those who were lost. Lead all to conversion of heart, to a true spirit of penance, and to a greater acceptance of God's mercy. Help us to welcome the stranger and to seek out those who are far off.

O Saint Gaspar, great apostle of charity, from childhood you fed the hungry and comforted the sick. Encourage us by the example of your holy life. Have compassion on us from your place at Jesus' side and obtain help for the poor, health for the sick, comfort for the abandoned, and aid for all in need.

O Saint Gaspar, intercessor, protector, and friend, bring the petitions we have placed before you to Jesus, along with the needs of all who have asked for our prayers.

MISSIONARIES OF THE PRECIOUS BLOOD

1786–1837: A priest who was exiled to Corsica for refusing to swear allegiance to Napoleon, Gaspar returned to France to found the first house of the Missioners of the Most Precious Blood, to serve as "missioners" in their own country.

—OCTOBER 22—

Saints Nunilo and Alodia

O Saints Nunilo and Alodia, intercede for all those whose parents refuse to accept their children for who they are, particularly those whose faith choice divides them. Pray for those who suffer persecution because of their faith, that God will send them the grace to persevere in joy.

Bless also those siblings who do not get along with one another, especially those where one is strong in the faith and the others rebellious or negligent or nonbelieving. Pray for these siblings, that they may come to enjoy the same solidarity in life on earth as you did, and be bonded forever in joy for eternity. We ask this through Jesus our Lord. Amen.

died 851: Nunilo and Alodia's Spanish Christian mother remarried a Muslim, who persecuted the two sisters for their Catholic faith. The girls fled when teenagers, seeking to preserve their virginity, and were among the first to be arrested when the persecutions of Christians began in their area of northeast Spain. The Moors sentenced them to a life of prostitution, but when the women refused, they were beheaded.

—OCTOBER 23—

Saint John of Capistrano

PATRON OF MILITARY CHAPLAINS

O Saint John, you profited from your term in prison to think about the affairs of your soul. I do not desire such enforced solitude, dear saint, but I would enjoy a time apart—a sabbatical, perhaps—during which I might reflect upon how I stand with God. So I ask you, dear saint, to pray to the Lord that I might be granted a short time of rest, that I may use the time to consider how I might need to change my life. And if my request is granted, dear John, bless me, that I may be able to focus on listening to what the Lord might have to say to me. I pray through Christ our Lord. Amen.

1385–1456: John, governor of Perugia, was betrayed and imprisoned during a war with a neighboring town. Upon his release, he entered a Franciscan community, was ordained, then traveled throughout the lands of Italy, Germany, Bohemia, Austria, Hungary, Poland, and Russia. At the age of seventy, when Mohammed II was threatening Vienna, Pope Callistus II commissioned John to lead a crusade against the invading Turks. John helped gain victory at the Battle of Belgrade. He died three months later.

—OCTOBER 24—

Saint Raphael

PATRON OF DRUGGISTS, HAPPY MEETINGS,
HEALTH INSPECTORS, LOVERS, TRAVELERS,
AND YOUNG PEOPLE LEAVING HOME;
INVOKED AGAINST BLINDNESS

Saint Raphael, archangel, you protected young Tobiah as he journeyed to a distant land. Protect all travelers and most especially those who go about near and far preaching the Gospel. Guide and inspire modern apostles who use the communications media to bring the Good News of Christ to many souls.

You also brought healing and joy to all you met. Help those who bring the Word of God to souls, that they may be as instruments in God's hands to draw many to lives of Christian holiness.

We ask this through Christ our Lord. Amen.

DAUGHTERS OF SAINT PAUL

One of the three angels venerated liturgically by name, Raphael appears in the Book of Tobit. His name means "the Healer of God," and he is associated with the angel of the sheep-pool in the Gospel of John.

—OCTOBER 25—

Forty Holy Martyrs of England and Wales

O blessed saints, martyrs for the faith, pray for me, that I may have the faith to follow Jesus and the courage to profess Christ always.

Please intercede for me, holy saints, as I call upon you now. Pray for me, Saints John Almond, Edmund Arrowsmith, Ambrose Barlow, John Boste, Alexander

Briant, Edmund Campion, Margaret Clitherow,
Philip Evans, Thomas Garnet, Edmund Gennings,
Richard Gwyn, John Houghton, Philip Howard,
John Jones, John Kemble, Luke Kirby, Robert
Lawrence, David Lewis, Anne Line, John Lloyd,
Cuthbert Mayne, Henry Morse, Nicholas Owen,
John Paine, Polydore Plasden, John Plessington,
Richard Reynolds, John Rigby, John Roberts, Alban
Roe, Ralph Sherwin, Robert Southwell, John
Southworth, John Stone, John Wall, Henry Walpole,
Margaret Ward, Augustine Webster, Swithun Wells,
and Eustace White.

O holy saints, martyrs for Jesus, pray for me, now
and at the hour of my death. Amen.

On October 25, 1970, Pope Paul VI canonized forty martyrs of England and Wales. These men and women were
representative of the English and Welsh Roman Catholics
who were put to death for the faith between 1535 and 1670.
Faced with the choice of remaining steadfast in the faith or
saving their lives, they joyfully embraced martyrdom in order to express their love of God. Despite their choice, these
martyrs continued to love their country as well, but they
knew the priority of their allegiance. Many of them have
their own feast day.

—OCTOBER 26—

Saint Cedd

Saint Cedd, my brother in Christ, when the king
wanted a new monastery, he gave you a piece of the
most undesirable land he could find. It was hardly
your idea of a fitting spot for a house of God. So
you sat down and prayed and fasted about the matter—for forty days, it is said. And in the end, the
monastery you founded there became one of the most
important religious centers in medieval England.

Dear Cedd, I must admit I don't have your perspective on such matters. When my boss or my
friends ask me to do something with insufficient
resources, I do get upset and question whether they
really want what they've asked for—or whether they
really want me to undertake the project in the first
place. Rarely do I step aside for a time to pray and
meditate about how to accomplish the task, and
rarely do I even insert God into my thinking about
the issue. Help me to remember God, and remind
me to take all my problems to the Lord. Not that
I'm asking for miraculous answers; just let me give
myself the time to listen to God's perspective on the
problem. So I ask you to remind me of this, dear
Cedd, on the many occasions when I won't be able
to remember myself. Amen.

died 664: Brother of Saint Chad of Lichfield, Cedd was a
monk of Lindisfarne who evangelized the Midlands; later,
he was appointed bishop of the East Saxons, whose chief
city was London. Cedd founded the abbeys of Tilbury and
Lastingham. At the Synod of Whitby, Cedd accepted the
Roman over the Celtic date for Easter, not wanting to cause
further disunity among the English churches. Cedd died from
the plague soon after.

—OCTOBER 27—

Blessed Contardo Ferrini

Most Blessed Contardo, I admire your pioneering
inclination, and I thank you for showing us how to
carry on our professional work in a Christian spirit.
You ordered your whole work to God, and I ask
you to help me order my entire professional life toward God too. No matter what my profession, no
matter whether I am satisfied in it or not, help me
to keep God in mind in all that I do, remembering

that the work itself is not so important as my attitude about it. Remind me that I work not for myself but as a servant of other children of God. Pray that I may learn to let everything I do reflect both my love of truth and my earnestness about it. And help me to keep my conversation sensible and logical and my actions above Christian reproach. I ask for your special blessing on *(mention name)*, who seems not to enjoy *his/her* work at this time; help *him/her* realize the joy of working with God in mind. I pray in Jesus' name. Amen.

1859–1902: As a young scientist and jurist, Contardo made a vow of lifelong celibacy while he was examining his professional options. He researched at all the major libraries in Europe and eventually became a professor of Roman law at the University of Pavia, meanwhile becoming a Franciscan tertiary and developing a deep prayer life.

—OCTOBER 28—

Saint Jude Thaddeus

PATRON INVOKED IN DESPERATE STRAITS

Glorious apostle Saint Jude Thaddeus, true lover of Jesus and Mary, I greet you. Through the Sacred Heart of Jesus I praise and thank God for all the graces...bestowed upon you. Humbly prostrated before you, I implore you to look down upon me with compassion. Despise not my poor prayer; let not my trust be confounded; to you God has granted the privilege of aiding humankind in the most desperate cases. Oh, come to my aid, that I may praise the mercies of God! All my life I will be grateful to you and will be your faithful devotee until I can thank you in heaven. Amen.

DAUGHTERS OF SAINT PAUL

first century: One of the twelve disciples, Jude is identified
in the Gospels as the brother of James (Gospel of Luke) or
the brother of Jesus (Gospel of Mark). He is considered to
be the writer of the Letter of Jude. According to tradition,
he preached in Mesopotamia and Persia.

—OCTOBER 29—

Saint Bartholomew
de las Casas

O Saint Bartholomew, why were you so slow to follow the convictions of your conscience? And why
am I so tardy in following through on what I know
is the right thing to do? Help me, dear saint, that I
may come to trust what my conscience is telling me
and do what I know I must do in a timely manner.

I ask as well, O holy saint, for your intercession
on behalf of all peoples who once suffered and still
suffer the indignities of slavery. Send your spirit to
us as we tardily attempt to heal the wounds that
still fester. Pray for us all, that we may all learn to
see beyond appearances and trust the good in all
people, no matter their ancestry or race or economic
position.

Help me especially to learn not to treat others as
servants or slaves, neither at work nor at home nor
at the store nor the hairdresser nor the garage. Teach
me to respect the human dignity of all persons, for
all of us are made in God's image. I ask this in the
name of Jesus our Savior, who sees God in each of
us. Amen.

1474–1566: A Spanish slave-owner on the island of
Hispaniola, Bartholomew realized the injustice of slavery
when he heard a Dominican friar preaching against it. However, even after Bartholomew converted and entered the

priesthood, he did not free his slaves, merely turning them over to a good friend. Not until eight years later, when he became a Dominican himself, did he free his slaves and become one of the great proponents of freedom for Native Americans.

—OCTOBER 30—

Blessed Dorothy of Montau

PATRON OF PRUSSIA

Most Blessed Dorothy, you experienced the great grief of watching your children die. Intercede for all parents who have lost their children. Comfort them in their grief, and ask the Holy Spirit to send them special graces so that they may understand that these children now rest in God's loving embrace.

Pray also for those men and women who lose their spouses. Implore the Lord to console them. Comfort them, that they may realize that God wants them to live a fruitful and joyful life despite their great loss. In Jesus' name I pray. Amen.

1347–1394: Married to an angry, domineering husband, Dorothy eventually won him over to the spiritual life. When he died, she lived as a recluse in a cell in Marienwerder, all of her nine children but one having died also. She gained great fame for holiness, healing, and good counsel and stressed devotion to the Blessed Sacrament. She is revered in Poland, Lithuania, Slovakia, and the Czech Republic.

—OCTOBER 31—

Saint Quentin

O holy Saint Quentin, your boldness in proclaiming the Gospel and your ability to speak the truth
brought you into mortal opposition with your enemies. Nevertheless, you persevered, and your reward is great in heaven.

Give me your spirit of boldness, that I may proclaim the truth to all. Remind me of the power of
words, that I may remember to choose them carefully with a view toward truthfulness. And keep me
mindful of the dangers still present to those who
speak truth. Protect me, and pray for me to the Lord
for his guidance and security.

I pray especially for *(mention name)*, who in
speaking about what *he/she* believes is angering
some people in the community. Protect *him/her* from
harm. And even if I don't agree with what *he/she* is
saying, make me bold in proclaiming *his/her* right
to say it. I ask this in the name of Jesus Christ, our
Lord and Savior. Amen.

died 287: According to tradition, Quentin was an army officer and the son of a Roman senator. When he became a
Christian, he journeyed as a missionary to western Gaul,
where he was martyred with unusual cruelty because of his
success as a bold preacher of the Christian Gospel. The city
of Saint-Quentin stands on the site of his first posthumous
miracle and the probable site of his martyrdom.

November

All Saints

O happy saints who rejoice in God: After having
passed through the tempestuous sea of this life, you
have merited to arrive at the port of eternal repose
and sovereign peace where, sheltered from tempests
and peril, you are made partakers of endless glory
and happiness. I beseech you, by the charity with
which your souls are replenished, to regard us with
a favorable eye. You are the brilliant portals of the
heavenly Jerusalem; grant us an entrance into that
holy city. You are on the mountain of the Lord; draw
toward you those who are yet in the valley of tears.
Your feet are firmly fixed upon the rock, according
to the words of holy Scripture, since you are confirmed in grace and charity; sustain those who still
walk in the slippery and perilous path of this life,
and who are continually exposed to the fatal falls
and mortal wounds of sin. In a word, you are the
saints and favorites of God; plead our cause before
[God] with so much force and ardor, and ask [God]
so earnestly to associate us with you, that we may
one day be so happy as to bless eternally [God's]
mercies, and testify to you our gratitude forever.

SAINT AUGUSTINE

—NOVEMBER 2—

Saint Marcian of Chalcis

Marcian, you wisely refused to do some miracles
when you knew they would increase the fame and
popularity that you never wanted in the first place.
I can't do miracles, but I am susceptible to popularity. Remind me that in God's eyes I do not need to
be popular and famous. My own life, even though
it be as narrow as your cell, can please [God].

TOM COWAN

died c. 387: Giving up a brilliant military career, Marcian
left the emperor's court to lead a solitary life in the desert of
Chalcis. He was known for the miracles that occurred
through his intercession.

—NOVEMBER 3—

Saint Martín de Porres

PATRON OF HAIRDRESSERS, PUBLIC-HEALTH
WORKERS, PERSONS OF MIXED RACE

O Saint Martín, teach us to be generous with the
gifts that God has given us. Make us sympathetic
toward those who are suffering and afflicted. Pray
to our Redeemer and to Our Lady of Mercy that
our hearts may not be hardened by sin and selfishness, but that we may always be kind and generous
to our neighbors because they are the children of
our heavenly Father. Amen.

DAUGHTERS OF SAINT PAUL

1569–1639: Born in Lima, Peru, Martín was the son of a
white Spanish knight and a freed black mother. Entering
the Dominican friary as a lay brother, Martin nursed the sick
and befriended the poor of the city, especially the African
slaves.

—NOVEMBER 4—

Saint Charles Borromeo

PATRON OF APPLE ORCHARDS, CATECHISTS,
SEMINARIANS, AND STARCH MAKERS;
INVOKED AGAINST STOMACHACHES AND ULCERS

Most holy Saint Charles, you used your immense power and considerable fortune to help the people in your archdiocese, building hospitals and schools, organizing famine relief, and caring so much for others that you exhausted yourself and ruined your health. And so, dear Charles, I ask you to be with me when I am made aware of the needs of others. Send me your spirit of generosity, so that I may not only give of my plenty but also stretch myself and give more than I feel able. As well, holy saint, remind me to thank the Lord for the bounty and abundance I enjoy daily, and remind me that this plenty belongs to God—that I am but caretaker, and accountable for how I dispense the Lord's goodness. Animate me, Saint Charles, with a joyously charitable spirit willing to take care of my sisters and brothers.

O Charles, I implore you to intercede also for those in dire need: the homeless, the hungry, the sick, the unemployed, the refugees from war or natural calamity. Especially remember *(mention request)*, who this day do not have food or shelter or clothing enough. Be with them. Protect them from harm—especially the children. And shower them with the love of God, whose providence will care for all. In Jesus' name I ask this boon of you. Amen.

1538–1584: The most imposing and influential figure of the Counter-Reformation in Italy, Charles did not receive priestly or episcopal orders until after his uncle Pope Pius IV appointed him archbishop of Milan. Charles was a model bishop, organizing relief efforts to alleviate famine and plague and exhausting himself in personally feeding famine victims. He also authored the final decrees at the Council of Trent.

—NOVEMBER 5—

Saint Elizabeth

PATRON OF PREGNANT WOMEN

O holy Saint Elizabeth, kinswoman of Mary and mother of Saint John the Baptist, though you gave up hope of ever conceiving a child, you were open to the power of God to do what mortals thought impossible. Pray for all those having difficulty conceiving, that they may remain open to all possibilities, for "nothing is impossible with God." Bless them when they despair and sorrow, and intercede for them, that they may conceive the child they so dearly desire. And once they have conceived, send your spirit to them so that they may cherish their child, and all children.

O holy saint, share with us also your love and friendship with the Blessed Virgin Mary. Teach us to rely on her, as you relied on her assistance during the difficult days of your pregnancy. Speak to her of us, that she may shower her loving care on us too. O help us to appreciate her tender love and her desire to be our friend. Thus we pray, through Christ our Lord. Amen.

first century: The mother of Saint John the Baptist, Elizabeth appears in the Gospel of Luke. She was kinswoman to Mary, the mother of Jesus.

—NOVEMBER 6—

Saint Illtud of Wales

Illtud, your calling to the spiritual life grew out of your loss of friends, and your pursuit of the spiritual life enticed you to leave your wife. I pray for guidance in knowing how to balance my own needs for solitude and contemplation with my obligations to family and friends. Help me make wise decisions that allow my love for God and my love for others to nurture each other.

TOM COWAN

died c. 505: Though the details of his life are obscure, Illtud is one of the most celebrated of the Welsh saints. A cousin of King Arthur, Illtud resigned his court posts and retreated with his wife, Trynid, to the wilderness to lead a life of contemplation after several of his friends were killed in a hunting accident. Soon after, he left his wife to enter a monastery. He is renowned for his miracles averting natural catastrophes.

—NOVEMBER 7—

Saint Willibrord of Echternach

PATRON OF THE NETHERLANDS;
INVOKED AGAINST CONVULSIONS

Saint Willibrord, you became aware of a need, and you took it upon yourself. And you were successful. And when you became aware of other needs, you took them upon yourself too. However, you reached your limit, and further enterprises proved unsuccessful. Thus you learned the extent of your capabilities.

Help me to recognize my limits. Teach me how to be reasonable in my expectations, particularly when it comes to my expenditures of time and effort, and especially when it comes to my relationships with other people.

At the same time, dear saint, teach me not to place limits upon myself. Don't let me admit I'm defeated even before I've begun.

Most gracious saint, help me to lead a full, productive life. Help me to place my energies and efforts at the Lord's disposal. Remind me to go to him for advice about where to direct my work, that I may do what is pleasing to him. I ask this through Christ our Lord. Amen.

c. 658–739: A Northumbrian who studied in France and Ireland, Willibrord set out with eleven companions to preach to the nonbelievers of Frisia. He was consecrated bishop and established his see at Utrecht. His efforts to evangelize the lands of Denmark were a failure. However, with the help of King Pepin, Willibrord established the monastery of Echternach, as the center of his missionary expeditions, whence he retired to pray from time to time and where he is buried.

—NOVEMBER 8—

Saint Godfrey of Amiens

O Godfrey, your way to holiness was through severe, inflexible discipline, but you learned that what worked for you was not necessarily what was best for others, for each person must find his or her own path to heaven. Help me to find my own path, then, and bless me with the perseverance to keep on searching until I arrive. Remind me that no one else can do things exactly my way; teach me tolerance, that I may give other people the freedom to find their own way too. And if I should ever try to force other people to do it my way, ask the Lord to block my efforts, for I would not wish to cause anyone spiritual harm. In this matter I pray especially for *(mention name)*, who is my *child/student;* pray that the Lord grants me the grace to be a good teacher and role model, allowing *her/him* to establish *her/his* own unique relationship with God.

O Saint Godfrey, pray for me. Amen.

c. 1066–1115: Godfrey was abbot of Nogent-sous-Coucy in Champagne, and his monastery flourished under his highly disciplined leadership. When he was appointed bishop of Amiens, he tried to apply the same discipline to the clergy there, yet he met with so much resistance that he was tempted to resign and become a monk, but his people would not allow it. He was a lifelong opponent of simony and unchastity.

—NOVEMBER 9—

Blessed Elizabeth of the Trinity Catez

Most Blessed Elizabeth, you called yourself *Laudem Gloriae,* the "Praise of Glory," and your life gave witness to a complete openness to the Word of God. Teach me to love God in my own way but after your example. Show me what it might mean for me to open myself completely to Jesus Christ. Help me to understand how I might praise the glory of God with my own unique voice and talents. Most of all, nourish my prayer life, that I may come to communicate with our Lord on an intimate basis and accept him into my heart. I ask this in the name of the Holy Trinity whose name you bear. Amen.

1880–1906: Elizabeth's spirituality of intense inner listening began with her first holy Communion. She took a vow of perpetual virginity at fourteen and, in opposition to her mother's wishes, entered the Carmel of Dijon. There, the Three Persons of the Trinity came to dwell in her soul. Though she died young, the mystical writings she left are considered spiritual treasures.

—NOVEMBER 10—

Pope Saint Leo the Great

Most blessed Saint Leo, God granted you the understanding of the Incarnation, and in turn you shared with your flock the great mystery of our redemption. Help me, then, in the times when my understanding is disturbed, to accept anew and adore the one Christ, true God and true man, neither divided from our human nature nor separated from the divine Being. And be with me also when others may question me about the Incarnation, that I may be able to clearly and truthfully explain God's plan of salvation, that I may be a faithful witness to our Lord, who suffered and died so that we might have eternal life. I ask for your help in the name of that same Lord, Jesus Christ, who lives and reigns, world without end. Amen.

died 461: Pope Leo I's defense of the Catholic faith against heresy and his intervention with Attila the Hun and Genseric the Vandal raised the prestige of the Holy See to great heights. One of only three popes called "the Great," he is a Doctor of the Church.

—NOVEMBER 11—

Saint Martin of Tours

PATRON OF ALCOHOLICS, BEGGARS,
INNKEEPERS, EQUESTRIANS, HARVESTS,
HORSES, THE MILITARY, NEW WINE,
AND TAILORS

With trust and faith I beg you, Blessed Saint Martin, to defend me against impure and evil thoughts that may stain my soul and come to thwart my desire for the true and complete satisfaction that is offered through perfect love. Rescue me from the mire lest I sink. Let not the deep swallow me up. Your mercy is great; draw near to me and lift me up, I pray.

Blessed Saint Martin, help me imitate your holy charity in giving of my own worldly goods to the poor and the homeless.

ANN BALL

c. 316–397: The son of a Roman officer, Martin enrolled in the imperial cavalry. He left the army after sharing his cloak with a poor beggar and receiving a heavenly vision, putting himself under the tutelage of Saint Hilary of Poitiers, living as a recluse, and founding a community of monk-hermits. Promoted to the see of Tours, he accepted with great reluctance and established a great monastic center at Marmoutier, where he lived while discharging his episcopal duties. He was the greatest pioneer of Western monasticism before Saint Benedict.

—NOVEMBER 12—

Saint Josaphat

PATRON OF UKRAINE

Josaphat, sometimes I am closed-minded about the value of other people's spiritual beliefs and practices. Like you, I have my own ideas about what is right and wrong. Help me to be understanding about the people whom I think are wrong, just as I would want them to be understanding about my beliefs, which to them appear equally wrongheaded. The Golden Rule must be paramount, and I ask for the ability to live by it.

TOM COWAN

1584–1623: A native of Poland, Josaphat became a monk of the Byzantine rite and abbot of Vilna, devoting himself unsparingly to union with the Holy See. He was eventually consecrated archbishop of Polotsk, Lithuania, but his rivals orchestrated his murder by an angry mob.

—NOVEMBER 13—

Saint Frances Xavier Cabrini

PATRON OF EMIGRANTS, HOSPITAL ADMINISTRATORS, AND IMMIGRANTS

O Saint Frances Xavier Cabrini, who found in the Divine Heart of Jesus the secret of sanctity and the strength to carry his message to many nations, look kindly upon me and hear my prayer.

Inspired by Christ's charity you went about helping many in their spiritual and temporal needs; from the glory of heaven, where your charity is not lessened nor your power weakened, grant my petition and obtain for me the grace I so urgently desire. *(Mention your request.)*

From the Sacred Heart of Jesus, obtain that his kingdom may be established in this world, now divided by hatred and dissensions; secure peace among nations, conversion of sinners, health to the sick, alleviation for the victims of war, deliverance of the souls in purgatory, and salvation for the human race redeemed by Christ our Savior. Amen.

MOTHER CABRINI LEAGUE

1850–1917: Born in Italy, Frances was the first U.S. citizen to be canonized. She founded the Missionary Sisters of the Sacred Heart at Codogno, Italy, then came to the United States to work with Italian immigrants in New York and Chicago. She extended her work to Nicaragua, Costa Rica, Chile, Brazil, and Argentina.

—NOVEMBER 14—

Saint Lawrence O'Toole

Holy Saint Lawrence, despite difficult times and open hostility, you brought as much peace as you could to your people. Bless the peacemakers, for ours is still a troubled world much in need of people who can bring opposites together in love. Remind us that we are responsible for our neighbors' welfare, and that sometimes we have to risk putting aside our own demands in order to grant others their rights. Teach us also, in the interest of peace, to forgive those who have injured us, that we may face all of our neighbors with calm and loving and peaceful hearts.

Dear saint, intercede especially on behalf of the people in *(mention place)*, for theirs is a violent and war-torn land desperately in need of peace. Bless all who are working for peace on their behalf. In Jesus' name, we pray. Amen.

1128–1180: From County Kildare, Ireland, Lawrence was kidnapped when he was ten years old. Two years later he was released to the bishop of Glendalough and became a monk. He was later abbot of Glendalough, then archbishop of Dublin. Despite upheaval and war, Lawrence's great goal was to keep the peace, and he was participating in negotiations on behalf of the Irish with King Henry II of England when he died.

—NOVEMBER 15—

Blessed Magdalena Catherine Morano

O Blessed Magdalena, you left beloved and familiar surroundings to be a model of faithful service to God and to your brothers and sisters in your new home. Bless all missionaries who follow the call of God to minister in foreign lands. Encourage them in their work, and wrap them in the Holy Spirit so that they may never feel lonely or unloved or afraid. Keep them safe and healthy as well. And pray that the rest of the Church never forgets the importance of their ministry but continues to support them with prayer, as well as with tangible material and financial assistance. Ask the Lord also to call more brothers and sisters to serve as missionaries, to bring the love of Christ to all people.

Blessed Magdalena, pray for us. Amen.

1847–1908: From the area of Turin, Magdalena taught elementary school before entering the Daughters of Mary Help of Christians. She was assigned to Catania, in Sicily, to administer an institute for women, where she founded new religious houses and educational and catechetical programs.

—NOVEMBER 16—

Saint Gertrude the Great

PATRON OF THE WEST INDIES

O holy virgin Gertrude, apostle of the Sacred Heart
of Jesus, chaste dove and sanctuary of the Holy
Spirit, the Lord has promised that no sinner who
honors and loves you will die a sudden and unprovided death. Pray to the Lord, I beseech you, for the
grace of forgiveness. O holy Saint Gertrude, help
me to so love God and repent of my sins that with
faith and confidence I may expect a happy death. In
Jesus' name, I pray. Amen.

c. 1256–c. 1302: Consecrated to God at the age of five,
Gertrude never left the convent. She had her first mystical
experience while in her early twenties, and from that year
her life was a continuous and familiar communing with
Christ. Her mystical writings have helped spread devotion
to the Sacred Heart.

—NOVEMBER 17—

Saint Elizabeth of Hungary

PATRON OF BAKERS;
INVOKED AGAINST THE PLAGUE

Saint Elizabeth, we venerate you for your compassion. Keep us loving and loyal to our families,
friends, and those in need. In our struggle for sanctity, help us maintain our charm of personality, for
true perfection is Beauty—Christ.

Intercede for us that we may have tenacity of
purpose when crushed beneath insupportable trials, a trust that exists against all human hope. When
we enter that drear desert where no earthly satis-

faction exists, and where pain rises to a crescendo resembling Christ's Passion, remind us that suffering is the food of saints. From your place of breathtaking bliss before the Beatific Vision, plead for us in your tender-hearted fashion to your Eternal Lover.

MARIE C. COMMINS

1207–1231: Daughter of King Andrew II of Hungary and niece of Saint Hedwig, Elizabeth married Louis IV of Thuringia and bore three children. Theirs was a happy married life until her husband went to the Crusades and died at Otranto. Elizabeth then became a Franciscan tertiary and devoted herself to the relief of the destitute. She died at age twenty-four.

—NOVEMBER 18—

Saint Rose Philippine Duchesne

O Saint Rose, your heart was wholly open to love God and God's people everywhere. Your special care for the Native American people continued through your old age, and they knew the Lord's divine power in spite of your helplessness. Inspire me with the generosity, detachment, and humility that marked your life. Give me a single-hearted dedication to God and to the mission to which I am called. Pray that I may remain faithful to the graces of the past and attentive to the Holy Spirit's action in my life today.

Dearest Saint Rose, inspire me with ways to incarnate my love for God and to live the message of the Gospel. And pray that I may act in concert with people everywhere, that all the world may come to know the love of the Sacred Heart of Jesus, in whose name I pray. Amen.

1769–1852: When the Visitation nuns were scattered during the Reign of Terror, Rose stayed with her family in Grenoble and gathered a community there, which she incorporated into the Society of the Sacred Heart. Rose went to New Orleans as a missionary, setting up a center in St. Charles, Missouri, and working among the Pottowatomies. She also worked in the Rocky Mountain mission area and established a school for Native American girls in Kansas.

—NOVEMBER 19—

Saint Nerses the Great

Holy Nerses, knowing that the reforms you wanted would arouse the ire of the authorities against you, you nevertheless followed the dictates of your conscience for the good of the Church. You knew well the power of pressure from other people, and you suffered the worst consequences of bucking that pressure. Intercede, then, on behalf of all those who face the pressure to conform. In particular, pray for all young people who are dealing with peer pressure. Help them to follow the dictates of their own hearts. Bless them with the confidence to resist the almost overwhelming temptation to follow the crowd. Remind them most of all to seek the counsel of our Lord in prayer, for he will reveal to them the way to go and strengthen their resolve to do his will. I pray particularly for *(mention name)*, who is having such difficulty with pressure from *his/her* so-called friends; strengthen *his/her* conviction to do the right thing, and protect *him/her* throughout this ordeal.

O Saint Nerses, pray for us. Amen.

died c. 373: After his wife was murdered by the king, Nerses became the chief bishop of the Armenian Church. He founded hospitals, supported monasticism, and implemented

the reforms he had learned from Saint Basil at the first national synod at Ashtishat. These reforms proved unpalat-
able to King Arshak, who exiled Nerses. King Pap recalled
Nerses but poisoned him at dinner after the bishop accused
the king of being demon possessed. Nerses was succeeded
by his son, Saint Isaac.

—NOVEMBER 20—

Saint Edmund of East Anglia

O Saint Edmund, martyr for the faith, your study
of Scripture and religious devotion prepared you
for your greatest trial—and brought you your greatest triumph. When I am inclined to gloss over the
importance of the Scriptures because I consider them
irrelevant to my life, remind me of how they enabled you to live a good life and prepared you for a
good death. Help me to find at least a few minutes
each day to read God's Word and store it in my
heart. And when the right time comes, bring it again
to my mind, that I may prove a worthy follower of
our Lord Jesus Christ. Amen.

849–870: Becoming king at the age of fourteen, Edmund
patterned his reign after that of the Hebrew King David.
When the Vikings mistakenly concluded that Edmund had
murdered their king, they invaded and roundly defeated
Edmund's army. To save his people, he offered himself as a
sacrifice to the enemy, and when he refused to renounce his
faith, he was scourged, shot with arrows, and finally beheaded. Legend relates that a wolf protected his severed head
until it could be miraculously rejoined to his incorrupt body.

—NOVEMBER 21—

Blessed María of Jesus the Good Shepherd
(Francisca Siedliska)

Blessed María, the source and reference point for your holy work was the hidden life of the Holy Family of Nazareth. For you and your sisters, the Holy Family represented unstinting service for those in immediate need, in particular children who were neglected or who had been abandoned. Teach me to defend children as you did. Inspire me to take action when I note innocence offended, to move quickly to protect children who are in danger, to aid children who cannot care for themselves. Intercede, I pray, on behalf of all children who daily stare death in the face, whether in the violence of war or crime or the devastation of famine or neglect. Particularly at this moment, bless the children of *(mention place)*. Protect them from harm, and inspire me to know how I and others might help them. This I pray in the name of the Holy Family of Nazareth. Amen.

1842–1902: Born into wealth near Warsaw, Francisca was a frail but brilliant child. Her parents attempted to discourage her religious vocation, but she was not to be sidetracked. Francisca became Mother María, began a series of charitable works for neglected and abandoned children, and founded the Sisters of the Holy Family of Nazareth, who had houses in Poland, Rome, London, and the United States by the time of her death.

—NOVEMBER 22—

Saint Cecilia

PATRON OF COMPOSERS, MUSIC,
AND MUSICIANS

O holy martyr Cecilia, the Lord blessed you with
the gift of music, and in return you consecrated
yourself to him. Bless all musicians, that they may
achieve the full potential of their gift of music, using it for the glory of God. Pray also for all those
who listen to music, that they may appreciate the
wonders of sound—melody and harmony, voice and
instrument, syncopation and rhythm—and through
music may come to know the glorious beauty of
our Creator, who wishes only and at all times our
complete well-being.

Intercede also for those who make promises and
vows. Help them uphold their word faithfully, and
help them seek Truth sincerely, that they may know
whither they are called and what God wants them
to do.

O Saint Cecilia, pray for us. Amen.

second–third century: Cecilia is one of the most famous of
martyred Roman maidens, though little about her is known
for certain. Legend has it that she could play any musical
instrument, sing any song, and hear angelic harmonies. She
married Valerian, convincing him to live chastely with her,
as she had consecrated her virginity to God. She is supposed
to have been killed for the faith while she was bathing.

—NOVEMBER 23—

Blessed Miguel Augustine Pro

Blessed Miguel, before your death you told your friend to ask you for favors when you were in heaven. I beg you to intercede for me, and in union with Our Lady and all the angels and saints, to ask our Lord to grant my petition *(mention request)*, provided that it be God's will. Amen.

ANN BALL

Blessed Miguel, high-spirited youth, pray for us.
Viva Cristo Rey.
Blessed Miguel, loving son and brother,
pray for us. Viva Cristo Rey.
Blessed Miguel, patient novice, pray for us.
Viva Cristo Rey.
Blessed Miguel, exile from your homeland,
pray for us. Viva Cristo Rey.
Blessed Miguel, prayerful religious, pray for us.
Viva Cristo Rey.
Blessed Miguel, sick and suffering, pray for us.
Viva Cristo Rey.
Blessed Miguel, defender of workers, pray for us.
Viva Cristo Rey.
Blessed Miguel, courageous priest in hiding,
pray for us. Viva Cristo Rey.
Blessed Miguel, prisoner in jail, pray for us.
Viva Cristo Rey.
Blessed Miguel, forgiver of persecutors,
pray for us. Viva Cristo Rey.
Blessed Miguel, holy martyr, pray for us.
Viva Cristo Rey.

ANN BALL

1891–1927: Born in Guadalupe, Mexico, Miguel was ordained a Jesuit in Belgium and returned to his home country at a time when priests in Mexico were being arrested and prosecuted. Betrayed, he was executed by firing squad for the crime of being a priest. He died with the words "Viva Cristo Rey!" (Long live Christ the King!) on his lips.

—NOVEMBER 24—

Saint Andrew Dung-Lac and Companions

Holy Saint Andrew, your life reminds us that the cross has long been a part of the lives of your people, and that the faith rooted in Vietnam's soil is hardier than the forces that would destroy it. Intercede, I pray, on behalf of all people who continue to suffer from religious persecution today. Strengthen and encourage them, that they may persevere and not lose their faith. And let them know—somehow, some way—that God has not forsaken them but holds them close in love. I ask especially for the people of *(mention place)*, who are especially beleaguered at this time.

As well, holy saint, remind me to thank the Lord daily for the religious freedom I enjoy, and to pray every day for the spirit of religious freedom and tolerance to blossom and flourish throughout the world.

O holy Saint Andrew, pray for me. Amen.

Father Andrew was one of 117 martyrs who met death in Vietnam between 1820 and 1862. During these decades, many missionaries and priests were martyred, and between 100,000 and 300,000 Catholics were killed or subjected to great persecutions, all in the effort to stamp out the faith in Vietnam.

—NOVEMBER 25—

Saint Catherine
of Alexandria

PATRON OF LAWYERS, LIBRARIANS, MILLERS,
NURSES, PHILOSOPHERS, ROPE MAKERS,
SECRETARIES, SCHOOLGIRLS, STUDENTS,
WHEELWRIGHTS, UNIVERSITIES,
AND UNMARRIED WOMEN; INVOKED
AGAINST DISEASES OF THE TONGUE

Saint Catherine, glorious virgin and martyr, resplendent in the luster of wisdom and purity: your wisdom refuted the adversaries of divine truth and covered them with confusion; your immaculate purity made you a spouse of Christ, so that after your glorious martyrdom angels carried your body to Mount Sinai. Implore for me progress in the science of the saints and the virtue of holy purity, that vanquishing the enemies of my soul, I may be victorious in my last combat and after death be conducted by the angels into the eternal beatitude of heaven. Amen.

TRADITIONAL

died c. 310: According to legend, Catherine was an Egyptian queen who preferred philosophy to marriage to the Roman emperor Maxentius. She had become a Christian when a desert hermit showed her a depiction of the Madonna and Child. Catherine won a debate with fifty non-Christian philosophers before being martyred at Alexandria. Her alleged relics have been enshrined in the Orthodox monastery of Mount Sinai.

Saint John Berchmans

PATRON OF ALTAR SERVERS AND TEENAGE BOYS

Most holy Saint John, you practiced perfection in little things. Help me to follow your example, that I may take care of the details of my faith life. Pray that I may remain love-filled in the actions I take each day, no matter how large or small they may be. Pray that my words—my every utterance—may proclaim my faith. Indeed, pray that my thoughts remain centered on God and on what God wants of me.

O holy saint, I pray also for young men. As you were obedient to your parents and submissive to your teachers, help our youth to follow the way of Love. Watch over them, keeping them safe from all harm. Protect them from temptation. And pray that they will have the courage to choose right over wrong.

O Saint John, please take my prayer to Jesus speedily. Amen.

1599–1621: A devoted altar boy from his earliest days, John joined the Jesuits but soon succumbed to the fever-inducing summer heat. After a short illness he fulfilled his childhood prophecy by dying at the age of twenty-two. Many miracles have been attributed to his intercession.

—NOVEMBER 27—

Saint Maximus of Riez

PATRON OF BABIES AND THE DYING

Saint Maximus, holy monk, you abhorred the idea of promotion, desiring only to lead a simple life of prayer and communion with God. As with you, it is sometimes hard for me to accept the will of my bosses as the will of God. Yet God had a miraculous plan for your life, and God has a wondrous plan for mine. So help me, dear saint, to put aside my own desires, my thoughts that I know what's best for me, and help me to be open to the new possibilities that come my way. Sometimes these are suggestions, sometimes commands, but all are worth my consideration, and all are worthy of being brought before the Lord in prayer. Help me to pray then, O Saint Maximus, when I am confronted with a promotion or a change that might not be to my liking, that I may seek the Lord's will in all things. I pray in the name of Jesus our Lord, whose love always wants the best for me. Amen.

died c. 460: As abbot of Lérins, Maximus had a wide reputation for sanctity and miracle-working. When he was appointed bishop, he fled to Italy and hid in a forest. Another story has him taking off across a lake in a rowboat to avoid his appointment. Ultimately, he was obliged to accept the miter, though he continued to live as a monk. He was known for his deathbed healings and conversions.

—NOVEMBER 28—
Saint Catherine Labouré

O great Saint Catherine, God gifted you with a wonderful vision and entrusted you with a holy mission. Pray for me, that I may be open to the visions and messages that God would like me to experience. Bless me with an understanding and courageous heart, that I may know and accept the assignments God may entrust to me. Help me in *(mention request)*, that I may follow God's will and persevere until the end.

O you who found favor with Our Lady, ask her
also to pray for me, to be a mother to me. Implore
her to favor me with her love, and to intercede with
her Son to comfort my fears and soothe my anxieties.
I pray for this boon through Jesus our Lord. Amen.

1806–1876: From a poor family in Châtillon-sur-Seine,
France, Catherine entered the Sisters of Charity and was
sent to the motherhouse at Rue du Bac, Paris. There she
received visions of the Blessed Mother, who showed her the
design for a medal. Catherine had the design reproduced,
and the millions of Miraculous Medals that have since been
distributed have been the cause of untold numbers of
miracles.

—NOVEMBER 29—

Saint Francis
Anthony Fasani

Dear Saint Francis, unselfish, committed educator,
you shine still as a beacon for new generations of
the faithful, illuminating the path for young people
so that they can be intellectually and morally prepared
for their Christian vocations. Bless all teachers, especially those who are charged with teaching faith
and morals. Inspire them to continue to seek the
truth, and to challenge their students to seek the
truth as well. Bless in particular *(mention names)*,
my *child's/children's/grandchildren's* teacher, that *he/
she* may always teach with compassion and sensitivity. This I ask through Christ our Lord. Amen.

1681–1742: Sent to study with the Friars Minor Conventual in Lucera, Italy, Francis eventually joined the
Franciscans, earned his doctorate, and became a professor
of philosophy, earning the title "Padre Maestro." He was

made superior and provincial of his order and was known as a remarkable preacher. He was one of the first to conduct novenas to the Blessed Virgin under her title of the Immaculate Conception.

—NOVEMBER 30—

Saint Andrew the Apostle

PATRON OF ANGLERS, SAILORS,
UNMARRIED WOMEN, GREECE, RUSSIA,
AND SCOTLAND; INVOKED AGAINST GOUT
AND NECK PROBLEMS

O great Saint Andrew, your name, a token of beauty, foretells your splendor in the glory of your holy cross.

The cross exalts you, the blessed cross loves you, the bitter cross prepares the joys of the light to come for you.

The mystery of the cross shines in you with a twofold beauty: for by the cross you vanquished insults and taught all [humankind] of the Divine Blood shed on the cross.

Give fervor to our languid hearts and take us under your care, that by the victory of the cross we may reach our home in heaven. Amen.

POPE SAINT DAMASUS

first century: A native of Bethsaida, Andrew was the brother of Saint Peter. A fisherman who left Saint John the Baptist to follow Jesus, Andrew is said to have evangelized Asia Minor and Greece and to have been crucified in Achaia.

December

Blessed Maria Clementine Anuarite Nengapete

Blessed Maria, you refused to give up the integrity of your own person, even though you knew the consequence would be your own death. Teach us all to treasure our own personal integrity, that we may establish our own holy limits and allow no trespass beyond them. Teach us also to honor the boundaries other people delineate for themselves, that we may treasure the decisions others make and not try to pressure them into doing things they don't want to do. Pray especially for our young people, who confront social and peer pressures on a daily basis, that they may understand the reasons for the boundaries they have mapped out. Encourage them not to allow other people to change those boundaries; help them to learn that they are in control; and bring them courage and wisdom to persevere, despite rejection or insult or worse. Blessed Maria, pray especially for *(mention name)*, who is distressed by peer pressure, that God may give *him/her* the grace necessary to persevere in doing the Lord's will. Amen.

1939–1964: Born in what is now Upper Zaire, Maria converted when she was just a child and entered the Holy Family Sisters at age fifteen. Political unrest and violence afflicted her land in the early 1960s, and an army colonel killed her when she rebuffed his sexual advances. Maria was instantly recognized as a martyr of purity and is revered as the "Martyr of Zaire."

—DECEMBER 2—

Blessed John Ruysbroeck

Blessed John Ruysbroeck, teach me by your example not to look for rest in things that pass, but to find in God alone my consolation and my joy. Keep before my eyes the life and death of my Savior, so that his glory may set me free from everything on earth, and every thought of him may set my heart on fire with love.

NATHALIE LIEFMANS

1293–1381: From the area of Brussels, John was canon at Sainte-Gudule. He founded and was first prior of the monastery of Groenendael. Here he composed numerous ascetical works, including *The Sparkling Stone* and *The Book of the Spiritual Tabernacle*.

—DECEMBER 3—

Saint Francis Xavier

PATRON OF FOREIGN MISSIONS, GOA, INDIA, JAPAN, OUTER MONGOLIA, AND TOURISM

Great Saint Francis Xavier, glorious apostle of the Indies, we are not discouraged at your illustrious example of becoming a saint in spite of yourself— through the overpowering grace of God—nor will we say that we cannot become as great as you, for we dare not put limits on God's mercies. Didn't God raise your converted [nonbelievers] from their grave of idolatry to the Light of the Beatific Vision? And haven't we been struggling all our lives to love God perfectly? Help us to emulate your zeal for souls insofar as circumstances permit. Our "ministry" allows alms, penance, suffering, good example, writing, prayer, and Church work. Ask that we be animated with your spirit, a spirit that has no cunning calculation. Enlighten our minds so that we will realize that the denial of the good within us brings pain. Stabilize our souls, making them unsusceptible to variation; independent of caprice, and the mood of the moment; regulating them in charity. May we keep the Lord and his excessive love as our only joy. Obtain for us the grace to be "watching" as you were when death comes. May we accept in advance all the events of that death, knowing that however lonely, unconsoled, agonizing it may be, it is still, like the deaths of all saints, "precious in the eyes of the Lord." For saints we intend to be, since it is the will of God, and our salvation is [God's] work. Pray for us!

MARIE C. COMMINS

1506–1552: Born a nobleman in Navarre, Francis, the second of Saint Ignatius Loyola's original seven followers, was a successful missionary in India, Ceylon (now Sri Lanka), Malaya (now Malaysia), and Japan. After Saint Paul, Francis is perhaps the greatest individual missionary of the Christian Church.

—DECEMBER 4—

Saint Barbara

PATRON OF ARCHITECTS, ARTILLERY,
FIRE FIGHTERS, FIREWORKS MAKERS, MINERS,
SAILORS; INVOKED AGAINST EXPLOSIONS,
FIRE, LIGHTNING, AND SUDDEN DEATH

Intrepid virgin and martyr, Saint Barbara, through your intercession come to my aid in all needs of my soul. Obtain for me the grace to be preserved from a sudden and unprovided death; assist me in my agony, when my senses are benumbed and I am in the throes of death. Then, O powerful patron of the dying, come to my aid! Repel from me all the assaults and temptations of the evil one, and obtain for me the grace to receive before death the holy sacraments, that I may breathe forth my soul confirmed in faith, hope, and charity, and be worthy to enter eternal glory. Amen.

Saint Barbara, at my last end, obtain for me the Sacrament; assist one in that direst need when I my God and judge must meet: that robed in sanctifying grace my soul may stand before God's face.

TRADITIONAL

c. fourth century: According to legend, Barbara was shut up in a tower by her father, who himself killed her for being a Christian. Immediately, he was struck dead by lightning.

—December 5—

Saint Sabas the Abbot

Holy Saint Sabas, like Moses before you, you needed time alone in the desert to recover from what life had put in your path. And like Jesus before you, you needed more time in the desert to prepare for what life had in store for you. When I find myself in intolerable situations, intercede on my behalf, that I may find the courage and the opportunity to run away, if only for an hour, just to be alone and talk with God and meditate upon my life. If other people accuse me of wasting time or putting things off, inspire me to remain firm, for, as you well know, this solitude is as important as communal activity. As well, remind me to seek out moments of solitude when things are going well with my life, that I may thank God and also reflect upon where the Spirit may be leading me now and in the future. O Saint Sabas, pray for me. Amen.

439–532: Sabas fled from a bad family situation in Cappadocia to Palestine, where for many years he lived a hermit's life in various places. He eventually founded a laura (Mar Saba) in the mountainous desert of Judaea between Jerusalem and the Dead Sea. He was appointed archimandrite over all the Palestinian houses and in that capacity played a prominent part in the campaign against the Eutychian heresy. He is regarded as one of the founders of Eastern monasticism.

—DECEMBER 6—

Saint Nicholas of Myra

PATRON OF ANGLERS, BAKERS,
BARREL MAKERS, BOOTBLACKS, BREWERS,
BRIDES, CHILDREN, DOCKWORKERS, GREECE,
MERCHANTS, PAWNBROKERS, PERFUMERS,
PRISONERS, RUSSIA, SAILORS, TRAVELERS,
AND UNMARRIED WOMEN

Saint Nicholas, I pray to you through [God,] who has made your name venerated throughout the world; do not refuse to help a needy suppliant. Why, sir, are you called upon by all people in all the world unless you are to be the advocate of all who pray to you? Why does this sound in all ears, "My lord, Saint Nicholas," "My lord, Saint Nicholas," unless it means, "My advocate, Saint Nicholas," "My advocate, Saint Nicholas"? Why is your name poured forth everywhere except that the world may have some great good poured into it? Your fame calls to me, your miracles send me to your intercession, your works draw me to seek your help.

SAINT ANSELM

died c. 350: Almost nothing is known for certain about the life of Nicholas except that he was a bishop of Myra in Turkey, that he was probably martyred during the Diocletian persecutions, and that Italian merchants stole his alleged relics in 1087 and enshrined them at Bari. According to legend, however, he saved three girls from lives of prostitution by giving their father the gold for their dowries. He is also supposed to have raised back to life three boys who had been pickled in a brine tub. Nicholas is considered the model for our Santa Claus.

—December 7—

Saint Ambrose

Saint Ambrose, God gave you such grace that you could eloquently proclaim the truth before all and fearlessly bear reproach from those who spurned God. Be with me as I encounter the storms of politics, war, and bigotry, and keep my soul calm and peaceful amid whatever turmoil or difficulties I personally may face today. Help me to keep faith in the Creator, who is above us all and loves us all and who will help us through all problems no matter how insurmountable they may seem. As well, intercede on behalf of all bishops and pastors, that God may grant them such excellence in preaching and faithfulness in ministering the Word that all people may come to know God and enjoy with you the glory that Jesus wants for all. I pray through Jesus Christ our Lord, who lives and reigns with God and the Holy Spirit, one God, now and forever. Amen.

340–397: Born in Gaul, Ambrose became a barrister at Rome, then was appointed governor of Liguria and Aemilia, with headquarters in Milan. When the bishop of Milan died, Ambrose went to the cathedral to ensure order during the new election, but he himself was elected bishop by acclamation. He is known for his excellence as an administrator, as a writer, as a protector of the poor, and as the "hammer of Arianism," the heresy in vogue at that time. He is one of the Fathers and Doctors of the Church.

—DECEMBER 8—

Blessed Josephine Bakhita

Most blessed Josephine, holy sister, God guided you through innumerable and unspeakable humiliations and sufferings, both physical and moral, to human freedom and to the freedom of faith, and you consecrated your whole life to God for the coming of the kingdom. I implore your intercession this day for all those who cry for freedom from slavery and all oppression. Beg the Lord, I pray, and work miracles, if necessary, to free all slaves, that all people may have the freedom to which they are entitled as children of God. And as they await the miracle of freedom, strengthen them, that they may persevere. Send them your spirit, that they may experience the sweet breath of freedom even now, even under the yoke of their captivity.

O holy Josephine, as well, send your spirit to me, not only that I may appreciate the freedom that I enjoy, but also that I may become aware of the little oppressions occurring all around me. And energize me, that I may have the courage to step forward and speak out against oppression wherever I see it. Activate me with the love of God, who called to you in the depths of your captivity and gave you the courage to prevail. I ask this in the name of Jesus, who is Love. Amen.

1869–1947: The trauma of being kidnapped and sold into slavery was so great that Josephine never remembered the name she received from her parents. Sold and re-sold in the slave markets of Sudan, she was finally purchased by an Italian consul, who treated her in a loving and cordial way. He eventually took her to Italy, where she was allowed to join the Institute of Saint Magdalene of Canossa. She was known to all as "our black Mother."

—DECEMBER 9—

Blessed Juan Diego

To humble Juan Diego: You who were chosen by Our Lady of Guadalupe as an instrument to show your people and the world that the way of Christianity is one of love, compassion, understanding, values, sacrifices, repentance of our sins, appreciation and respect for God's creation, and most of all one of humility and obedience. You who we know is now in the kingdom of the Lord and close to our Mother, be our angel and protect us, stay with us as we struggle in this modern life not knowing most of the time where to set our priorities. Help us to pray to our God to obtain the gifts of the Holy Spirit and use them for the good of humanity and the good of our Church, through the heart of Our Lady of Guadalupe to the heart of Jesus. Amen.

MARIA E. BOUEY

1474–1548: A poor Aztec who lived near Mexico City, Juan received a vision of the Virgin Mary. When the bishop refused to believe Juan's story, the Virgin miraculously transformed a bunch of roses she told Juan to gather inside his cloak into an image of herself. The image, on Juan's cloak, still hangs in the Basilica of Our Lady of Guadalupe.

—DECEMBER 10—

Saint Eulalia of Mérida

PATRON OF BARCELONA, SAILORS, SEA VOYAGERS, AND WOMEN IN LABOR; INVOKED AGAINST DROUGHT AND STORMS AT SEA

O holy Saint Eulalia, you boldly professed your faith in God before hostile judges. Ask God to give me the strength to overcome my fear of looking ridiculous. Inspire me, that I may speak Truth to those who stand against God. Be with me especially when professing my love of our Lord may be dangerous. Protect me from danger; protect me also from forsaking my love. Pray that my actions may bring others to love God; but if not, pray that my responses may inspire others to profess their faith so that all the world may know the strength of God's love for all people. I pray this through Christ our Lord. Amen.

died 304: The most famous virgin martyr of Spain, Eulalia was only twelve when the edict condemning to death those who did not sacrifice to the Roman gods was issued. Instead of hiding, as her mother urged, Eulalia presented herself before the judge of Mérida to witness to him about the faith. In response to her scorn of the required sacrifice, the judge had her body torn with hooks and burned. As she was dying, a white dove came from her mouth.

—DECEMBER 11—

Blessed Maravillas of Jesus

Blessed Maravillas, you put on the meekness and humility of Jesus' heart. Intercede for me now, that the example of your virtues may stimulate the desire within my soul to follow the Way, the Truth, and the Life, as you did. Ask the Lord to give me the graces I need to serve the needy with gentleness and joy. Guide me in my prayers, and hear the requests I bring before you today. *(Mention requests.)* O Blessed Maravillas, pray for me. Amen.

1891–1974: Born in Madrid, Maravillas entered a Discalced Carmelite community and then founded the Carmel of Cerro de los Angeles. Nine other foundations in Spain and one in India followed. She gave first place to prayer and sacrifice, initiating and supporting apostolic, social, and charitable works to help those in need.

—DECEMBER 12—

Saint Jane Frances de Chantal

Holy Saint Jane, under the guidance of Saint Francis de Sales, you surrendered your life to God's love and will. Like you, I thank God for those persons in my life who support me on my spiritual journeys. Pray that the Spirit of Wisdom and Love be with all of my companions, that they may support and love me as I need.

Dearest Saint, you said that we must "remain in the state where God puts us." Grant that I may live in the present moment and accept it as God's gift. Help me to accept the circumstances of my life as an invitation to deeper union with the God who lures me on the way to wholeness. And give me faith to believe, in times of darkness, that the Spirit prays within me when I am unable to pray.

O Saint Jane, help me also not to take myself too seriously, but to trust in God's love and infinite mercy. I ask this in Jesus' name. Amen.

1572–1641: Born in Dijon, France, Jane married the Baron de Chantal, with whom she had four children. After his death, under the spiritual direction of Saint Francis de Sales, she founded the Visitation Nuns. The congregation welcomed widows and those in poor health and consequently met with strong opposition during her lifetime but flourished nevertheless.

—DECEMBER 13—

Saint Lucy

PATRON OF GONDOLIERS, GLAZIERS,
AND LAMPLIGHTERS; INVOKED AGAINST
DYSENTERY, EYE DISEASE, HEMORRHAGE,
AND THROAT DISEASE

Dear Saint Lucy, whose name signifies the light: to you we come full of confidence, and we beseech you to obtain for us a holy light that will make us careful not to walk in the path of sin, nor to remain surrounded by the darkness of error. We ask also, through your intercession, for the preservation of the light of our eyes and an abundance of grace that we may use our sight according to the divine will without any harm to our soul. Grant, O dear Lucy, that, after venerating and thanking you for your powerful protection here on earth, we may finally share your joy in paradise in the eternal light of the Lamb of God, your beloved Bridegroom, our Lord Jesus Christ. Amen.

DAUGHTERS OF SAINT PAUL

died c. 304: A wealthy maiden of Syracuse, Sicily, Lucy vowed herself to chastity and decided to give all her goods to the poor when her mother was cured of a sickness at the shrine of Saint Agnes. Lucy's charity distressed her fiancé, who denounced her to the authorities. She was condemned to a brothel, but not even a team of oxen could move her from the place where she stood. She also survived a burning at the stake but was killed when her throat was slashed.

—DECEMBER 14—

Saint John of the Cross

O glorious Saint John of the Cross, great Doctor of the Church, who, from very longing to be configured to Jesus crucified, desired nothing more ardently, even to the last moment of your holy life, than to suffer and to be despised and rejected of all people; and so great was your thirst for suffering that your generous heart was filled with joy in the midst of most painful torments and afflictions; I beseech you, dear saint, by the glory you merited by your manifold sufferings, intercede for me with Almighty God and obtain for me love of suffering, together with grace and strength to endure all tribulations and adversities with dauntless courage; for these are the sure means of coming into the possession of that crown of glory that is prepared for me in heaven. Ah yes, dear saint, from that high and glorious throne where you sit triumphant, hear, I beseech you, my earnest entreaties, that, following you, I may become a lover of the Cross and of suffering and thus may merit to be your companion in glory. Amen.

THE RACCOLTA

1542–1591: Born John de Yepes in Old Castile, Spain, this Carmelite friar was selected by Saint Teresa of Ávila as the first member of the first friary of the reformed observance. Establishing this reform among the male Carmelites, he endured persecution, including imprisonment at Toledo. He is a Doctor of the Church for his supreme mysticism, and his writings include *The Ascent of Mount Carmel, The Dark Night of the Soul,* and *The Spiritual Canticle.*

—DECEMBER 15—

Saint Mary di Rosa

Mary di Rosa, help me find the energy to stay involved in the needs of those around me, supporting them whenever I can be of assistance. It is so easy to turn to my own affairs and ignore the suffering of others, but remind me of our obligations to be caretakers for one another, especially for those who are less fortunate. Give me the will to be of service.

TOM COWAN

1813–1855: Born into a wealthy family in Brescia, Italy, Mary convinced her father to allow her to remain single so that she could dedicate herself to caring for others. She volunteered for hospital duty during the cholera epidemic of 1836 and nursed wounded soldiers on the battlefield during the fighting of 1848. She established a school for girls who could not hear nor speak and eventually founded the Handmaids of Charity.

—DECEMBER 16—

Saint Adelaide

O holy Saint Adelaide, you experienced familial strife that sundered your family and made life miserable for all. We pray you, intercede for extended families who allow strife to divide them. Ask God to send them the Holy Spirit, that they may seek and be granted forgiveness—and that they may forgive as well. Bring them, we pray, the holy spirit of reconciliation, and help them to live in harmony among themselves. We ask this through Christ our Lord. Amen.

931–999: A princess of Burgundy, Adelaide was married to Lothaire II of Italy, upon whose death she was treated with

great brutality by her husband's assassins. Emperor Otto
the Great rescued and married her, and they had five children. When he died, she was ill-treated by her son the king
and his wife. Eventually, they reconciled, and after other
deaths Adelaide became regent. She is revered for her forgiveness of her enemies.

—DECEMBER 17—

Saint Lazarus

Dear patron and assistant of the poor and sick. With
this prayer I request your assistance, and with the
aid of the Holy Spirit may the Lord always protect
me during sickness or in health.

Saint Lazarus, give me the strength to overcome
all the temptations on earth, in the name of the Father, the Son, and the Holy Spirit. Amen.

TRADITIONAL

first century: The disciple and friend of Jesus, Lazarus was
the brother of Mary and Martha of Bethany. Some traditions hold that he died from leprosy, and the story of how
Jesus raised Lazarus from the dead is told in the Gospel of
John. According to Greek tradition, Lazarus became bishop
of Kition in Cyprus. Other legends connect him with Marseilles.

—DECEMBER 18—

Saint Flannan of Killaloe

Flannan, help me to be resourceful in finding ways
to stick to my goals. I pray that I will find the courage to do what I know I must do, even if others
have different plans for me.

TOM COWAN

seventh century: An Irish monk, Flannan was consecrated bishop by Pope John IV in Rome, despite the dangers and difficulties of travel. He invented the practice of praying the Psalter while immersed to the neck in icy water, to banish carnal temptations. To avoid the possibility that his own father, King Turlough of Killaloe, would make him a king as well, Flannan appealed to an old Celtic tradition that required a blemished king to abdicate and prayed to be made physically repulsive. God answered the prayers by sending Flannan rashes, boils, and scars, enabling him to live out his days as a man of the Church.

—DECEMBER 19—

Saint Safan

Holy Saint Safan, wise mother and counselor, I come to you with a heart that desires to learn how to pray. As you taught nuns and monks in your own time, teach me how to pray whether standing or sitting—at every time of day—in all that I say and do. Teach me as well how to address my prayers—that is, where to seek God and where to direct my thoughts. Bless me with your understanding of God's presence in every place and every time. Reveal to me the kingdom of heaven that can be reached from every land, so that I may not only pray to our Lord but abide with him always.

I ask your special intercession for *(mention person)*, who seems to have such difficulty with prayer at this time; be with *him/her*, and carry all prayers to the Lord. I ask this in the name of Jesus, who is with us always, even to the end of the age. Amen.

died 739: Raised in important circles in Ireland, Safan was married briefly before becoming a nun. Traditions link her with the founding of the monastery at Clonbroney, where she served as abbess. She is known for her wise advice about how to pray and how to find God.

—DECEMBER 20—

Saint Abraham

Holy Father Abraham, God called you out of the comfort of your senior lifestyle and sent you to a new land, for God had great plans for you and your descendants that you could not foresee. Be with all those who must make decisions about emigration. Calm them, strengthen them, and encourage them, that they may be able to pay attention to the voice of God talking to them in the still, deep recesses of their hearts, so that they may know what to do. Protect them on their journeys, and send angels and people of goodwill to help them upon their arrival in their new homes.

I also implore your help as I embark on a new life in a new place. Now that I am *(going away to school, graduating from college, taking a new job in another city, being transferred to a new location, retiring to another location,....)*, I am afraid of the uncertainties, and I am having difficulty coping with all the details involved. I ask for your reassurance and encouragement; please send me your spirit of trust in the Lord, that I may come to understand that all will be well, in accordance with the Lord's plans. Please also send people of goodwill—and angels, if necessary—to greet me and help me settle into my new home. I ask this in the name of the Almighty, who called you forth to a new life. Amen.

twentieth century B.C.: Born at Ur in Chaldea, Abram—whom God renamed Abraham—migrated at God's command to Canaan. Here he lived a pastoral and nomadic life. From him descended the Twelve Tribes of Israel, for which he is known as the Father of all believers and progenitor of the Hebrew nation.

—December 21—

Saint Peter Canisius

Saint Peter Canisius, you saw the good in even the most troublesome of people. You found their talents and used them. Help me to see beyond the behavior of others that may bother me to the gifts God has given them. Amen.

TERRY MATZ

1521–1597: From Nijmegen, the Netherlands, Peter was part of a movement for religious reform as a very young man and was the eighth professed member of the Society of Jesus. He was eventually assigned as the first superior of the German province of the Jesuits, and he restored and founded colleges, attracted vocations, and supported reforms, becoming a leading force in the Counter-Reformation. He is a Doctor of the Church.

—December 22—

Saint Chaeremon

Most holy Saint Chaeremon, you know personally the terror of having to flee for your very life from your own home, without knowing if you will live to see another day's dawn. Intercede, then, for all people who flee from war or persecution or tyranny. Protect them from all harm, and guide them to freedom and peace. Calm their fears, and help them to act wisely in the midst of terror. Approach Saint Joseph on their behalf too, and ask for his assistance, for he, as well as you, knows the terror of the nighttime escape from the soldier's sword. Dear Saint Chaeremon, inspire us to be "good Samaritans" to any refugees by helping them in whatever way they need, and implore the Lord to send them many such

neighbors—people of goodwill, partisans, even angels. We ask especially for your intercession on behalf
of the people of *(mention place)*. In the name of Jesus
our Lord, who exhorts us all to be "good Samaritans" to those in need, we make this prayer. Amen.

died c. 250: Bishop of Nilopolis in Egypt, Chaeremon was
already a very old man when the emperor Decius began his
persecution of Christians. Chaeremon fled to the mountainous district of the Arabian desert with several companions,
and none was ever seen or heard of again.

—DECEMBER 23—

Saint Marguerite d'Youville

Saint Marguerite d'Youville, we turn to you in
humble prayer because your life speaks to us of
goodness, compassion, and love in a world of suffering, anguish, and pain. It is not unlike the world
you knew as you went about doing good with a
great love for the human family, with preference for
the poorest of all. Your dream of universal charity
became a mission in the Church. We give thanks to
you for the inspiring vision that is ours today as
your dream lives on. May we learn as you did the
life-giving power of love, the profound peace of
unfailing trust, the deep mystery of suffering and
pain, the strength-giving solace of prayer.

Saint Marguerite, teach us to listen, in the silence
of our hearts, to the God of Mercy and Compassion, that we too may be signs of God's love to all
peoples of our world. Amen.

THE SISTERS OF CHARITY OF MONTREAL

1701–1771: Born in Quebec, Marguerite became a widow
with three children to support. She founded the Grey Nuns
and directed the General Hospital in Montreal.

Saint Charbel Makhlouf

O holy and glorified Saint Charbel, saint monk, you led the perfect life of a hermit. God blessed you with the strength to detach yourself from the world so that the heroism of the monastic virtues of poverty, chastity, and obedience might triumph in your hermitage. I beseech you, aid me in loving and serving God, following your example of hospitality and self-sacrifice. Ask the Lord to turn my heart of stone to a heart of flesh. And look kindly on my request *(mention request)*, favoring me with a miracle, if necessary, as you have favored countless others. Grant me this grace, which I request from God through your intercession. Amen.

1828–1898: A Maronite monk from Lebanon, Charbel suffered a stroke while saying Mass the day before Christmas and died a few hours later. A light from his tomb attracted the local villagers, and miracles of healing began to occur. His body was exhumed four months later and is still incorrupt, and miracles continue to occur through his intercession.

Saint Eugenia

Holy Saint Eugenia, your love of the Lord and love of your own father, together with your example of self-sacrifice for your faith, eventually led to the conversion of your entire family. Pray for all daughters whose fathers do not believe in God. Strengthen these women and girls in their faith, that they may be witnesses of faith to the men who first gave them life.

As well, O wonderful saint, bless all children whose parents do not understand them. Help them to be true to themselves and to Truth. Keep them strong in their faith, and intercede for them that they may, with your prayers and assistance, convert their parents to the Way, the Truth, and the Life.

Saint Eugenia, pray for us. Amen.

died 257?: Eugenia was the daughter of Philip of Alexandria. According to legend, she was eager to become a nun, but because of her father's disapproval she is supposed to have disguised herself as a man and fled to an abbey. No one ever discovered her ruse, and she was eventually elected abbot. A woman decided to accuse Eugenia of adultery when she refused the woman's seductions, and Philip imprisoned Eugenia. When she removed her disguise, her father converted to Christianity and moved to Rome. Eugenia was finally martyred under the Valerian persecutions.

—DECEMBER 26—

Saint Stephen

PATRON OF BRICKLAYERS, BUILDERS, HORSES, AND MASONS

Holy Stephen, blessed Stephen, loving Stephen, mighty soldier of God, first of the blessed army of the martyrs of God, powerful prince, one of the great lords of heaven. I call upon you, sir, with joy, because I believe this of you: when you were on earth such light of holiness glowed within you that your venerable face shone with the nobility of an angel, for purity made your heart so clear that your blessed eyes saw God in [God's] glory; and you were on fire with so much love that in your goodness you prayed for the evil men that surrounded you. It was so, good Stephen, it was indeed so, and I rejoice, praise, and exult that I know this of you.

For I am fearful, knowing the wrath of the strict judge, for I am a sinner, a prisoner deserving punishment, and I need someone to help me. In love and assurance I send you as my intercessor, that you may make peace between me and your powerful friend, the Lord and Creator of both you and me. For I am quite certain, sir, that by your great merits you can do this, and I am sure that out of your great charity you will do this. I hope in the immense mercy of the Judge that [God] will not refuse you. So anxious and trembling, I come to you for refuge, only too well aware that I am a sinner. So, good Stephen, behold my wretchedness and pour over it your love.

SAINT ANSELM

died c. 33: Chosen by the apostles as the first of the seven deacons, Stephen was stoned to death at the instigation of the Sanhedrin. He is the first Christian martyr, and his dying prayer is supposed to have led to the conversion of Saint Paul, who actively participated in Stephen's murder.

—DECEMBER 27—

Saint John the Evangelist

PATRON OF TURKEY AND OF WRITERS;
INVOKED AGAINST POISON

O most blessed John! beloved friend of Jesus, who was chosen in your purity by our Lord, and because of your purity more tenderly beloved, and more deeply imbued with high and heavenly mysteries than your brethren: O most glorious apostle and evangelist, I invoke you together with Mary the Mother of the same, our Lord Jesus Christ, and beseech you that you would, in union with her, bestow upon me your aid....

Demand for me, I beseech you, the salvation of my soul and of my body. Grant, I implore you, oh,

grant that through your glorious prayers, the good
and gentle Spirit, bounteous giver of all Grace, may
cleanse me from all the defilements of my sins, may
enlighten and adorn me with all holy virtues, and
enable me to stand steadfast and to persevere unto
the end in the love of God and of my neighbors,
and when I have finished my course, may the most
gracious Paraclete lead me up to [heavenly joy]: who
with the Father and the Son lives and reigns, One
God, forevermore. Amen.

SAINT EDMUND

died c. 100: The son of Zebedee and brother of Saint James
the Greater, John was a fisherman until called by Jesus to be
an apostle. John was "the disciple whom Jesus loved" and
to whom Jesus gave over care of his mother. John is considered the author of the fourth Gospel, three canonical epistles,
and the Book of Revelation. After Jesus' death, John lived
at Ephesus and Patmos.

—DECEMBER 28—

Holy Innocents

Most Holy Innocents of Bethlehem, the pure joy of
your existence was cut short by a fearful, ignorant
king. I implore you, pray for all innocent victims,
that the Lord will greet them with arms of mercy
open wide. I beseech you, frustrate the designs of
evil tyrants, that the Lord may establish his rule of
justice, love, and peace. I beg your special prayers
for the victims of child abuse: ask the Lord to send
them his healing spirit, that they may find peace
and love in this life.

Most of all, I beg your continued prayers for the
victims of abortion. For the children whose joyful
lives are cut short, that they may be with God now.
For the parents who will never know the joy of hold-

ing these children in their arms, that the Lord will heal their lives and bring them peace. For doctors and nurses and health-care professionals, that the Lord may open their eyes to the truth of their business. For politicians and political advocates, that the Lord may grant them the wisdom to find better ways to solve the problems that lead people to abortion. And for the rest of us, that we may come to understand what we can do personally to end the tragedy of abortion.

In the name of the baby Jesus, I pray. Amen.

The Gospel of Matthew relates the tragedy of the Holy Innocents. When Jesus was born in Bethlehem, King Herod, fearing for his throne, ordered that all the male infants of Bethlehem be killed. These children are the first martyrs for the Gospel.

—DECEMBER 29—

Saint Thomas à Becket

INVOKED AGAINST BLINDNESS

Saint Thomas, the Lord gave you the courage to witness to the Gospel of Christ, even to the point of giving your life for it. By your prayers, help me to endure all suffering for love of God and to seek the Lord with all my heart, for God alone is the source of my life. Be mindful of my needs, dear saint, and grant my petition *(mention request)*, that through your intercession I may be made whole. I ask this through our Lord Jesus Christ, who lives and reigns for ever and ever. Amen.

1118–1170: As archbishop of Canterbury, Thomas opposed the encroachments of his friend King Henry II on the liberties of the clergy and the rights of the Church. The king's

imprudent words, let fall in a fit of rage, prompted four of
his knights to murder Thomas in the cathedral. His shrine
at Canterbury is one of the most important and famous in
Christendom.

—DECEMBER 30—

Blessed John Maria Boccardo

Blessed Father John, you were a pastor in the truest
sense, a good shepherd who pastored his flock with
compassion and deep dedication. Bless all parish
priests, that they may learn from and follow your
example. Teach them the lesson that Jesus taught
his apostles when he washed their feet at the Last
Supper. Ask the Lord to give them love, wisdom,
and discernment. Inspire them to spend their energies in imitating Christ the Good Shepherd. Bless
especially *(mention names)*, our priests. In Jesus'
name we pray. Amen.

1848–1913: John spent most of his life as a parish priest at
Pancalieri, Italy, where he cared for the sick and started an
apostolate to aid the abandoned aged, the orphaned, and
the homeless. He established the Hospice of Charity and
founded the Congregation of the Poor Daughters of Saint
Cajetan.

—DECEMBER 31—

Saint Sylvester I

Holy Saint Sylvester, you witnessed great changes in your lifetime, for you experienced great persecution of Christianity and then, happily, its full acceptance into the Roman Empire. You well understood the great stress that can accompany big changes, even if those changes are long-hoped-for and welcome, so please pray for me now at this time of great change in my life. Sometimes it seems as if my entire world has been turned upside-down; what I expected has disappeared, and in its place I find situations and events that I never anticipated and for which I feel completely unprepared. Send your spirit to me, to guide me through the uncertainty. Bless my efforts, especially those made in faith. And encourage me with the sure knowledge that all will turn out to be in accord with God's will. I ask in particular for your help with *(mention request)*. In Jesus' name, I pray. Amen.

died 335: A Roman, Sylvester reigned as pope just after Emperor Constantine granted toleration to Christianity by means of the Edict of Milan. Though little is known for certain about Sylvester, the first general council was held during his reign at Nicaea to deal with the Arian heresy.

Alphabetical Listing of Saints, Indicating Feast Days

Abraham Kidunaia, St.: 3/16
Abraham, St.: 12/20
Adelaide, St.: 12/16
Adrian of Canterbury, St.: 1/9
Aegidius Mary of Saint Joseph
   Pontillo, St.: 2/7
Aelred of Rievaulx, St.: 2/3
Agape, Chionia, and Irene, Sts.: 4/3
Agatha, St.: 2/5
Agnes, St.: 1/21
Albert Chmielowski, St.: 6/17
All Saints: 11/1
Aloysius Gonzaga, St.: 6/21
Alphonsa Muttathupandatu,
   Bl.: 7/28
Alphonsus Maria dei Liguori,
   St.: 8/1
Ambrose, St.: 12/7
André Bessette, Bl.: 1/6
Andrew Dung-Lac and
   Companions, Sts.: 11/24
Andrew the Apostle, St.: 11/30
Angela Merici, St.: 1/27
Anne-Marie Javouhey, Bl.: 7/15
Annemarie Taigi, Bl.: 6/9
Anselm of Canterbury, St.: 4/21
Anthony of Egypt, St.: 1/17
Anthony of Padua, St.: 6/13
Ardalion, St.: 4/14
Athanasius of Athos, St.: 7/5
Augustine (or Austin) of
   Canterbury, St.: 5/27
Augustine, St.: 8/28

Barbara, St.: 12/4
Bartholomew de las Casas,
   St.: 10/29
Basil the Great and Gregory
   Nazianzen, Sts.: 1/2
Bathildis, St.: 1/30
Benedict of Nursia, St.: 7/11
Benedict the Moor, St.: 4/4
Bernadette Soubirous of Lourdes,
   St.: 4/16

Bernard of Clairvaux, St.: 8/20
Bernard Tolomei, Bl.: 8/22
Bernardine of Siena, St.: 5/20
Blandina Merten, Bl.: 5/18
Boleslawa Maria Lament, Bl.: 1/29
Boniface of Mainz, St.: 6/5
Brendan, St.: 5/16
Brigida of Jesus Morello, Bl.: 9/3
Brigid of Kildare, St.: 2/1
Bruno of Segni, St.: 7/18

Casimir, St.: 3/4
Castora Gabrielli, Bl.: 6/14
Catherine Labouré, St.: 11/28
Catherine of Alexandria, St.: 11/25
Catherine of Bologna, St.: 3/9
Catherine of Genoa, St.: 9/15
Catherine of Siena, St.: 4/29
Cecilia, St.: 11/22
Cedd, St.: 10/26
Ceferino Gimenez Malla, Bl.: 8/2
Chaeremon, St.: 12/22
Charbel Makhlouf, St.: 12/24
Charles Borromeo, St.: 11/4
Charles Lwanga and Companions,
   Martyrs of Uganda, Sts.: 6/3
Charles the Good, Bl.: 3/2
Christina Ciccarelli, Bl.: 1/18
Clare Bosatta, Bl.: 4/20
Claude de la Colombière, St.: 2/15
Clelia Barbieri, St.: 7/13
Clement Maria Hofbauer, St.: 3/15
Colette, St.: 3/6
Conrad of Piacenza, St.: 2/19
Contardo Ferrini, Bl.: 10/27
Cuthbert of Lindisfarne, St.: 3/20
Cyril and Methodius, Sts.: 2/14
Cyril of Jerusalem, St.: 3/18

Damien de Veuster, Bl.: 4/15
Daniel Brottier, Bl.: 2/28
Daniel Comboni, Bl.: 10/10
David (Dewi), St.: 3/1
Denis, St.: 10/9
Dismas, St.: 3/25

Permissions,
Acknowledgments,
and Sources

I thank the following people for all their help, without which this book would not have been possible: Joanne Bartoli, Judy Bauer, John Cleary, Patricia Kossmann, and Cecelia Portlock. My special thanks go out to Rayner W. Hesse, Jr., for his assistance with proofreading, his practical suggestions, his invaluable insights, and, most of all, his sincere interest in my work.

Every effort has been made to locate and secure permission for the inclusion of all copyrighted material in this book. If any such acknowledgments have been inadvertently omitted, the publisher would appreciate receiving full information so that proper credit may be given in future editions.

The author wishes to express his gratitude as follows for permission to reproduce copyrighted materials:

Prayers to Abraham Kidunaia, Albert Chmielowski, Anselm of Canterbury, Athanasius of Athos, David, Edward the Confessor, Emily de Rodat, Enda of Arranmore, Flannan of Killaloe, Guy of Anderlecht, Illtud of Wales, Josaphat, Joseph of Cupertino, Marcian of Chalcis, Mary di Rosa, Mechtildis of Edelstetten, Nicholas of Tolentino, Stephen Harding, Stephen of Perm, Thais, Thomas of Villanueva, William of York: from *The Way of the Saints*, copyright © 1998 by Tom Cowan. Used by permissioin of Putnam Berkley, a division of Penguin Putnam Inc. New York: G. P. Putnam's Sons, 1998.

Prayers to All Saints (by Saint Augustine), Martin of Tours: Ann Ball, *A Litany of Saints*. Huntington, Ind.: Our Sunday Visitor, 1993. The permission to reproduce copyrighted materials for use was extended by Our Sunday Visitor, 200 Noll Plaza, Huntington, IN, 1-800-348-2440. Website: www.osv.com. No other use of this material is authorized. Printed matter only.

Prayer to All Saints: John Henry Newman, *Meditations and Devotions*, as found in Barry Ulanov, comp., *On Death: Wisdom and Consolation from the World's Great Writers*. Liguori, Mo.: Triumph, 1996.

Prayer to Aloysius Gonzaga: William Hart McNichols, S.J. in *Aloysius*, ed. by Clifford Stevens and William Hart McNichols. Huntington, Ind.: Our Sunday Visitor, 1993.

Prayers to Alphonsus dei Liguori, Clement Maria Hofbauer: Courtesy of The Redemptorists, c/o Liguori Publications, One Liguori Drive, Liguori, MO 63057.

Prayers to André Bessette, Peter Canisius: Copyright © 1999 by Terry Matz.

Prayer to Andrew the Apostle: Pope Saint Damasus, as found in Rev. Charles Dollen, comp. and ed., *Prayer Book of the Saints*. Huntington, Ind.: Our Sunday Visitor, 1984.

Prayers to Annemarie Taigi, Brendan, James the Greater, Martha, Monica, Peregrine Laziosi, Pius X: Daughters of Saint Paul, *Queen of Apostles Prayerbook*. Boston: St. Paul Books & Media, 1991.

Prayers to Anthony of Egypt, Bernardine of Siena, Fidelis of Sigmaringen, John Baptist de la Salle, John Bosco, John of the Cross, Lawrence, Michael of the Saints, Pancras, Paschal Baylon, Paul, Tarcisius, Vincent Ferrer: Joseph P. Christopher, Charles E. Spence, and John F. Rowan, eds. *The Raccolta*. New York: Benziger Brothers, 1952.

Prayer to Anthony of Padua: Patricia Soper, in John Cumming and Paul Burns, eds., *Prayers for Our Times*. New York: Crossroad, 1983.

Prayer to Augustine: Albert J. Hebert, S.M., comp., *A Prayerbook of Favorite Litanies*. Rockford, Ill.: TAN Books and Publishers, 1985.

Prayers to Catherine of Genoa, Dismas, Elizabeth of Hungary, Francis Xavier, Jerome, Louis Marie Grignion de Montfort, Mary Magdalene: Marie C. Commins, *Be a Saint: In Spite of Yourself*. Milwaukee: The Bruce Publishing Company, 1956.

Prayers to Barbara, Catherine of Alexandria, Denis, Elmo of Formiae, Eustace, George the Great, Giles, Holy Helpers, Margaret, Pantaleon: Fr. Bonaventure Hammer, O.F.M., comp. *The Fourteen Holy Helpers: Early Christian Saints Who Are Powerful with God*. Rockford, Ill.: TAN Books and Publishers, 1995 (Benziger Brothers, 1909).

Prayer to Benedict of Nursia: Saint Gregory the Great, *The Life of St. Benedict*. Rockford, Ill.: TAN Books and Publishers, 1995.

Prayer to Bernadette Soubirous of Lourdes: *The Catholic Family Book of Novenas.* Harrison, N.Y.: Roman Catholic Books, 1956.

Prayers to Cyril and Methodius, Stanislaus Szczepanow: Karol Wojtyla, *Prayers of Pope John Paul II,* ed. by John F. McDonald. New York: Crossroad, 1982.

Prayer to Dominic de Guzmán: Blessed Jordan of Saxony, courtesy Monastery of Saint Dominic, 375 Thirteenth Ave., Newark, NJ 07103.

Prayers to Dymphna, Thomas More: Leaflet Missal Company, *A Holy Card Prayer Book,* vol. 1 & 2. Saint Paul: The Leaflet Missal Co., 1992.

Prayers to Elizabeth Ann Seton, Vincent Pallotti: Pope John XXIII, *Journal of a Soul.* trans. Dorothy White. New York: McGraw-Hill, 1964. Copyright © 1964. Reproduced with the permission of the McGraw-Hill Companies.

Prayer to Faustina Kowalska: Marians of the Immaculate Conception, Eden Hill, Stockbridge, MA 01263.

Prayer to Frances Xavier Cabrini: Mother Cabrini League, MSC Word Ministry, 434 W. Deming Place, Chicago, IL 60614-1719.

Prayer to Francis Caracciolo: Adorno Fathers, 575 Darlington Ave., Ramsey, NJ 07446.

Prayer to Francis of Assisi: "Our Parish, Our Patron: Saint Francis of Assisi." Liguori, Mo.: Liguori Publications, 1999.

Prayer to Francis of Paola: "Mariners' Prayer," Minim Fathers, All Saints Church, 3431 Portola Ave., Los Angeles, CA 90032-2215.

Prayer to Gaspar Bertoni: Stigmatine Fathers and Brothers, 554 Lexington St., Waltham, MA 02154-3097.

Prayer to Gaspar del Bufalo, Maria de Mattias: Missionaries of the Precious Blood, 1427 Sixth St., Alameda, CA 94501-3760.

Prayers to Gerard Majella: Thomas E. Tobin, C.Ss.R. *St. Gerard Majella: The Mothers' Saint.* Ligouri, Mo.: Liguori Publications, 1997.

Prayer to Heavenly Patron: M. Basil Pennington, O.C.S.O. *Pocket Book of Prayers.* New York: Doubleday, 1987.

Prayer to Jacob Netsvetov: Holy Trinity Cathedral, San Francisco, CA.

Prayer to John Neumann: The National Shrine of Saint John Neumann, 1019 North 5th St., Philadelphia, PA 19123.

Prayer to John of God: Rev. Lawrence G. Lovasik, S.V.D., *The Heart Saint: St. John of God.* 1988.

Prayer to John Ruysbroeck: Nathalie Liefmans, courtesy The Augustinians in the United States, Augustinian Provincialate, Province of Saint Thomas of Villanova, 214 Ashwood Road, P.O. Box 340, Villanova, PA 19085-0340.

Prayer to John-Baptist-Marie Vianney: Anthony Manuppella, *Novena to St. John Vianney*. Boston: Pauline Books & Media, 1975.

Prayer to Joseph: *The Raccolta*, 10th ed., ed. Ambrose St. John. London: Burns Oates & Washbourne, Ltd., 1924.

Prayer to Juan Diego: Maria E. Bouey.

Prayer to Jude Thaddeus: Daughters of St. Paul, *St. Jude—Helper in Great Need*. Boston: St. Paul Books & Media, 1977, 1992.

Prayer to Kateri Tekakwitha: Pauly Fongemie.

Prayer to Louis IX of France: Mother Saint Louis, S.C.S.L., courtesy Sisters of Charity of Saint Louis, 4907 South Catherine St., Plattsbrgh, NY 12901.

Prayer to Lucy: Daughters of Saint Paul, *Devotion to St. Lucy*. Boston: Pauline Books & Media, 1977.

Prayer to Margaret of Castello, Rose of Viterbo: From *Treasury of Women Saints*, © 1991 by Ronda De Sola Chervin. Published by Servant Publications, Box 8617, Ann Arbor, Michigan, 48107. Used with permission.

Prayer to Marguerite d'Youville: The Sisters of Charity of Montreal, 138, rue Saint-Pierre, Montreal, Quebec, H2Y 2L7, Canada.

Prayer to María Soledad Torres Acosta: The Sisters, Servants of Mary, 800 N. 18th St., Kansas City, KS 66102-4291.

Prayer to Martín de Porres: Daughters of Saint Paul, *Novena to St. Martín de Porres*. Boston: St. Paul Books & Media, 1980.

Prayer to Mary Domenica Mazzarello: Daughters of Mary Help of Christians, Salesian Sisters of Saint John Bosco, Office of the Provincial, 655 Belmont Ave., Haledon, NJ 07508-2398.

Prayer to Mary MacKillop: Kathleen T. Boschetti, M.S.C.

Prayer to Mary, the Mother of God: Mother Teresa of Calcutta, in Eileen Egan, *At Prayer with Mother Teresa*, ed. Judy Bauer. Liguori, Mo.: Liguori Publications, 1999.

Prayer to Mercedes Prat: Society of Saint Teresa of Jesus, 18080 St. Joseph Way, Covington, LA 70435-5623.

Prayer to Miguel Augustine Pro: Ann Ball, ProVision, 4906 Highway 6 North, Houston, TX 77084.

Prayer to Mother Maria Skobtsóva: Raymond J. Mastroberte, iconographer and cantor, East Stroudsburg, Penn., 1997. Permission granted for reprint by the author.

Prayers to Nicholas of Myra, Stephen: Saint Anselm, *The Prayers and Meditations of Saint Anselm, with the Proslogion.* trans. Sr. Benedicta Ward. New York and London: Penguin, 1973. Reproduced by permission of Penguin Books Ltd.

Prayer to Nilus of Sora (Nil Sorky): Br. Isaac E. Lambertsen, 75 East 93rd St., New York, NY 10128.

Prayer to Patrick: Richard Cardinal Cushing, *Devotion to St. Patrick.* Boston: Pauline Books & Media, 1982.

Prayer to Raphael: Daughters of Saint Paul, *The Archangel Raphael—Sent by God.* Boston: Pauline Books & Media, 1983.

Prayer to Rita of Cascia: Marianne Lorraine Trouvé, F.S.P., ed., *My Favorite Prayers and Novenas.* Boston: Pauline Books & Media, 1997.

Prayer to Romuald: Camaldolese Hermits of Monte Corona, Holy Family Hermitage, 1501 Fairplay Road, Bloomingdale, OH 43910-7971.

Prayer to Thomas à Becket: Daughters of Saint Paul, *Christian Prayer: The Liturgy of the Hours.* Boston: St. Paul Editions, 1976.

Prayers to Thomas Aquinas: Marianne Lorraine Trouvé, FSP, *Novena to St. Thomas Aquinas: Patron of Students and Catholic Schools.* Boston: Pauline Books & Media, 1997; Karl Rahner, *Prayers for a Lifetime,* ed. Albert Raffelt. New York: Crossroad, 1984.

Prayer to Vito: Church of St. Vito, 816 Underhill Ave., Mamaroneck, NY 10543; trans. by Joanne Bartoli.

Other Sources

Ball, Ann, *A Litany of Saints.* Huntington, Ind.: Our Sunday Visitor, 1993.

Benedictine Monks of St. Augustine's Abbey, Ramsgate, *The Book of Saints,* 4th ed. New York: Macmillan, 1947.

Bunson, Matthew, et al., *John Paul II's Book of Saints.* Huntington, Ind.: Our Sunday Visitor, 1999.

Chervin, Ronda De Sola, *Treasury of Women Saints.* Ann Arbor: Servant, 1991.

Chiffolo, Anthony F., comp. *At Prayer with the Saints.* Liguori, Mo.: Liguori Publications, 1998.

Commins, Marie C., *Be a Saint: In Spite of Yourself.* Milwaukee: The Bruce Publishing Company, 1956.

Congregation of the Daughters of St. Mary of Providence, *Prayers of the Daughters of St. Mary of Providence.* Chicago: 1995.

Cowan, Tom, *The Way of the Saints*. New York: G. P. Putnam's Sons, 1998.

Donaghy, Thomas J., *Lives of the Saints II: For Every Day of the Year*. New York: Catholic Book Publishing Co., 1998.

Ellsberg, Robert, *All Saints: Daily Reflections on Saints, Prophets, and Witnesses for Our Time*. New York: Crossroad Publishing, 1997.

Foley, Leonard, O.F.M., ed., *Saint of the Day: Lives and Lessons for Saints and Feasts of the New Missal*, rev. ed. Cincinnati: St. Anthony Messenger, 1990.

Hammer, Bonaventure, O.F.M., comp. *The Fourteen Holy Helpers: Early Christian Saints Who Are Powerful with God*. Rockford, Ill.: TAN Books and Publishers, 1995 (Benziger Brothers, 1909).

Hebert, Albert J., S.M., comp. *A Prayerbook of Favorite Litanies*. Rockford, Ill.: TAN Books and Publishers, 1985.

Heffernan, Eileen, FSP, *Fifty-Seven Saints*, second ed. Boston: Pauline Books & Media, 1994.

Hoever, Hugo, S.O.Cist., *Lives of the Saints: For Every Day of the Year*, rev. ed. Catholic Book Publishing Co., 1999.

Kelly, Sean, and Rosemary Rogers, *Saints Preserve Us!* New York: Random House, 1993.

Koenig-Bricker, Woodeene, *365 Saints: Your Daily Guide to the Wisdom and Wonder of Their Lives*. New York: HarperSanFrancisco, 1995.

Larssen, Raymond E. F., comp. and ed. *Saints at Prayer*. New York: Coward-McCann, Inc., 1942.

Quintiliani, Patricia S., comp. *My Treasury of Chaplets*, sixth ed. Still River, Mass.: The Ravengate Press, 1986, 1998.

Stevens, Clifford, *The One Year Book of Saints*. Huntington, Ind.: Our Sunday Visitor, 1989.

The Woman's Prayer Companion. Indianapolis: The Carmelites of Indianapolis, 1994.

Water, Mark, *A Year with the Saints*. Liguori, Mo.: Liguori Publications, 1997.